"Any reader who dabbles a toe into Chapter 1 will be instantly swept up into Bangs's vivid tales of whitewater rafting and his adrenaline-pumping prose."

—msnbc.com

"While Richard Bangs's reputation as an explorer and writer is well established, rarely has he documented a story of such intense personal drama as this."

—*Sports Afield*

"Bangs . . . tells his tale with the ease of a worldly relative who swoops in for Thanksgiving dinner and regales the table with stories that keep everyone's attention."

—*Publishers Weekly*

"Bangs's writing effectively captures the thrills, chills, and spills that make rafting such a popular, albeit sometimes dangerous, recreation."

—*Library Journal*

# THE
# LOST
# RIVER

OTHER WORKS BY RICHARD BANGS

*Rivergods*

*Islands of Fire, Islands of Spice*

*Paths Less Traveled*

*Riding the Dragon's Back*

*Islandgods*

*Peaks*

*Whitewater Adventure*

*Adventure Vacations*

*The Adventure Book*

*1001 Adventures*

*SOBEK's Adventure Vacations*

# THE
# LOST
# RIVER

*A Memoir of Life, Death,*
*and Transformation on Wild Water*

# Richard Bangs

SIERRA CLUB BOOKS
SAN FRANCISCO

The Sierra Club, founded in 1892 by John Muir, has devoted itself to the study and protection of the Earth's scenic and ecological resources—mountains, wetlands, woodlands, wild shores and rivers, deserts and plains. The publishing program of the Sierra Club offers books to the public as a nonprofit educational service in the hope that they may enlarge the public's understanding of the Club's basic concerns. The point of view expressed in each book, however, does not necessarily represent that of the Club. The Sierra Club has some sixty chapters coast to coast, in Canada, Hawaii, and Alaska. For information about how you may participate in its programs to preserve wilderness and the quality of life, please address inquiries to Sierra Club, 85 Second Street, San Francisco, CA 94105.

www.Sierra.org/books

Published by Sierra Club Books in conjunction with Crown Publishers, New York, New York. Member of the Crown Publishing Group.

Random House, Inc. New York, Toronto, London, Sydney, Auckland
www.randomhouse.com

SIERRA CLUB, SIERRA CLUB BOOKS, and Sierra Club design logos are registered trademarks of the Sierra Club.

Originally published in hardcover by Sierra Club Books in 1999.

Design by Caroline Cunningham

Library of Congress Cataloging-in-Publication Data
Bangs, Richard
    The lost river: a memoir of life, death, and transformation on
wild water/by Richard Bangs.
    1. Bangs, Richard—Journeys.   2. Rafting (Sports)
3. Adventure and adventures—United States Biography.   I. Title.
GV780.B36   1999         796.1'21'092—dc21         99-13287
[B]

ISBN 1-57805-063-4

10  9  8  7  6  5  4  3  2  1

First Paperback Edition

To Lawrence Cutler Bangs, who caught the first accents of my tongue and joined in that innocent glee—who taught me to be a dragon seeker

# CONTENTS

# ACKNOWLEDGMENTS

The character, spirit, and course of a river are determined as much by the minerals it carries as by the rock and sediment through which it passes. So it is with this book. Spanning half a lifetime, the story has been made by people who have traveled with me, people who supported me, people who pointed the way. Many are mentioned within this book, and many more are not—it would take a catalog to give full tribute where it is deserved. So, instead, I have chosen to mention a few organizations and companies with whom I have worked, whose excellence and right-mindedness have mapped a good way to get downstream, and who were involved specifically in making the dream of the Tekeze Expedition come true.

If you are going to trek to the headwaters of great rivers nothing is as important as footwear, and I want to thank the Dexter Shoe Company, whose boots I have worn on many expeditions over the years. I want to thank Ex Officio for the best-designed adventure shirts in the world (those who work with me see me wearing them almost every day of the year). I want to thank Eagle Creek for the tough, yet smart, travel luggage, and The North Face for the quality sleeping bags, clothing, and tents. Thanks also to the Eastman Kodak Company, which supplied us with the DCS 460, the DCS 420, and the DC 50 digital cameras used on the Tekeze. Lufthansa Airlines and Ethiopian Airlines, who flew many of the members of the Tekeze Expedition to far-flung airports. Mountain Travel★SOBEK, the Adventure Company, which supported the expedition in every way. Cascade Designs for the comfortable air mattresses and thoroughly dry dry bags. Wing Inflatables for the self-bailing rafts that kept us upright. Turner Original Productions, who produced the documentary film version of this book. Camera World of Oregon who supplied Fuji and Kodak film. The Coleman Company who provided stoves and lanterns for the expedition. Extrasport, Inc., who supplied the life vests that kept bodies and spirits afloat. Intégral Peripherals' whose Viper 340 PC Card hard drives were used in the high-end Kodak digital cameras, including the DCS 460 and DCS 420. The Leatherman Tool Group, Inc., who supplied each expedition member with pliers, knife, file, screwdrivers, and more, all in a compact, stainless steel unit called the Pocket Survival Tool. Magellan Systems, who supplied our Global Positioning System (GPS) receivers so we always sort of knew where we were. Pelican Products, Inc., who supplied our technologically advanced flashlights and tough, watertight equipment protector cases. Prima International, which supplied the PCMCIA Type II cards upon which we were able to store our digital images. Play Incorporated, which supplied us with the Snappy Video Snapshot that allowed capturing video images and porting them to our computers. Toshiba, who supplied the field laptops that kept on tickin'. Teva Sandals, the longtime innovator in the adventure sport sandal market. Wild and Scenic River Tours of Seattle, who helped in training missions for the Tekeze. The International Rivers Network in Berkeley, California, is the organization that will lead the charge to save the Tekeze when the inevitable dams are being financed. The Sierra Club, for whom this is my third book, will be there as well. And last, the Microsoft Corporation and Expedia.com, the on-line travel service, who published the pioneering web magazine *Mungo Park* that covered the Tekeze Expedition live via the Internet and the World Wide Web.

# PREFACE

My father never really cared much for the outdoors. He preferred a cozy chair and a fat book, a night at the movies, maybe a ball game on TV, certainly restaurant food. But one weekend when I was a small boy he took me camping. I don't remember where he took me, but it was by a river, a swift-flowing stream, clear and crisp. I have a faint memory now that my dad had a difficult time setting up the tent, but somehow worked it out and he was proud of the task. With some soda pop and our fishing poles, we went down to the river to have one of those seminal father-son bonding experiences.

The air told me first that we were someplace special. It whooshed, delivering the cool message of a fast river on a hot summer day. Then a muffled sound came from behind, back at camp, and we turned around and could see through the trees that the tent had collapsed. My dad said something under his breath and started up the hill, then turned back to me and said, "Don't go in the river!"

They were the wrong words.

At first I put my hand in the water to swish it around and was fascinated by the vitality, the power that coursed through my arm, into my chest, and up into my brain. I looked in the middle of the stream, where tiny waves burst into a million gems and then disappeared. It was magic, pure magic. I stepped into the river to my waist and felt the water wrap around and hug me and then tug at me like a dog pulling a blanket. Another step and the water reached my chest and pulled me down wholly into its vigorous embrace. I was being washed downstream.

Effortlessly, the current was carrying me away from confinement, toward new and unknown adventures. I looked down and watched as a color wheel of pebbles passed beneath me like a cascade of hard candy. After a few seconds I kicked my way to shore, perhaps a hundred yards downstream. When I crawled back to land I had changed. My little trip down the river had been the most exhilarating experience of my life. I felt charged with energy, giddy, cleansed, and fresh, more alive than I could remember. I practically skipped back to the fishing poles and sat down with a whole new attitude, and a secret.

When my father came back, he never noticed anything different. And I didn't volunteer anything. The August sun had dried my shorts and hair, and I was holding my pole as though it had grown as an extension of my arm since he left. Only my smile was different—larger, knowing. I grew in that little trip like corn in the night.

We didn't catch any fish that day, but I caught something that would stay with me for years: a knowledge that the clearest way into the universe is off the path, upside down, and downstream. . . .

# THE
# LOST
# RIVER

CHAPTER 1

# RETURN TO EDEN

"I want this adventure that is the context of my life to go on without end."
—Simone de Beauvoir

*September 1996*

Stepping from the tarmac into the terminal is like swallowing a time pill. The low-watt fluorescent lights, the cell-block architecture, the greetings with palms that slide like beadwork. Smells are the handmaidens of memory, and the edgy smell that is a mixture of eucalyptus and uric acid brings back a dizzying rush. These are sensations locked away with a twenty-three-year interregnum, unleased with the moist embrace of Africa.

There is such a collation of joy and fear. While the Bole Road from the airport looks exactly as it did when I first visited Africa, at the age of twenty-two, so much has happened in my life in the intervening years—and in all lives, especially in this *ancien régime.* To me it seems Ethiopia has been asleep all this time. I recognize posters, shops, restaurants, the Total petrol stations, the fluttering green, red, and yellow Ethiopian flags, the same rusted blue-and-white Fiat 1100-D taxis churning out black soot, and even, it seems, faces, the drawn faces of beggars, shoe shiners, ragged street children, as we wind into Addis Ababa—a city that has grown, despite the mass killings during the revolution, to some five million souls.

But memory palters with truth; differences cry out. Where once we would pass the odd Mercedes, the badge of a successful black marketer or minister, now there are shiny new Range Rovers (with 107 percent import duty) competing with donkeys, laden with twisted, multiform firewood and charcoal, on potholed roads. And beyond the pocked roads are the odd reminders of an era just ended, the quickly fading red stars and hammers and sickles, the distorted and defiled faces of Marx and Mengistu.

But with the rain that washed away a brutal time, there is also a palpable sense of hope and renewal. When I left Ethiopia at the start of the revolution in 1974, it was a scary moment; the country crouched in fear and despair. Now it's as though a heavy rock has rolled from the shoulders of the country, and it is crowing and stretching with relief. I wish my mood were as jubilant, but it has been tilted onto its darkest edge. Many thoughts have kept me restless over the last few days. The reports of record floods on the Nile in the Sudan and Egypt don't bode well. I'm here to attempt the first descent of the Tekeze River, a major tributary of the Nile, flowing into the hot plains of the Sudan downstream of Khartoum, past Elephantine and Luxor, past Abydos and Cairo, and finally into the Mediterranean, over 2,500 miles from source to sea. The great majority of the waters that feed the Nile proper come from the highlands of Ethiopia, a wrinkled tableland formed forty million years ago from massive volcanic eruptions. I'm also haunted by the news that my father is ill, undergoing a risky cranial subdermal hematoma operation as I'm preparing to risk my life for God knows why once again. He doesn't even know I'm here.

The Awash, the first river I ran in Ethiopia in 1973, was also in the news a few days ago. It is the drainage for Addis Ababa and adjacent to the Tekeze watershed. It, too, has been experiencing record floods—so much so that the Koka dam, built in 1960, the largest in Ethiopia, has been on the verge of bursting. In fact, the military helicopter we were to charter is now unavailable, as it is in service rescuing some of the twenty thousand flood victims in the town of Wonji, southeast of here. What does this mean for the Tekeze? Well, despite the creeping thought that this exploration somehow seems frivolous in the wake of natural disaster, it also speaks of dangers I don't want to face again. I have already knelt at the altar of mischance one too many times.

It was during the second season of my first year in Africa that I tackled a river in flood, the Baro, another tributary of the Nile, and it was the wrong spate at the wrong time. Everything went horribly wrong on this river, too strong for even the best boaters, in peak condition, in prime time. We had no business being there, and I can't help but wonder if we have any business here, especially in older bodies, minds that may know too much, baggage that is stained with blood.

Then there is George Fuller, the carmine-haired epidemiologist and physician I met in Addis in 1973, who became a lifelong friend. Together we authored first descents of rivers in Sumatra, New Guinea, and Alaska. We trekked across the Amazon, climbed Krakatau and other active volcanoes of Java, sailed the coast of Antarctica. But on the eve of departure for this exercise, George called to say he was bowing out. He had many good reasons: he had crushed his foot in a recent car accident and couldn't walk any distance; he could make some good money staying in California and working his shift at the emergency room; he could tend his garden.

But one reason chilled me. George said he had a bad premonition about this expedition. He mumbled that the closest he ever came to death was near the Tekeze, down by the Sudanese border, below our proposed take-out, when a group of machine-gun-wielding soldiers stopped him on a bridge after dark. He believes he was within seconds of being split apart by gunfire, in a pestilential place he described as god-awful. He also revealed to me he had had similar premonitions before the Baro expedition, and again before the Blue Nile, the river that will forever in my mind evoke the death of a friend, and of a part of me.

After hours of phone calls, George relented and promised to join the trip, but only "out of friendship," and under the condition that he expressly not be the trip doctor. "I don't want to be attending to every cut and scratch, every loose bowel movement." I was relieved he recanted, but my own qualms were swarming. I had given George every argument I could muster as to why his atavistic fears were unfounded, yet as I spun them out, my own doubts crawled in.

Now, at last, some of the crew who survived our early SOBEK expeditions are back in Ethiopia: George Fuller, Bart Henderson, Jim Slade, and myself, and we're joined by a film team from Turner Original Productions, and by a squad from *Mungo Park,* Microsoft's on-line travel magazine. The media want to document our reunion attempt to explore the Tekeze River, and see if we are up to the task after all these years. Not so secretly, they are hoping for some blood.

Bart and I spend the day visiting old haunts: the patisserie off the piazza where we would nosh sweet cakes and sip cappuccino (my first exposure to exotic coffee, long before Starbucks was even a bean of a concept) and plot our next expeditions; the compound in the red-light district I rented for $50 a month where ten of us would sprawl on the cement floor and sort our expedition gear; the Filowa hot mineral baths, where we would soak for hours in tiled tubs after a fortnight or more in the bush. All were exactly as when we left, as if preserved in aspic. And despite my pall of gloom, I can't squelch a rising sense of excitement, a quickening of the pulse as memories return. Moments of shared discovery in a special time echo, and the realization that a long-held dream, to run through this deep, deep canyon on its racing river, may be on the verge of really happening.

I've heard the reasons not to go forward a hundred times. There are a thousand sane, intelligent, and well-articulated grounds for not running an unrun river, for not climbing a peak, for not venturing into space, for not exploring, for not evolving. But then, what's the point? There is something downstream around the unseen bend that calls. It's been calling for twenty-three years, and I'm obliged and compelled and thrilled to answer. Even as the amanuensis of death on the river resoaks my soul and won't dry out, a dam breaks in my memory, and the flood of beginnings overwhelms.

CHAPTER 2

# WHITE MAGIC

"For every problem there is one solution which is simple, neat and wrong."
—H. L. Mencken

It's a singularly American rite of passage, reading Mark Twain's masterpiece, *The Adventures of Huckleberry Finn*. I was a junior at Walt Whitman High School in Bethesda, Maryland, in 1967, and the story of Huck and Jim and their raft trip down the Mississippi affected me in a way that Jay Gatsby and his silk shirts, or John Marcher and his figurative beast, or George Babbit's conformity, or even Natty Bumppo's "noble savage" ever would. Huck discovered adventure, beauty, self-reliance, peace, and true human values by rafting down the river. "It's lovely to live on a raft," Huck said, and I believed him. I wanted to raft a river.

I lived just a few miles from the Potomac, the "River of the Traders," as the seventeenth-century Indians who bartered tobacco and catfish near my house called it. One Sunday in May my father, at my urgings, reluctantly took me on a hike on the towpath of the Chesapeake and Ohio (C&O) canal up near Great Falls, fifteen miles above Washington where the broad river is squeezed through an obstacle course of massive boulders and in just a half mile roars downward some seventy-five feet.

Juno, our golden retriever, saw a squirrel and made a beeline down a tight path through a welter of vegetation. I followed, leaving my father on the towpath, and found myself on the edge of a two-hundred-foot-high cliff overlooking the Potomac as she swirled through Mather Gorge, a granite defile that was described at the turn of the century as "the Grand Canyon of the East."

The sight was dazzling, the fast currents spinning the reflecting light as though thousands of silver pinwheels were washing downstream. I was hypnotized, drawn toward the shimmering water, and I knew I had to get on that river.

Monday morning I announced to Miss Hammond, my English teacher, I wanted to build a raft and journey down the Potomac just like Huckleberry Finn. She said fine, as long as I didn't miss any school. The three-day Memorial Day weekend was coming up, so I thought that would be the chance. I recruited my camping friends John Yost, Ricky Vierbuchen, and John Kramer. John Yost was something of a prodigy, two years younger than the rest of us, having skipped two grades before reaching high school. He was in the German and French Honor Societies, a National Merit semifinalist, a Mathlete, and on the varsity soccer team and in the Mountaineering Club. He was also on the in-school publicity committee. I had met John at the Bethesda River Bowl, where I accused him of cheating when I looked at the score sheet he was handling and saw that some of my strikes and spares had disappeared. He made a nervous, high-pitched laugh and put the points back, and we became friends. John Kramer was a dancer, a member of National Thespians, the swim team, and the president of the Mountaineering Club. He was a fluid athlete, nimble and long-muscled as a cat, with a soul capable of boundless verve. Kramer took me caving and showed me the joys of the underground. Ricky Vierbuchen was taller, stronger, and more studious than anyone in our circle, also a member of the Mountaineering Club, as well as the cross-country ski team, but he shared a glee for the mischievous. Together we pranked through high school, including running a fake candidate for student body president (J. H. Plumb . . . he came in a respectable third), and taking off on various outdoor adventures.

For the Huck Finn raft redux I also brought in friends Dave Nurney, Fred Higgins, and Steve Hatleberg, and together we started gathering the equipment we'd need to build our raft and float the Potomac. None of us had ever been in a kayak or canoe, let alone a raft. We picked out an eight-mile run through Mather Gorge, one that expert kayakers had been running for years. Though, as we talked to the experts, including a scuba rescue team who routinely retrieved drowned bodies from the river, the prognosis was we wouldn't make it through in a log raft; the rapids were too treacherous.

Word of our expedition spread through the student body, and the editor of the *Black and White,* the school newspaper, Dan Reifsnyder, approached me for the exclusive story. At seventeen Dan was already hard-boiled, and he smelled disaster in my little plan. He made no pretense of his looking for blood, or a spectacular failure, to fill column space in an upcoming issue. I said I was happy to give him the story, but I was certain he'd be disappointed: we planned to make it down the river on time, and intact.

On Friday afternoon we all set up camp not far below Great Falls and, with axes, started cutting the timber we needed. We rolled the logs to our assembly spot down by the river and began binding them with cross pieces and eight-inch gutter nails.

Our raft was about half finished when a stentorian voice echoed across the canyon. "Have you ever messed with a German shepherd?" It was a park ranger, calling from atop a palisade of gneiss on the Virginia side, a huge German shepherd at his side. "You're on national park land. You can't cut down trees, you can't build a raft, and you can't camp. Now get outta there before I come get ya."

It was the end of our dream trip. We slowly packed up and trudged back to the parking lot. On the drive out we passed a ranger vehicle coming in with a dog in the back, and guessed it was our friend with the German shepherd.

We still had two days of the Memorial Day weekend left and couldn't go back home; not with everyone expecting us to have at least attempted our raft expedition. So, we headed for Bear Island, a popular camping spot below Mather Gorge, and holed up there for the rest of the long weekend, swimming, fishing, and trying to forget our failure.

Monday night we were all back at my house cleaning the camping gear when the phone rang. It was Dan Reifsnyder, and he wanted the scoop on our expedition.

I put my hand over the receiver and talked to our team. "Let's tell him we did it," I proposed with a grin. "We can't," Steve Hatleberg countered. "It's not the Christian thing to do." In *The Adventures of Huckleberry Finn,* Huck had to battle with his conscience, because according to the morality of society and the church, he should have reported Jim, whom he had come to love as a brother, as a runaway slave. His final decision in Jim's favor was concluded with his famous reflection, "All right, then. I'll go to hell!" I looked around at our group, then back at Steve, and said, "All right, then. I'll go to hell!" and put the receiver to my mouth and started to tell Dan about our raft trip.

On June 9, the article appeared, titled "Rapids Capsize Craft; Raftsmen Score First." It went on to say, "The raft had to be scrapped in the middle of Yellow Rapids. 'We scrambled for the inner tubes and kept going,' boasted junior Richard Bangs. 'You wondered if you were going to live.' 'Man, was I scared.' 'It was out of sight, like an LSD trip.' These were just a few of the emotions described by the group, all of whom made the entire passage alive."

The article gave us some notoriety and inspired us to form the Raft Club, which was the seed from which would sprout SOBEK, the international rafting and adventure travel company I would later cofound. Steve Hatleberg couldn't live with our secret, though, and one day told Dan the full and true story. To Dan's credit, he never pursued it in print, but whenever I passed him in the hall he gave me that drop-dead stare editors around the world have mastered. And, it made me want to make good on the Potomac.

It was still early summer when I saw an ad on the bulletin board at the grocery store. It told of a seventeen-and-a-half-foot fiberglass Old Town canoe for sale, for $150. I called all the members of the Raft Club and asked if anyone would go in with me on halves. Ricky Vierbuchen had the $75, so we bought the canoe, painted R&R on the stern (we flipped a coin for top billing), and toted our new toy down to Bear Island. We launched and headed upstream, toward the crystalline mouth of Mather Gorge.

We were awkward paddlers and the canoe crankled through the water as though drunk. We bobbed and weaved upstream and slowly picked up some proficiency as we angled toward Difficult Run Rapids, marking the end of the gorge. The white-breasted water got faster as we got closer, and my blood accelerated correspondingly.

This was exciting. Then we were in the roostertails of the rapids, being flung up and down on a dizzy aquatic seesaw, paddling with all our strength. "Let's go higher," I screamed over the rapid's roar, and we sunk our blades deeper and lunged forward. Then the bow snapped to its side, abruptly capsizing the canoe, and precipitating us into the spume. We'd been christened as river runners.

〰〰〰

Ricky and I spent all our free time the summers of 1967 and 1968 in our blue canoe, exploring new routes, refining techniques, scoring the bottom of our boat with a matrix of scratches and dents. We made many of the classic runs, including the coup de grâce run of the Potomac beginning at the base of the Great Falls, where the Potomac spectacularly drops over the edge of the continental bedrock onto the sedimentary soil of the coastal plain.

Above Great Falls the river stretches to a half mile in width; below it pinches into the sixty-foot-wide Mather Gorge, where we would negotiate through S-Turn Rapids, Rocky Island Rapids, Wet Bottom Chute, and past the ancient rocks that formed the exit gate to the canyon. We would continue downstream on a wider, but no less magnificent river, through Yellow Rapids and Stubblefield Falls, underneath the Cabin John Bridge carrying the Capital Beltway (I-495) past the Carderock Picnic Area, where climbers crawl like flies on impossible faces, down to Sycamore Island and the Brookmont dam. Constructed in the 1950s for the city water supply with no thought for the safety of boaters, the deceptively innocuous weir is a death trap for upset paddlers, with a perpetual hydraulic that, like a black hole with stray light, sucks in boats and bodies, never to let them go. A rust-spotted sign adjacent to the pumping station stated that an average of seven people a year drowned in this area. Its nickname was "the Drowning Machine." Below Brookmont was the most hair-raising mile of navigable whitewater along the entire 383-mile course of the Potomac, culminating in the explosive Little Falls, in which the entire river is funneled from parking-lot width to a Grand Prix raceway, then spectacularly split in two by a sharp, granite-slab island. It was here Captain John Smith, in his search for the elusive Northwest Passage, was stopped in his upriver journey in 1608. Little Falls is the last whitewater, or the first, depending on which way you're traveling, on the Potomac. In the massive flood of 1936 the velocity of the water was recorded as the fastest ever in nature. Just below is Chain Bridge. A short ways beyond the river becomes tidewater, and the nation's capital begins to spread its concrete tentacles along the banks.

Ricky and I never canoed the Little Falls section; it was beyond our abilities. But, that didn't mean we couldn't run it. With the money I'd saved working as a carhop at the local Kentucky Fried Chicken outlet, I purchased a yellow Taiwanese-made four-man raft from Sunny's Surplus. And with it we paddled out to Snake Island, across from the Brookmont pumping station, and slipped over the killer weir where we thought the one clear passage, down a fish ladder, was supposed to be. But we missed and were suddenly in the backwashing hydraulic, capsized, bouncing about in the aerated water along with beach balls, chunks of

Styrofoam cooler, rubber sandals, branches, and other debris stuck in the eternal washing machine. I remembered reading the only way to escape a strong recirculating hydraulic was to abandon one's life jacket, and dive beneath the surface, where the water makes its deep exit. But I couldn't bring myself to take off my flotation, which was propping my mouth just above the terrible soapy froth. I looked over to Ricky, who was choking from water splashed into his throat. "Swim toward the island," I yelled to Ricky above the weir's gargling. And though it was slow going, we found it possible to dog-paddle perpendicular to the current, along the hydraulic line, back toward Snake Island. I towed our little yellow raft, and after several scary minutes we reached the edge of the island, where a chute emptied water in a straight shot downstream. We were out and into the next section, where the water accelerated as the river narrowed, and the waves grew thicker with each stroke.

Then the final pitch presented itself, with the river piling up onto the anvil-shaped island, spilling off either side into huge, impermeable, complex rapids. We blasted straight down the middle, plowed into the saber-toothed island, spun backward, then collapsed over the falls on the Virginia side, the worst side. The first drop catapulted Ricky into the air. When he fell back into the bilge, the floor of the raft peeled back like a sardine can, depositing Ricky into the depths. I continued to paddle alone, my feet dragging in the current where the floor had been, my neck spinning looking for signs of Ricky. The roar of the rapid muffled as I strained to hear Ricky's cry. Hours later, or so the seconds seemed, Ricky resurfaced fifty yards downstream, slick as an eel, all smiles. Climbing back on board, we drove our paddles deep to our take-out at Chain Bridge on the Virginia side, where my mother was waiting with the 1966 Oldsmobile and a prayer. My father had stayed home to read.

I discovered the lack of floor didn't make much difference in the tiny Taiwanese boat, and continued to use it for runs down Little Falls the following weeks with the various members of the Raft Club, even Steve Hatleberg, who thought he saw God during one capsize. For us it was a grand thrill in a suburban existence conspicuously short of such.

〜〜〜

I fell in love with the Potomac that summer and wanted to know everything about her—every dimple, every curve, where she came from, and where she was going. I began to study her serpentine mysteries in my free time. She trickles forth at an altitude of 3,140 feet just downhill from the crest of Backbone Mountain in a deep fold of the Allegheny Mountains in West Virginia. There she seeps from a spring beneath a chunk of rock, called the Fairfax Stone after the colonial landowner Lord Fairfax. The fledgling river soon becomes the Maryland–West Virginia border, loops back and forth around Appalachian ridges in the region of the Paw Paw bends, and then bursts through the Blue Ridge Mountains at Harpers Ferry, where she is joined by the Shenandoah. Here the plunging slopes and roiling rapids make "perhaps one of the most stupendous scenes in nature," Thomas Jefferson wrote, "worth a voyage across the Atlantic." Continuing her journey, the Potomac levels off, now alive with geese and eagles, oysters and shad. She eventually becomes a seven-mile tidal giant, easing majestically into Chesapeake Bay as she stretches between the Maryland and Virginia shores.

As summer faded to fall the frequency of our trips decreased, because of the cooler weather, school commitments, and a new diversion: women. Ricky and I were both taken by a tall blonde named Arlene Wergen. The air surged with the dull clacking sound of soft, young antlers in nervous ritual combat. Since he shared homeroom and some classes with her, Ricky had the advantage, and he exploited it. He took Arlene caving, camping, and bought her an expensive friendship ring. I had an ace up my sleeve, however . . . the river. I just had to wait for the right moment.

〰〰

That moment came mid-December. We were in the midst of an unseasonable heat wave, and the weatherman said the upcoming weekend would be warm enough for outdoor activities. I asked Arlene if she'd like to go canoeing.

I picked out a run I had always wanted to do, a stretch beginning at Bloomery, West Virginia, on the Shenandoah, running to the confluence with the Potomac, and continuing below Harpers Ferry, the place where John Brown's body lies a-molderin' in the grave. The ten-mile run was supposed to be beautiful, with some challenging rapids and good camping, all-important ingredients in what I perceived to be an important weekend.

Saturday morning was clear and crisp as we loaded the blue canoe and headed downriver through a navelike arch of sycamores and silver maples. The river here had sawed away at the mountains as they rose up beneath it, imbedding itself 1,200 feet or more in the Blue Ridge. I was wearing my new letter jacket, which I had been awarded for the dubious honor of managing the soccer team. Still, it was a badge, and I wore it proudly with hopes it would impress Arlene. It was a beautiful day, brimming with a sense of adventure and romance, and I could tell Arlene shared the thrill of a live vessel beneath us sliding silently over brawling water. An ad for Canadian Club had been running that fall showing a couple canoeing the rapids. The woman in the bow looked very much like Arlene, and though I bore no resemblance, I felt like the man in the stern in that ad.

As we eased our way down the river the sun's rays reflected off water the color of copper, and I started to get warm. I took off my letter jacket and bundled it in front of my knees. At lunch we pulled over beneath a spreading willow, and I prepared a sumptuous repast with Pouilly-Fuissé and Brie and French bread. As we took our first bites, a pint-sized bark came from behind, and a little puppy bounded into our picnic. He was a mongrel, but with the biggest brown eyes I'd ever seen, and a wiggly, irresistible appeal for affection. For Arlene it was puppy love at first sight. She fed the little mutt all of her meal, and then some of mine, and then asked if we could bring him along. "But he must belong to somebody," I protested. "Please go check," she implored, and I got up to make a search. Sure enough I could find no evidence of owners within a half mile of our mooring and came to the conclusion that the puppy was, indeed, hopelessly lost. So we perched the puppy on my letter jacket, and continued downriver.

As the day wore on, it began to cloud and the temperature dropped. The puppy was asleep, so I didn't bother to put on my letter jacket, but instead paddled harder to keep warm. By late afternoon we approached the river-wide ledge of Bull Falls, which the guidebook rated as difficult, but doable, and recommended a portage for less-than-expert boaters. Checking my watch I saw we were at least an hour behind schedule; the puppy incident had taken up precious time. The guidebook said the portage around Bull Falls took an hour, an hour we didn't have on a short, midwinter day. If we portaged, we'd have to paddle the final miles after dark, a dangerous proposition in the cold of December.

And, after a full summer of canoeing I figured I was more than less-than-expert and could make the run. So, we rammed ahead into Bull Falls. The entry was perfect, gliding between the boulders as though on a track, slipping down the drop as though by design. At the bottom I held the canoe paddle above my head and screamed, "We made it!" But I was a bit premature. The tail waves at the bottom of the rapid continued to wash over the bow of the canoe, and the boat filled with turbid river water. By the time we reached the last wave, we were swamped, and the canoe phlegmatically rolled over, dispatching us into the icy river. The current was swift here, and the cold punched my breath away. With one hand I hung onto the canoe; with the other I tried to paddle, all the while yelling for Arlene to swim to shore. Then I saw my letter jacket surface a few feet away. The jacket meant the world to me, so I started paddling toward it. Then, a feeble yelp came from the opposite direction. The puppy was spinning in an area of circling water with a center like an inverted shield-boss: a strong, sucking eddy. For a quick second I weighed options. I could retrieve only one. I went for the puppy.

A few hundred yards downstream I managed to grapple the canoe to shore, the puppy still held above my head with my free hand. Arlene was there, shivering violently, yet she gave the puppy a hug that would crush a bear.

Both Arlene and I had lost our paddles in the capsize, though I had one spare strapped to the center thwart. I emptied the canoe, turned it over, and tried to tell Arlene to get back in . . . but my speech was slurred; I could barely form words. I was becoming hypothermic. So was Arlene. I knew we couldn't stop here—we had nothing dry, it was getting dark. We'd die if we stayed. I pressed Arlene into the bow of the canoe, and she crouched over the trembling puppy, while I pushed us off. I had just the one paddle, but I dug like an antbear. The sun dipped behind the trees, and a chilling wind blew up the valley, filling it with dusk. Barely able to see the rocks, I propelled us into the last rapids, the mile-long Staircase. We scraped and bumped and banged every few seconds, but somehow emerged in one piece at the Route 340 bridge below Harpers Ferry, where my car awaited.

My plans for a romantic campout were scrapped that night. Rather than a hero, I was a bungler who almost cost us our lives, and worse, the life of the puppy, who won the contest for Arlene's heart and became her constant companion.

〰〰

Still, I remained hung up on Arlene, as did Ricky. But it was unrequited love. As the school year wound down Arlene started dating a Young Republican, a radical act in the Vietnam era. When Ricky and I independently asked Arlene to the senior prom, she turned us both down for the right-wing radical.

We'd been left high and dry. Neither of us found alternative dates for the most socially significant event of a teenager's life. So, we turned to each other and said, "Let's go run a river."

We picked the Smoke Hole Canyon section of the South Branch of the Potomac in West Virginia for two reasons: we'd never done it before, and it was as far away from the prom as we could get and still be on our favorite river. It was a section described by George Washington as "two ledges of Mountain Impassable running side by side together for above 7 or 8 miles and ye River down between them." So, as the senior class was slipping into crinoline and tuxedos, we were fitting our knee pads and kapok life jackets. And as carnations were being exchanged, we were trading strokes on the upper Potomac. Mockingbirds called from the woods cathedral through which we passed, hardly giving us solace. It was springtime, and the delicate pink blossoms of the laurel and the notched white flowers of the dogwood dappled the greening banks. We moved to music, but not the Motown our peers were enjoying, rather the haunting whistle of the lordly cardinal. The river here was shallow, stinging cold from the spring runoff. Some miles below our launch we struck a moss-encrusted rock, jutting out into the current like some miniature Lorelei. The siren rock punched a hole the size of my fist into our fiberglass hull.

We didn't have the materials or the time to properly repair the hole in our boat, so we stuffed the puncture with spare clothing and continued downstream. It was slow going. We'd paddle ten minutes, then pull over the same to bail. When we emptied the canoe at camp at twilight we discovered our neoprene duffel bag had not been waterproof; that all our gear, sleeping bags, tents, and food had been soaked. We dragged everything up a knoll of weathered limestone overlooking the Potomac, erected the wet tent, and lay the rest of our effects out to dry in the waning minutes of daylight. It was quickly evident our attempts to dry the gear by natural means would not work, and that it was to be a nippy night. We had several packs of matches, but they were all saturated and wouldn't light. We gathered wood and, with our knives, trimmed paper-thin shavings that would light at the least spark. But we went through several packs of matches and couldn't get the spark. With nightfall the air became brittle, and we jumped up and down, slapping our sides, to keep warm. Our classmates were doing the Jerk in the Whitman gym, and we felt like the dance as we flapped in the dark. But it wasn't working, and I knew we couldn't do the Freddy all night. We needed to build a fire, as much as Jack London ever did.

If we didn't, we could perish, and we both knew it.

Then Ricky literally got a bright idea. The flashlight still worked, so why not unscrew the lens covering the bulb and put the remaining matches inside the glass, against the filament bulb, where they could dry from the heat of the light? We had five matches left, and inside they went. The flashlight remained on for twenty minutes as we continued our jumping jacks; then it started to fade. The flashlight was going dead. We unscrewed the top, took out the matches, and tried to light the first one. In my haste I tore off the head of the match. The second actually lit, but before I could touch it to the kindling it blew out in the cold wind. I cupped my hand around the third as I struck. It spat to life, and as I touched it to the shavings, the fire took. In minutes we had a bonfire. We curled our backs to a log and held up our clothes and sleeping bags to dry. All night we continued to feed the fire and bathe in its warmth, occasionally looking down the hill at the Potomac meandering in the moonlight, in curves that somehow looked like Arlene's.

As with our classmates, that was a special night, one filled with danger and promise, with rites of passage, with friendship and warmth. The Potomac had dealt some blows since our first assignation, but she had given me some of the most exciting, most exquisite moments of my existence. On that prom night, high on a limestone ridge, I realized how much I loved the river, deeply, wholly, and that I had found a consort for life. I discovered, as Tom Sawyer finally said to Huckleberry Finn, that all I really wanted to do was "have adventures plumb to the mouth of the river." On that prom night I lost and found a certain innocence, and readied for the adventures of tomorrow, the great adventures cached just around the next bend, just out of sight, on the river.

What I didn't know in the summer of 1968 was that just as I was charting the river road for my life, another man on the other side of the world, a young man named Ian Macleod was about to lose his life to the Blue Nile of Ethiopia. The loss would be one among many on the rivers of Ethiopia, including ones that would jolt my life.

CHAPTER 3

# TIME BANDITS

"Any life, no matter how long and complex it may be, is made up of a single moment—the moment in which a man finds out, once and for all, who he is."

—Jorge Luis Borges

Afloat down the Colorado through the Grand Canyon is a stark descent through light and density and time. From the soft sandstones and flamingo limestones of the Kaibab Plateau, exposed at river level at Lees Ferry, the Colorado cuts through rock that progressively ages, hardens, and darkens. It plunges through the eons and the strata, through shales, conglomerates, and basalts, residues of primordial seas and cataclysmic eruptions and upheavals. Until, at last, in the Inner Gorge, in the deepest corridor of the canyon, the river washes against the oldest, blackest, and hardest rock of all: Vishnu schist. Dark as Dante's Inferno, almost two billion years old, the rock is a relic of a time when the earth's molten center disturbed its surface, imposing unfathomable heat and pressure that recrystallized sediments into new minerals. So dark it seems to swallow light, Vishnu schist is named for the Hindu deity worshiped as the protector, a syncretic personality composed of many lesser cult figures and associated with the sun. The rock, like depictions of the god, is darkskinned and noble. From sandstone to schist, the voyage down the Colorado is one of dramatic change, a metamorphic journey. And like the peels of stone that compose the walls, the people who pass through the Grand Canyon change with each mile. They grow darker, harder, older. And some make the apotheosis to Vishnu himself.

I cozened my way onto the Colorado. Like any eighteen-year-old, I was searching for the fantasy summer job during college, and when I learned people could get paid to raft tourists down the Colorado, I knew that was for me, my lack of big-water boating notwithstanding. So, I drew up a résumé featuring my experience on the Potomac, Shenandoah, and other Eastern Seaboard rivers, but also listing some of the classic western rivers as intimates, although I had never seen them beyond a book or a slide show. My cover letter was as colorful a piece of creative sophistry as ever penned: rafted twenty-two major rivers, guided professionally for three years, knew all the ropes (when, in fact, I couldn't even tie a decent bowline).

In 1968 the rafting business was barely that, but rapid growth was just around the corner. Bobby Kennedy had floated the Colorado with Hatch River Expeditions, the company to which I applied, and through the wizardry of Press Secretary Pierre Salinger, the story was a worldwide pickup. Between 1869, when John Wesley Powell made his exploratory voyage, and 1949, a grand total of one hundred people had floated through the Grand Canyon. By 1965 some 547 people had rafted the Colorado; in the summer of 1972 the numbers had swelled to 16,432, and the Park Service stepped in and froze the use at that level. But in the late 1960s and early 1970s the wave of popularity was becoming tidal, and the few concessionaires servicing the budding industry had to find guides to meet the growing demand. My timing couldn't have been better, and Ted Hatch, the largest outfitter on the Colorado, hired me for the following season the day he received my missive. It was Halloween, 1968. I encouraged John Yost, who had become my best friend, to apply as well, but he had an even sexier opportunity. His father was a Foreign Service officer at the State Department and was just posted to Ethiopia as DCM (deputy chief of mission, or vice ambassador). So, while I was to go rafting, John was going to visit his parents in Africa, at the U.S. government's expense, and explore exotic landscapes. I knew nothing whatsoever about Ethiopia, but asked John to look around and see if there might be any rivers worth rafting.

Six months later I was circling over the Glen Canyon Dam, the 710-foot-high plug that creates the 186-mile-long Lake Powell, before we began our descent into Page, Arizona, a town erected in the red dust of nothingness to accommodate dam workers. Within minutes I was standing in the parking lot of the Page Boy Motel, where I met Ted Hatch, scion to rafting royalty (his father, Bus, had pioneered many rafting runs in Utah and Colorado in the 1930s and 1940s). Ted extended a puffy, freckled hand in greeting, but he couldn't mask his disappointment as my skinny hand met his. Here he had hired a gangly, pale Atlantic Seaboarder who appeared as guidelike as Ichabod Crane. But he rolled with it.

"You're swamping tomorrow's trip. We have the Four Corners Geological Society, one hundred ten people, ten rafts. Drive the winch truck down to the ferry as soon as you change out of that blazer and try and help the boatmen rig. Welcome aboard, kid. You'll be a good swamper."

"Ahhh, one question, Mr. Hatch."

"Call me Ted. Now, what's your question?"

"What's a swamper?"

Ted reared his Cabbage Patch doll head in laughter before explaining. "You dig the toilet hole at camp, help the boatmen cook, wash the dishes, bail the rafts. And assist the guides in every way. Now, get on it."

He handed me the keys and pointed to the truck. When I sidled into the cab, I knew I was in trouble—it was a stick shift. I'd grown up in an automatic suburb. I'd never even been in a manual. I studied the diagram on the knob.

Holding my breath, I turned the key. It hummed. Fine. Toeing the clutch, I maneuvered the stick to first position and the truck eased forward. Beautiful. I finessed across the parking lot, then headed down the motel driveway, a wave of pride washing over me. I slipped into second. No problem. Then, a thunderclap and plastic shrapnel sprayed the windshield as the truck jerked to a halt and stalled. Leaping from the cab, I ran for cover, finally looking back to survey the scene. I had driven the winch, which stood a good five feet above the truck roof, smack into the middle of the Page Boy Motel sign hanging above the driveway. The motel owner, with Hatch in tow, bolted to my side, issuing obscenities at floodgate rate.

"Can you take it out of my pay?" I meekly asked my new boss.

"Forget it, kid. I'll cover it. But don't screw up again."

That was the beginning of a miraculous metamorphosis from sandstone to schist, boy to boatman, river ingenue to river god. And it took its toll.

Somehow I managed to negotiate the truck down the fifty-mile route to Lees Ferry. One of the only access sites for the length of the canyon, it was named for John Doyle Lee, a Mormon fugitive who had ferried passersby across the river, after being implicated in the Mountain

Meadow massacre of 1857 in which 123 non-Mormon pioneers were mysteriously murdered in southwest Utah. Lee was one of the first known non-Indians to find a new identity here, far from the persecution of Salt Lake City and civilization. Or so he thought. He was tracked down and arrested in 1874, apparently a scapegoat for the massacre, and executed in 1877. Perhaps progenitor to the waves of river guides who would come a century later, Lee was a man who had found his place in the sun on the river and was finally eclipsed because of it. He was also the Anglo embodiment of the fate of hundreds of Native Americans over the centuries—Havasupai, Hopi, Hualapai, Navajo, and Paiute—who had sought sanctuary and new lives in the rarified environs of the Grand Canyon, far from rival tribes, conquistadors, marauding white settlers, and Colonel Kit Carson.

Lees Ferry is now designated Mile Zero of the 277-mile Grand Canyon experience, launching pad for all river trips. It was here, in April of 1969, I took my assigned spot on the pontoon raft and held on tight as we pushed into the Kool-Aid green that passes for the Colorado, so colored since the silt settles out in the reservoir 15.5 miles upstream and the remaining microplankton refract their dominate hue. In the first mile I spun my head around frantically, taking in a view as otherworldly as a landscape out of a Frank Herbert novel.

As we passed into the buff-colored, cross-bedded cliffs of the Coconino sandstone and into the gates of Marble Canyon (not yet officially part of the Grand Canyon; that would come in 1975), propelled by a 20-hp Mercury outboard attached to the orange transom of our baloney boat, I desperately gripped a line, fearful that if I let go I'd be flung back to reality. We slipped into the soft red-and-maroon walls known as Hermit shale, clifftops soaring two thousand feet on either side. The din of a rapid, sonorous and deep in timbre, thickened as we eased toward Badger Creek, named for the mammal shot by Mormon explorer Jacob Hamblin.

This was thrilling. After six months of anticipation, of poring over picture books, I was on the lip of a major rapid of the Colorado. Glancing to the stern, where Dave Bledsoe controlled the tiller, I saw nonchalance unrivaled, a face fairly dancing with the aplomb of a centurion. As we slid down the coconut-butter tongue into the yaw of Badger Rapid, the crisp 47-degree water slapped me, and the pontoon pranced like a dolphin in flight. It was over in ten seconds and we pulled to shore to set up camp.

As we went about our tasks, erecting tables, filling buckets, clearing the beach of tamarisk (a loathsome weedlike tree encroaching on the beaches since the dam closed its gates in 1964, gates that denied the annual spring floods that once washed away such nonsense), Dave Bledsoe made a discovery—there were no paper plates. His veneer of pluck seemed to crack ever so slightly as he rifled the commissary boxes for a second look. "This is terrible," his words floated up the walls. "How can we serve one hundred and ten geologists without plates? We need plates."

Seeing we were camped at the mouth of a tributary canyon (Jackass Creek), I asked Dave if it exited to a road, and if so, then perhaps I could hike out and fetch some plates. He thought the canyon emerged somewhere near Highway 89A, connecting Flagstaff and the North Rim. He figured I could hike out, hitch to the Hatch warehouse near Lees Ferry, hire a jetboat capable of traveling down to the lip of Badger and back to the Ferry, and get the plates to camp by dinner. So, with canteen filled, I took off up the twisting side canyon.

After an hour's hiking, the mazelike canyon divided into passages of equal size. Flipping a mental coin, I took heads, the left route, and continued. It divided again and again and again. By the time I pulled myself up onto the flat plateau, I was completely disoriented, utterly lost. I could only guess the direction the highway passed. Kicking the red dust, passing a few Engelmann prickly pear cacti, I started east, away from the sun. But after half a mile I came to a sheer defile a hundred feet deep. Turning north, I came to another steep cut in the tableland. West, the same. It was Sartre-esque; no exit. Finally, toward the south, a spit of level ground streaked between two gorges, and led to the shimmering asphalt of 89A.

On the climb out I had ripped my shorts, leaving a slightly obscene appearance, which didn't help the hitchhiking cause. It also didn't help that even in rush hour this highway served less than a car every quarter hour. Despite my frantic waves, the first four autos, all crammed with vacationing families, passed me by. Salvation came in the fifth, a Navajo in a pickup who delivered me to the warehouse, where I found several cartons of paper plates. I tracked down Fred Burke, who operated the Park Service jetboat, and in the waning light, we surged downstream.

As we approached Badger, I caught a queer sight on the right bank. On the spit of a sandbar, backed by a vertical limestone wall, a solitary man was hysterically waving his overshorts at us. Fred spun the boat around and picked up the marooned man, who was on a few inches of dry land that was disappearing as the river rose. This Daniel Defoe character was part of the Four Corners expedition. Several hours earlier when the group had stopped for lunch on what was then a broad beach, this Canyon Crusoe had decided to take a quick snooze behind a rock. He awoke hours later to find the cold Colorado nipping at his toes and the rest of the party gone. As one of the consequences of progress, the Colorado would rise and fall many vertical feet each day in an artificial tide created by the diurnal differences in electrical demands, flushing the four turbines that spin in the belly of one of the world's highest dams, Glen Canyon. In another hour, Crusoe would have had no place to stand, no place to go, save downstream, without a life jacket.

Reunited, just after soup, we passed out the plates in time for the salad and entrée. I was treated like a hero for my derring-do hike, and for the first time I had a sense of how it felt to be a river guide. The marooned client settled into the group little worse for wear, and I took my first repast in the canyon.

I remember little of the next few days. As is not uncommon to first timers on the river, I picked up a bug and spent much of my time heaving over the gunwales or in delirium, collapsed on the duffel as we caromed through rapids, swept past unconformities, synclines, and other geological anarchy. At trip's end, I expected to be fired. I thought I had been a lousy swamper—sick for the majority of the passage, sluggish in my chores, not used to the harsh sun and physically demanding days.

But Hatch, in a moment of leniency, kept me on. He assigned me to the boat-patching detail at Marble Canyon Lodge, a ramshackle motel near Navajo Bridge. For a month I lived the life of a desert rat, filling my days with Barge cement and neoprene patching material, and reading old adventure magazines like *Argosy* and *Saga*. Every few days another trip went out, and I stood aching at the Lees Ferry ramp, waving as the rafts dipped into the Paria Riffle just downstream. Out of boredom and desperation one afternoon, after uncovering a supply box filled with cartons of rotten eggs left from a previous trip, I drove down the Lees Ferry road and plastered each road sign with a battery of omelets. Waiting at road's end was John Chapman, the ranger, who promptly sent me retracing my yellow trail with wire brush and soap and water. It took me two days to clean the baked-on eggs off the metal signs.

Finally, miraculously, a trip was departing that was short on help, and Dave Bledsoe requested me. This was my big chance and I hustled at every turn. I watched Dave's every move; I hung on his every word. He was fatherly to me in a way my own had never been. Where my dad was cerebral and couldn't fix a broken widget, Dave was a doer and could take apart a Mercury outboard while floating through a rapid; while my dad was governed by a keen morality, Dave was expedient and bent the rules to get things done. While my father was a quiet soul, Dave was an artful storyteller. His lecture hall filled with stories of hermits such as Louis Boucher, who operated a copper mine from 1891 to 1912, and of prevaricators such as "Captain" John Hance, who claimed to have crossed the dense clouds from the South Rim to the North on snow-shoes. But the lesson that sunk in deepest was the history in the making, the story of river guides.

My ascension up the Hatch hierarchy was not mercurial. I swamped seven trips the summer of 1969—a record, I believe, before being made river guide. Some newcomers—Perry Owens, Jim Ernst—were piloting by their third trip. I wasn't disappointed, though. I loved the river. I lived for each trip and socked away my $20-per-day earnings while on the river.

At last, on my eighth descent, I was given my badge and my own boat to steer. I was a river guide. Now, peculiar things happened to me. My tan deepened, my chest filled out, my hair grew lighter and more lustrous. But beyond that, a heretofore unplumbed confidence surfaced and I found people reacting to me in an entirely different manner. At North-western, where I was attending undergraduate studies in winters, I was undistinguished academically, athletically, socially. I was painfully shy with women and had never dared venture alone into a bar. But, on the river, everything changed. I brandished the rudder through the rapids, affect-ing the stern, purposeful look I'd picked up from Bledsoe. I lectured eru-ditely about the likes of John Wesley Powell and other explorers, and about the deltaic sedimentary Hermit shale. I stirred Dutch ovens over the campfire like an outdoor Julia Child. People looked to me for guid-ance, wisdom, direction, political opinions, even sex.

My second year, the summer of 1970, I guided the president of MGM, a celebrated political journalist, the editor of the Chicago *Sun-Times,* writers from *Newsweek* and *The New York Times,* Broadway actors, television stars, successful professionals of every sort. I was in awe of these folks. I would never be able to speak with these people in the winter months, let alone eat, laugh, and play with them. But here, they were in awe of me, kowtowing, following my every direction, hanging on my every word. It was sobering, unbelievable. When the president of MGM sheepishly asked me to help him set up his tent (he couldn't figure it out), I felt like the roaring lion in the famous logo.

And this was happening to every other guide on the river, every coun-try-roughneck-cowboy-Vietnam-vet-farmhand who somehow back-eddied into this nouveau elite club. At night, women—single, coupled, married—sneaked over to the guides' sleeping bags under the cover of darkness. River romances were as common and flighty and full of trills as canyon wrens. Back at Northwestern, I couldn't get a date to save my life. But on the river, I couldn't find an evening alone. Klutzy romantics in December transformed to lusty Don Juans in June, and egos soared.

Most boatmen were quick to capitalize on this center stage and let loose bottled histrionics, and I was no exception. We sang off-key before appreciative audiences, told bad jokes that sent laughter reverberating between the Supai sandstone, played rudimentary recorder as passengers swayed. Every guide took advantage of the rapids, all 161 of them. Those pieces of effervescence in the long, emerald band of the river were chances to shine, to showcase mettle and stuff, to enhance the legend of dauntless river guide. Of course, we boatmen would never admit to the rapids' tendency toward impunity to visitors. We could flip, wrap, broach, jackknife, catch a crab, lose an oar, tubestand, endo, and swim the rapids and be relatively assured of emerging intact in the calm water below. But that was classified information.

All this theater was heightened in 1970 with the motor-driven pontoon raft. Nobody had yet figured out how to get through Lava Falls— the Colorado's biggest rapid and one of the last on the trip—with the engine running. The few attempts ended in broken shear pins, bent shafts, or outright loss of outboards, as the propeller invariably hit a rock soon after entry. So, two sets of twelve-foot oars, desuetude on a typical trip, were lifted from their straps on the sides of the raft and mounted on the thoe pins marking the orange frame that gridded the pontoon's center. Then, the outboard was lifted and tied flat, like a roped calf, to the stern floorboard.

All the passengers then walked around the rapid (Ted Hatch deemed the run too dangerous in those days) and watched and photographed in horror as two boatmen, one seated behind the other, entered the rapid, madly pumping the huge oars while being pitched and folded like laundry in a spin cycle. Then, as the last roostertail was broached on the back side of the crest, the rear captain had to leap to the stern and, in a genuinely risky maneuver, pull out a knife, cut the ropes binding the outboard, pull the eighty-pound motor up, slide it onto the transom mount, clamp it down, and pull the starter cord.

Time allowed just three or four chances to kick the engine to life (and it was sometimes too swamped to catch) in order to power the raft to a wisp of an eddy at the mouth of Prospect Canyon, where the passengers could reboard. If the engine didn't start in those few seconds, the raft would dive into the next rapid, Lower Lava, which was walled by a seventy-five-foot cliff on the south bank that prevented passengers from hiking farther downstream. They would have to wait for the next raft and crowd onto it as it taxied them down to their own carrier, bobbing in a large eddy a mile downstream on the north bank. If the last raft in the party didn't make the critical landing or if all the boats on a trip were swept into Lower Lava—and this happened occasionally—the passengers would have to hike a half mile upstream, swim across the cold river, knowing that if they cramped they could be sucked into Lava, and then hike a primitive path down the north bank to the waiting rafts. Or they could wait for the next rafting company to come by.

All this action made a great spectacle for those on shore. What I soon learned was that rowing through Lava was really nothing more than a show. No matter what you did with the oars, be it snapping hard strokes throughout or freezing the blades in place, the results would most often be the same. It was, more than anything else, a piece of theater, and I learned to play it with Kabuki-like stagecraft.

This dashing, somewhat pretentious rowing ritual was also employed, at some water levels, at the two other rapids rated 9–10 (the Grand Canyon has its own 1–10 classification scale for rapids): Hance and Crystal. A new addition to the fold, Crystal was created in December 1966 when a massive flood bulldozed a boulder-debris fan into the river at Mile 98. But at the cusp of the 1970s, motor routes were being pioneered, many by Hatch honcho Dennis Massey, regarded by some as King of the River, the man who could make his raft dance in any wave, hole, or eddy on the Colorado.

Whether Massey, or guides named Brick, Snake, Whale, or Bear, once below The Rapid, the boatmen would be feted as heroes, hailed as Galahads, Lindberghs, champions charged with extraordinary backbone and bravery. Prior to my guiding, my only work experience was as a bellboy and carhop, and that didn't quite prepare me for idolatry. The river guides, me included, were exalted. The problem was some began to believe it, creating a duality in personality and self-perception, an almost schizophrenic state that was not easy to cope with or resolve. We were walking, rowing oxymorons. All of us relished those moments of Canyon adulation, but reality always returned at summer's end. Some turned to the slopes, some to carpentry or other crafts or service jobs. I went back to school. Still others dipped into their black books of summer clients, those, who tugged from the beach after lingering embraces, said through tear-stained smiles, "Whenever you're in town, you must look me up.

Come stay with me. . . ." Following those words, many boatmen roamed from client home to home, reliving the summer through slides, scrapbooks, and Super-8 movies, and wearing out welcomes. But wherever we wandered, whatever we did, it seemed mundane by comparison to our summer work and identities.

The Colorado irrevocably changed me, as it does everyone. It fanned a false ego, then doused the fire. The boatman subculture was a strong one, a brotherhood bond formed in the summer months, and we kept in touch in the off-season, compared notes. Everyone seemed to suffer the same fate and searched in vain for a winter's equivalent of the astral light that caressed us in the Canyon. But few found it. One bleak winter Dennis Massey, King of the River, was driving a pizza delivery truck, and he shot himself in the head. Years later, Whale, a ski-lift operator, did the same, on the eve of a boatmen reunion party. These were the extremes. Sometimes, though, the spool rolled the other way. Some people who were undistinguished in their normal lives, perhaps shy, or living with untapped potential, found an unplumbed confidence while guiding, and that allowed them to stretch, assert, and experiment, and sometimes become extraordinary in ways they otherwise might never have been. A few guides went on to become celebrated photographers, film directors, businessmen, politicians, and one, perhaps the most envied, became the road manager for The Grateful Dead. And there was one who went on a quarter-century global quest to find the perfect river, and the endless summer.

〜〜〜

For the 1971 rafting season I convinced high school Raft Club friend John Kramer to come out to the Colorado and be my swamper, with intent to graduate to guide under my tutelage. He proved a quick study, becoming a lead guide in near record time. I had also tried to recruit John Yost, but he was heading back to Africa, with his own ambitions of setting up an import business. I also met a kindred spirit in Bart Henderson, from Vernal, Utah, where Ted Hatch lived. Bart came from riverrunning royalty (his Christian name was Royal), and was finally breaking into the Colorado. His uncle was with Bus Hatch in 1938 on the famous first descent of the Green River, a trip sometimes cited as the birth of modern river running. His father bought a pile of surplus ten-man rafts in the early fifties and started river running, often taking his young son on the water. Bart was guiding by the time he was thirteen. An artful athlete blessed with chiseled good looks and a lion's mane of blond hair,

Bart was a great guy, and the first boatman I had met who would consistently beat me in chess. I taught Bart the ropes, but within a month he surpassed his teacher with sheer native ability and smarts, and ended the season as one of the finest guides on the river.

By the end of the summer, my third as a river coxswain, I came to realize a common current ran through all those who drifted into the life of a guide on the Colorado River—it was the knowledge that the cosmos could be reduced to a cool, wrapping white wave, to the pull of an oar or the twist of a tiller, to the crest of a wave—and at that moment, the top of the world was reached, all magic was white, and all was good and great.

Once that knowledge soaked in, every guide, no matter how far his pursuits carried him, came back to the river.

CHAPTER 4

# THE ROOF OF AFRICA

"The universe is change, life is understanding."

—Marcus Aurelius

I n the winter of 1971 I came across an old copy of *Argosy* magazine
that reported on a 1968 expedition down the Blue Nile by a British
Army team. The article told of superfinancing and over-the-top publicity, of an expedition that compared in pomp and stature with the British
naval campaigns of two hundred years earlier. With seventy men, a budget in the hundreds of thousands of pounds, and no whitewater experience per se, the army, seemingly out of fear of atrophy, marched forth to
accomplish what it self-named "The Last Great First."

Though the righteous zeal seemed a bit impertinent, the photographs
in the piece sold me. Looking at those pictures was like peeking through
a window into the bedroom of a sleeping demon, peering into the pure
soul of a river, glimpsing a divine afflatus. The Blue Nile somehow
seemed special, untainted by commercial guiding, but naughty, all at once.
It coiled through a mile-deep gorge, and by a member's own description
it was a seething cauldron of giant boils, whirlpools, and hydraulic jumps.

Despite meticulous planning of the industrious operation (they practiced capsizing on land with color-coordinated paddles and helmets),
things went awry. There were capsizes, missed airdrops, lost boats, in-

juries, and fatalities. It still called itself a success, and indeed members did gather a glut of scientific data and specimens. However, there was a section they had not rafted as they deemed it too difficult . . . and that missing piece on their map inspired me. I showed the article to John Yost, who had just returned from a visit to Ethiopia, and he was charged with the possibilities. He said Ethiopia was the Tibet of Africa, a high plateau boiling with big, fast rivers, ripe for running, and that he was up for an expedition, if I could ever organize such a thing. This was a challenge I was ready to take.

I spent spare time that winter researching the Blue Nile. I found it had intrigued inquiring minds for centuries. Napoleon hoped to conquer it; Egypt feared it, for if it ever dried up, or were dammed, the Nile proper would lose most of the precious silt that has annually fertilized the land since time immemorial.

Rising from Lake Tana in the Ethiopian highlands, the river plummets off the Afro-alpine plateau and snakes its way through a mile-deep gorge. Its waters travel nearly three thousand miles before reaching the Mediterranean. The biography of the river held scores of dauntless attempts to navigate its wild waters. There was the wealthy American big-game hunter, W. N. McMillian, who in 1903 sailed less than five miles before his metal boats were destroyed in the rapids; Herbert Rittlinger and party, who in 1954 made thirty-five miles in kayaks before being attacked three times by giant crocodiles; Kuno Steuben, who in 1959 tried to make it alone down the river on a makeshift raft of logs and empty oil drums, but was wounded in a skirmish with local people and hiked out; Arne Rubin, who in 1965 canoed an upper section and then climbed out after a capsize lost his camera and maps; and the two Germans who in 1970 tried to float it in an oversized plastic bathtub (they actually made ten miles before losing the craft in a cataract). And there were a dozen other daring, if not eccentric, explorers who answered the call to conquer the "Mount Everest of Rivers," the Blue Nile.

The British called the Blue Nile gorge "the Grand Canyon of Africa," and that image resonated with me. The American Grand Canyon, where I had guided now for three seasons, was such a powerful place, it had become the pivot of my identity, around which everything else spun and was measured. As I read the account of the British attempt I became appalled at their inexperience and bungles, and their insensitivity to the land. Two men died on their expedition, one from a car accident. The other, a man named Ian Macleod, tried to cross a swollen tributary of the Blue Nile while attached to a rope around his waist, secured to a tree on shore. As he was swept downstream, the rope went taut, and he was pulled under and drowned. It was a stupid mistake, a violation of a simple rule of water mechanics. As I read about their blunderings and misadventures, I couldn't help but think I should be there. I understood whitewater; I knew the Grand Canyon; and for some twisted reason, I loved the notion of running rapids on a river with crocodiles.

Now sucked in, I couldn't read enough about Ethiopia. It was like a drug. I became obsessed not just with the Blue Nile, but with all the rivers of the Hidden Empire, and with the country itself. Locked away in remote mountains, Ethiopia, which means "burnt face" in Greek, had a three-thousand-year history. The Semites of present-day Ethiopia arrived from Arabia. They intermarried with local Cushites and later organized themselves into the kingdom of Axum. The Axum Empire was converted to Christianity in the fourth century, and the new religion was institutionalized as the Ethiopian Orthodox Church. For thousands of years the rich land, watered by the Blue Nile basin, and the watershed of a sister river farther north called the Tekeze, was tilled for self-sustenance. But as Ethiopia began to reach out beyond its borders in the 1960s, agronomists looked at its abundant rivers and predicted the country would transform itself into the breadbasket of Africa. Yet, at the time of my research, the early seventies, it was one of the world's poorest and hungriest countries.

Once known as Abyssinia, Ethiopia was the land of Prester John, the nation of Cush, the last resting place of the Ark of the Covenant, the vault for King Solomon's Mines, the repository for the true cross of Christ, the site of the Garden of Eden, the tomb of Adam, and other legends and medieval myths. The bulk of the country occupied a vast, fissured plateau that for half the year soaked up tremendous rains that fell during two rainy seasons, creating the huge rivers that spilled off the "roof of Africa" to the cardinal points, into thirsty deserts and lowlands. The biggest of the rivers were the Blue Nile, the Omo, the Baro, the Awash, and the Tekeze. On antique maps the waters were set in highlands called "Lunae Montes." I was able to get a set of CIA-published satellite maps, and these gave the rivers definition, beginnings, and mouths. But I could find little of their character, what was in their water and along their banks. I lusted to run all five. The Blue Nile was, of course, the most famous, but the Tekeze ultimately had the most allure. It drained the Simien Mountains in the north, curled around the Ethiopian Everest, snowcapped Ras Dashan, fourth highest peak in Africa, the tallest mountain in Ethiopia, soaring to 15,158 feet. And there were myths that it was the river highway up which the stolen Ark of the Covenant was carried, where it lay hidden in a guarded church called St. Mary's, or Beta Maryam. Other myths suggested the fabled Ark never made it out of the Tekeze canyons, and it was there still, lost. This was the golden Ark that was built at the foot of Mount Sinai, containing the two tablets of stone upon which the Ten Commandments were inscribed by the finger of God; that was carried through the wilderness and across the river Jordan; that brought victory to the Israelites in their struggle to win the Promised Land; that was taken up to Jerusalem by King David; and that, around 955 B.C., was deposited by King Solomon in the Holy of Holies of the First Temple. This was the same Ark that would kill the unpure by fire or melting if they gazed upon it. Legend had it that Moses' mercenary brother was burnt to a crisp when exposed to the Ark, and that it, not Jacob's trumpet, brought down the walls at Jericho. This was the same Ark that was stolen and, by local legend, brought into Ethiopia. The story of the epic looting begins with the meeting of King Solomon with Maqueda, the Queen of Sheba, who ruled Ethiopia. On a diplomatic mission she crossed the Red Sea, and was awed by Solomon's court. She gave Solomon four and a half tons of gold for his temple, which housed the Ark of the Covenant, and Solomon gave her "all her desire"— whereupon she returned to Ethiopia, pregnant. The story continues that her son, Menelik I, grew up and went to Israel, where he stole the Ark of the Covenant, carried it up the Nile to its confluence with the Tekeze (there called the Atbara), and then spirited it up the Tekeze canyons to a secret resting place, where it remains hidden to this day. This would be worth seeking, especially along a major unnavigated, unexplored river.

These were the dreams of a river boy, but in actuality I had no idea how to make them real. I had no overseas experience, no equipment, and no money. Only an ever-deepening desire.

〰〰〰

When the summer of 1972 arrived, John Yost was free and joined me for a few trips through the Grand Canyon as my swamper, as John Kramer had the year before. Throughout the season I made many new friends, guides and clients both, but none who bonded as tightly as a man I met on the final tour—a young man, just a few years older than I, who reminded me a bit of my father in the rigidness of his ethical compass, and in the awkwardness of his wilderness ways. But he also seemed a mirror of my being, with an insatiable curiosity, an enthusiastic willingness to try new things, and a waking thirst for adventure.

The man was Lew Greenwald, who with his wife, Karen, joined my raft on a ten-day run. Lew had a B.A. in psychology from the University of Connecticut and was working as a sociologist along with his wife. He was overweight, prematurely bald at twenty-six, pasty and pale from too much time indoors. On the first day of the trip he tried to set up a tent, but it collapsed with a whoosh as we were all eating dinner by the river. But as the trip progressed, Lew loosened, and a dry humor emerged, as well as a wild whoop as we rolled through the rapids. At one point, I taught him how to skip polished stones into the river, and the simple act gave him great joy. By the second week of the trip Lew was jumping off the raft into the bigger rapids and floating through with reckless abandon, as other clients looked on jealously. By trip's end we were good friends and talked of getting together in Los Angeles in a couple weeks before he had to head back to Connecticut and his job.

When the season ended, things were different. I had graduated college, and though graduate or law school was in the plan, I wanted to take a little time off first. Africa was still a dream, but seemingly inaccessible, at least for now.

So, I did what so many boatmen had done before me. I opened my black book of clients and picked the most delicious: Patti Gales, a girl met earlier in the season when her family vacationed on one of my trips. It was a potent river romance, and I was keen to follow up. So, John Yost and I hitched to San Diego and spent a week at Patti's house, waterskiing, hiking, and body surfing. One day walking on the beach Patti pulled out a brochure she had received in the mail from another river guide. It was titled "River Trip of the Century," and it was advertising a *National Geographic*–sponsored expedition down Ethiopia's Omo River. It was to be led by Ron Smith, owner of Grand Canyon Expeditions, the company that had outfitted a *National Geographic* team down the Colorado in 1968 for a feature that ran in the magazine in 1969. Adventurers were invited to join the first descent of this great river for $3,000, more than three times my annual income as a river guide. And that didn't include airfare. But I suspected they needed guides for an expedition of this magnitude, and I fancied I was one of the best around. John Yost had more energy than a pot of cowboy coffee, so I thought we might propose ourselves as staff. Why not take a year off for a last yahoo before getting serious about life?

I called Ron Smith and asked if we might get together and talk over prospects. He said sure, come on by after his next trip, which would get him back to headquarters in a couple weeks. It was an easier invitation to extend than to fulfill, as Ron lived in Kanab, Utah, a tiny town two days' drive away, and we had no car. But there were drive-away companies in Los Angeles, so we decided to hitchhike to the big city and find transportation north. I again pulled out my address book of past passengers. Stuart Bruce, a past client who was a descendant of the great eighteenth-century Ethiopian explorer James Bruce, lived in San Marino, fashionably northeast of Los Angeles, and he accepted my request to come stay for a while. I also knew that Lew Greenwald would be in town, and called the number he had left me.

〰〰〰

John and I got together with Lew one afternoon in L.A. and shared a beer, and also some of our Ethiopian plans, and Lew's eyes lit up. He wanted to know everything. But neither John nor I took it too seriously. Lew had a real job, a wife, a car, responsibilities. That evening we all decided to attend the film *Deliverance,* which had just opened. James Dickey's tour de force of violent adventure and inner discovery on a southeastern river had become an instant classic with its publishing in 1970, and for river runners it was the Talmud. Now, John Boorman had brought the tale to the big screen, and the world premiere was at the Cinerama Dome on Sunset Boulevard in Hollywood.

The entrance to the theater was decked out with ravaged river gear, splintered paddles, and ripped life jackets. From the ceiling hung aluminum Grummans, severely bashed and dented. As we surrendered to the darkness of the theater, the story was so real, so powerful that the images singed my mind. I identified with Ed, played by Jon Voight, the WASPish city boy-man, who was one of life's sliders until he found a concealed inner strength through his confrontation with the river. I saw my new friend Lew as the Lewis of the film, who plows into the experience with abandon, believing he is immortal, and is near-fatally injured in the process. When we emerged from the theater we turned to one another and John and I almost simultaneously asked the same question: "Where was that river?" It was the Chattooga, Lew volunteered, having read some background on the making of the film. "We gotta run it!" I proposed. Lew and John agreed, and we shook hands on it.

Lew flew back to Connecticut the next day. He could afford a flight. He had a regular job. John and I cast about for a drive-away company that wanted a car driven east, and that would risk the required bond on us, as we didn't exactly have established credit. We found one, AAA Drive-Away, that needed a Gremlin delivered to Annapolis. So, we took it, and three days later we were at Ron Smith's warehouse looking at slides he had taken on a reconnoiter of the Omo several months previous. They looked so exotic I almost fell into the photos. Ron said they planned on making the first descent of the Omo in August of 1973, eleven months away, and that he hadn't yet selected the crew. I listened to Ron, swallowing his words like water. Why, we would be good candidates, I volunteered, and he looked us up and down, and suggested I start a workout program and call him in a couple months. I took that as a good sign, and as we bowled across country John and I plotted and shared dream-streak talk of running the Omo and other great rivers of Africa.

As soon as we landed in Bethesda I signed up at the local gym for a buff-up program, and spent two hours a day lifting weights and running in place. The rest of the day I usually spent at the Library of Congress, drinking down information about the rivers of Africa.

Then, in late October, chest and thighs expanded in a way never before, I called Ron and said we were ready to go. He hemmed and hawed, then explained he had decided to hire his younger brother and some of his friends for the crew, so, sorry, there wouldn't be a place for us. Unless we wanted to pay . . .

This was a blow. But I called John Yost and threw out an idea. Why don't we do this ourselves? Why don't we just go over the first of the year and head down some river? I knew as much as anyone about white-water rafting, and he had embassy connections. John was intrigued, but he had committed the winter to opening an import store on Long Island with his college roommate, David Bohn, so he suggested I go over and get things started and he could join me later. That sounded fine with me, except that I had less than $500 in life savings, so my first order was to see if we could find sponsors. I wrote to all the rafting manufacturers in the country . . . both of them; Rubber Fabricators of West Virginia, who were making boats for Ron Smith, and didn't reply; and Holcombe Industries of Redwood, California, who had just started building a vinyl version of a rubber raft, and were eager to promote it. The rafts would sell for $1,000 each, but the owner of the company, intrigued with my proposal, offered to sell me two for a total of $400. This was good news, except it was beyond my budget. It was clear I needed another partner. So, I started calling my river-running friends.

First was John Kramer. Kramer lived a short ways away in Bethesda, and when I approached him about running rivers in Ethiopia he threw in his hat, but not his money. He would love to join the expedition, but he had plans for graduate school in geology the following fall and didn't want to invest in a raft. The next call was to Tom Cromer, another Hatch guide, who hailed from Los Alamos, New Mexico. Tom's older brother, Roy, had started rafting the Colorado in the late sixties, and brought Tom into the fold. In our three seasons guiding together, we became close friends and shared a love of books rare at that time among the river community. We even talked of going into partnership, opening a bookstore together in the mountains, as a career, when not plunging down rivers. Tom was also slated to go to graduate school the following fall, in mathematics, and was saving his money, so he didn't want to invest in the concept, but he wanted to join up. Bart Henderson was very enthusiastic about the concept, but had family obligations for the winter months, and asked that I call again if I made it to a second season in Africa. The subsequent call was to Lew Greenwald. When I asked, he admitted things were pretty boring. When I said I finally had a proposition for him about river running in Africa, he invited me up to present it in person.

So, I took a long weekend and drove my father's Oldsmobile to Connecticut. Lew said he didn't recognize me at the door, I was so buffed up. He still looked like an indoorsman, and was even a bit balder, paunchier, and paler than when I last saw him in Los Angeles—but his wild eyes radiated a puckish sense of fun. Once inside his small den, Lew turned up his tape deck and put on his favorite artist, Van Morrison, and we sat back with a few beers to talk about music, about the film *Deliverance,* about how special the time we shared on the Colorado was, and about how little time there is to pursue dreams. When I made my proposition, asking for the money to buy a raft to become part of this scheme, he stuck out his hand to shake. He was my partner. Outside, the tips of a golden crescent moon pointed east to Africa.

CHAPTER 5

# THE GOD SOBEK

"It is a hideous blot upon the creation: the crocodile."
—Reginald Maugham, *Wild Game in Zambesia*

L ew and I spent the next several weeks seeking sponsors and doing more research. One weekend I met Lew in New York City and we went to the Museum of Natural History, where we saw the skull of Phobosuchus, the Fearsome Crocodile, an ancient relative to the Nile crocs that had been forty-five feet long, weighing fifteen tons. The skull was six feet long by three and a half feet across. Some of the teeth were six inches long and two inches deep. The crocs we would encounter would be at best a third that size. Nonetheless, the display gave us pause.

I knew there would be a lot of bugs where we were going, and that some perhaps were unclassified, so that gave me an idea. I called the Smithsonian Institution's department of entomology and asked if they might be interested in a sponsorship in exchange for collecting bugs. They thought it an interesting idea and suggested I come in for a meet.

This put the pressure on for a name. I felt we couldn't present ourselves to potential sponsors without a proper name, and after some deliberation I came up with one I thought quite clever. I had recently seen the Thor Heyerdahl documentary on the Ra expedition, his attempt to cross the Atlantic from Africa on a papyrus reed boat (Ra was the ancient

Egyptian sun god). So, I figured we would be the RAW Expedition. It would be an acronym: Reconnaissance of African Waterways; it would be a play on Heyerdahl's high-profile expedition; it was a celebration of the times (streaking was a rage, as was nude rafting); and it evoked the state of our enterprise, lean, crude, raw.

But when I wound my way through the inner corridors of the Smithsonian, found myself facing a line of white lab coats, and announced I was with the RAW Expedition, I was met with blank stares. The most senior of the researchers, Dr. Spangler, put his arm across my shoulder and walked me to a corner. There he gave me some advice: lose the name. If we wanted the Smithsonian, or any prestigious organization to be involved, we needed a more earnest name.

So, I spent the next several days at the Library of Congress, poring over books describing the many ways we could die while rafting in Ethiopia, and thinking about a name. I learned there were a raft of nasty obstacles that might do damage. The rapids were certainly a given—they were likely big and dangerous. But then there were hippos, second largest land mammals after elephants, and infamous for turning over boats and snapping occupants in two. The wild buffalo in the region had a reputation for charging unprovoked. I read about puff adders, black mambas, and spitting cobras, and about legendary twenty-foot pythons that capsized canoes. And there were a score of documented exotic tropical diseases, from onchocerciasis (River Blindness) to elephantiasis; from trypanosomiasis (Sleeping Sickness) to trichuriosis (whipworm); from yaws to several fatal forms of malaria. There were the local peoples, some with fierce reputations. The Blue Nile, the only river previously run in Ethiopia, had taken a toll of victims who fell prey to the ruthless *shiftas,* the roaming bandits who ruled the outback. In 1962 a Swiss-French canoeing expedition was attacked in the middle of the night. Four of the party escaped in a single canoe under a hail of gunfire, while the rest lay dead in the campsite. And during the 1968 British Blue Nile expedition there was a similar shifta attack, but the expedition members escaped without serious injury.

But the one danger repeated over and over, in print and voice, underlined and accented, was the risk of death by crocodile attack. The ancient Greeks called the beast *kroko-drilo,* "pebble worm"—a scaly thing that shuffled and lurked in low places. The most deadly existing reptile, the man-eating Nile crocodile has always been on the "man's worst enemies" list. It evolved 170 million years ago from the primordial soup as an efficient killing machine. More people are killed and eaten by crocodiles each year in Africa than by all other animals combined. Their instinct is predation, to kill any meat that floats their way, be it fish, hippo, antelope, or human. To crocs, we are just part of the food chain. Crocodile hunters, upon cutting open stomachs of their prey, often discover bracelets and bits of jewelry and human remains. Huge, ravening predators, armed with massive, teeth-studded jaws, strong, unrestrainable, indestructible, and destructive, crocodiles, if given the chance, eat people. It's their nature. The river is their turf, and we would be trespassing. I found myself in cold-sweat nightmares imagining the yellow, chisel-sharp teeth of a giant croc ripping my skin apart. This would be the most awful way to die. But I thought about the alternative—law or graduate school leading to a real job—and facing crocodiles seemed the delightful evil of two lessers.

I read as much as I could find about crocodiles that month, though I quickly discovered not many people had ever navigated whitewater in Africa, and of the few who had, and survived, less than a handful left reliable accounts of their experiences with crocs. I discovered there were two major schools of thought about how to cope while floating a crocodile-infested river: 1) Be as noisy as possible when passing through a crocodile pool to scare them off. 2) Be as silent as possible when passing through a croc-infested area so as not to attract attention. The rationale for the latter method was that since crocodiles have fixed-focused eyesight—meaning they can see things clearly at only one specific distance—a noiseless boat floating past at the proper distance could probably go unnoticed. One expert at the National Zoo even warned us not to laugh in a certain manner, as it resembled the sound of an infant croc in trouble, and the noise would alert all larger crocs within hearing distance to rush to the rescue. He demonstrated the laugh, and it sounded eerily like John Yost's high-pitched, nervous laugh, so I silently vowed to keep topics serious if sharing a raft with John.

Another account was graphically presented in the book *Eyelids of Morning, the mingled destinies of crocodiles and men,* by Alistair Graham, and photographed by Peter Beard. It told of a Peace Corps volunteer, Bill Olsen, twenty-five, a recent graduate of Cornell, who decided to take a swim in Ethiopia's Baro River, one of my targets, against the advice of locals. He swam to a sandbar on the far side of the muddy river, and sat there, his feet on a submerged rock. He was leaning into the current to keep his balance, a rippled vee of water trailing behind him, his arms folded across his chest as he was staring ahead, lost in thought. A few minutes later his friends saw that Bill had vanished without trace or sound. A few more minutes later a big croc surfaced with a large, white, partially submerged object in its jaws, whose identity was in no doubt. The next morning a hunter on safari, a Colonel Dow, sneaked up on the croc, shot it, and then dragged the carcass to the beach. He cut it open, and inside found Bill Olsen's legs, intact from the knees down, still joined together at the pelvis. His head, crushed into small chunks, was a barely recognizable mass of hair and flesh. A black-and-white photo of Bill's twisted, bloody legs dumped in a torn cardboard box drilled into my paraconsciousness, and for days I would shut my eyes and shiver at the image.

In the end, I was not comforted by what I learned in my research—if anything, I was a good deal more afraid.

〜〜〜

It was while casting about for a name that a thin book in the Library of Congress on the gods and goddesses of ancient Egypt wrought inspiration. There was Ra, the sun god, but that had been taken. There was Hesamut, the hippo goddess depicted in the act of demolishing a crocodile. But Hesamut Expeditions didn't resonate. One chapter spoke of the crocodile god SOBEK, worshiped along the middle Nile. A temple was built to the deity on the island of Kom Ombo between Aswan and Luxor, where mothers of children eaten by crocodiles felt privileged to have provided something for SOBEK's delectation. And there were sacrificial pools on another island called Crocodilopolis. The story went that once upon a time Menes, first king of all the Egyptians, was set upon by his own dogs while out hunting. In his flight he came to the Nile, where lay a large croc baking in the sun. The croc, rapidly sizing up the situation, offered to ferry the desperate king across the river. With all saurian ceremony, Menes was sculled over to found the city of Crocodilopolis, about 3000 years B.C. Henceforth, it was believed that if SOBEK was appeased, he would allow the fragile papyrus boats used to ply the Nile to remain unharmed. About 300 B.C., when the army of Perdiccas was crossing the Nile at Memphis, it forgot to pay SOBEK homage, and one thousand soldiers were killed and eaten. Naming our enterprise after a deity that would protect boats from sharp-toothed serpents seemed like a good idea to me, so SOBEK we became.

And with my return visit to the Smithsonian, I announced our name, and it seemed fine to the insect men. Dr. Spangler said they would officially sponsor our little expedition. This was quite exciting news, and I asked exactly what that meant, dollarwise.

"Nothing" was the reply. It meant the institute would supply us with a load of bulky and delicate insect collecting gear, for which we would be responsible. It meant if I found some new genus of bug, they might name it after me. And it meant we could use the good Smithsonian name in soliciting from more commercial concerns. But it didn't mean money. Nonetheless, SOBEK it would be.

With this start Lew, John Kramer, and I set out on a letter-writing campaign, and we ended up with a respectable list of sponsors, though none with cash. *Saga* magazine supplied us with film; Peter Storm, a British life jacket company, supplied flotation; and my mother threw in a poncho, a mess kit, flashlight, and a harmonica. But, we were stuck with our cash at hand.

Shipping could have been a problem; certainly duty and customs. But here contacts made all the difference. Even though John Yost would not be joining our first expeditions, as the son of a diplomat, he arranged for us to use the diplomatic pouch, and several hundred pounds of rafts and gear went flying to Addis Ababa on U.S. military transport. Getting ourselves there was another thing altogether. The commercial air ticket price was over $1,000, way beyond my budget. So, I went to a bucket shop.

These were the days before airline deregulation, and pretty much all carriers charged the same high prices to fly internationally. The one exception was for affinity groups, which were allowed to charter planes and charge whatever seemed fair. This spawned a whole underground airline industry, in which bogus affinity groups were created. Anyone could join for a small fee and receive a backdated membership card (you had to be an affinity member for six months to qualify for these special fares). So, I sought out a bucket shop in downtown Washington, D.C., paid my $25, and became a right guard on a rugby team. Tom Cromer became a goalie, and together we would fly February 10, 1973, to Nairobi for a sporting match, for $150 round trip. John Kramer and Lew Greenwald would take a later flight and meet us in Addis Ababa, where together we would put the pieces together to run some African whitewater.

Before getting on the plane, however, we had to undergo the indignity of pre-African travel: inoculations. In the days before departure I was perforated with immunization serums for Poliomyelitis, cholera, tetanus, smallpox, yellow fever, diphtheria, typhus, and infective hepatitis, both A and B. It was an uncomfortable flight.

Our charter flight first landed in London for an overnight, and so Tom and I took a train to the Royal Military Academy, Sandhurst, to meet Richard Snailham, chronicler of the official account of the British Blue

Nile Expedition. He was proper and preppy, smoked a Holmesian pipe, and warned us of shiftas and crocodiles. Then we caught the next leg of our flight and landed in Nairobi.

Nairobi was thick with new smells, jacarandas and flame trees, grilled corn and meats. We checked into the local YMCA and went off to explore. We visited a snake farm, where we learned of another dozen types of snakes that might do us in. We rented a taxi and headed out toward the Tana River, which I had heard from Geoffrey Kent, a young safari outfitter, might be runnable. The only attempt, I was told, had been in a single rowboat, but it made only a short passage before spooking a grazing hippo high up on shore, which then stampeded straight over a ten-foot mud embankment and belly-flopped, all five thousand pounds of it, onto the small boat, crushing it and its passengers. The story only fueled our curiosity, so we pooled resources and gave the driver a fixed amount to take us as far as he could and back, hoping we could reach the river. When the meter was halfway there, so were we, so back we came.

That evening, craving a touchstone of familiarity, I wandered over to the Hilton while Tom stayed behind in a bath. I went to the coffee shop, where I ordered a cheeseburger and coffee. While chomping into the watery ground meat, I looked up and saw a familiar face, a very glamorous face, with an aquiline nose, framed with striking blond hair, a camera draped around her neck. She asked if she might sit with me, as I was the only Westerner in sight. Of course, and then I recognized her as Candice Bergen. She proceeded to tell me she was hoping to switch careers and become a professional photographer, and that she was on assignment for a woman's magazine to shoot Jane Goodall and her chimps. She rambled on about how unfulfilling acting was, that her last couple films had taken a toll, and finally ended by asking me if she was making the right decision. Of course, I counseled; she probably would never make it as an actress, and her prospects as a photographer were much brighter. "Thanks," she flashed her great white smile and left to pursue her destiny.

My destiny was north, and I spent a restless night rolling around my small bed in orthogonal thoughts: the excitement that courses on the eve of a great adventure intersecting with the anxiety about all the things that could go wrong.

〜〜〜

The next morning Tom Cromer and I caught the flight to Addis Ababa, on the western ridge of the Great Rift Valley, at eight thousand feet the third highest capital city in the world. Addis Ababa means "new flower" in Amharic, and coming in for a landing I imagined the tin-roofed shanties were its petals, the tall buildings its stalks, and the eucalyptus groves its leaves. It was founded by Emperor Menelik II in 1896, both for its central location and its therapeutic hot mineral waters. It was a city of hills and endless rows of eucalyptus, planted in the 1920s for fuel wood and construction material. And construction was everywhere. Skyscrapers and modern buildings were being erected at every turn, yet at their feet were the shacks of the poor. Still, it seemed a city of hope, a city on the march, a city of new sights and sounds, and of pure exotica for me.

With arrival we sought out the local YMCA once again, and while wandering about like lost puppies, an attractive Western woman with dark hair motioned us across the street, leashed us in. Without preamble, she introduced herself as Diane Fuller, a public health nurse, said we looked disoriented, and asked where we were headed. When we told our tale, she offered to guide us to the Y. Along the way we described our reason for being in Ethiopia—wild rivers—and she suggested we meet her husband, Dr. George Fuller, an anthropologist, artist, and medical doctor with a special degree in tropical medicine and hygiene, who was also a hobby rafter.

That night we had dinner with George and Diane Fuller, and they filled us in as to why they were there. Fresh from postgraduate studies at the London School of Tropical Medicine, George accepted an ambulatory medicine fellowship sponsored by the Smith, Klien and French drug company in 1971. The program took him to Kenya for three months, then Nepal for six weeks. A former ranch hand who had spent his youth herding cattle and mending fences in Nebraska, George was now hooked on foreign travel; he'd seen Paris and would never return to the farm. Immediately after his fellowship, he signed for a three-month stint in Ethiopia to conduct backcountry research on *Kālā āzār,* a protozoan organism that transmits a disease related to malaria and sleeping sickness. He was into his second year.

George's boss, Aklelu Lemma of Haile Selassie University, hated the uncomfortable conditions and high temperatures of lowland Ethiopia and was pleased to find in George an enthusiastic researcher willing to embrace the hardships of the field. "They pay me expenses to go to places nobody else will go, which is fine with me, because I love those places," George explained over spaghetti cooked by Diane. "I'm attracted to the hot and humid. What most people call miserable, I love." He sounded like my kind of guy, and when he told me he had lost his raft while running California's Stanislaus River during medical school, I asked if he wanted to join our expedition. By evening's end, the small freckled man with the thick glasses of a schoolboy who tinkers with bugs was officially signed on as trip doctor.

At this point, we still weren't sure which river to attempt first. The Blue Nile was the most celebrated, and was the original seductress. The Omo was the river *National Geographic* had identified as the "River Trip of the Century," and we were in Ethiopia with gear and crew a good six months before the officially scheduled attempt. And the Tekeze, the most mysterious, myth-shrouded, and erotically appealing—with its deep gorges and wide bend—beckoned from the north. But, I realized a more modest and accessible flow might be the place to start, and that looked to me to be a river called the Awash, draining Addis Ababa and emptying into the sinkhole of the sun, the Danakil Depression, lowest point in Africa, where it sank into the sands. If we survived, we would try the bigger flows.

A couple days later Tom and I took the local bus down to the Awash River, a dusty, bumpy 140-mile, seven-hour journey with a radio blaring forth an unceasing stream of local music at earsplitting pitch. We scraped down the edge of the escarpment into the Great Rift, the giant geological fault that runs from Galilee down the River Jordan and the Dead Sea to the Gulf of Akaba, across the Red Sea, then down a furrow of Ethiopia into Kenya, Tanzania, Zambia, and what was then Rhodesia.

We got out at a small *buna beit* (coffeehouse) alone at the edge of the desert. We pushed aside a curtain of bottle tops on strings. Inside a portrait of Haile Selassie hung on a wall of mud and chopped grass, blackened with candle smoke. The proprietor stood behind a wooden counter, fanning away flies with a horsehair whisk. We ordered hot tea and asked where the river was. The owner pointed over a small rise, and off we went in search of moving water. As we approached what looked to be a crack in the earth, an animal snorted and shot out from behind a rock, galloping toward us. It had huge curved tusks, a flatiron face, and was charging at top speed, with a tail upright as a radio antenna. Turning on our heels, we ran as fast as we could toward the canyon rim. When we got to the edge, we stopped, as it was four hundred feet straight down the canyon wall. And the animal, which we now saw was a warthog, kept jinking toward us . . . but twenty feet in front of our path, it veered sharply to the right and ran right off the cliff. We heard an awful thump a few seconds later, a noise like a mallet driving in a tent peg. We then peered over the edge to see what looked like a crumpled paper bag containing a broken bottle of red wine. The poor animal was flattened on a rock, encircled in a pool of blood. It was an eerie first contact with African wildlife. As we gazed down at the dead beast, a soft afternoon breeze, laden with the fragrance of the desert, blew up the canyon, circulated around our heads, and soared to the first battlements of the escarpment behind us.

We repaired to Addis Ababa and met up with John Kramer and Lew, who had just arrived. As a full-fledged guide, John Kramer was brimming with brio and leapt into the culture with both feet. Lew was more hesitant, reflective, and cautious. I enjoyed showing Lew the ropes, how to get around, the rudiments of the language, where to get the best mango shakes. But one piece of advice he refused to take concerned the beggars. Over dinner one night before Lew arrived George Fuller went into a rant about the evils of begging. He postulated that naive, bleeding-heart tourists help perpetuate a system that demotivates street people to work—a casual quarter thrown to a panhandler is more than he would make in a few hours of hard labor. George steadfastly refused to give a beggar a break, and he brought me into his orbit, even if it was with a bit of cognitive dissonance. When I explained this higher thinking to Lew he rebuffed it. Wherever we walked about town he always had a few *birr,* the local currency, for a street urchin or codger, and a part of me always felt guilty that he did.

The next couple weeks were spent in Addis Ababa, securing the necessary laissez-passers, buying food and supplies in the Mercato, wandering among the tumultuous color, the exotic fruits, spices, and narcotics (such as *chat,* the glistening green leaf of *Cattula aedulis* that provokes a caffeine-mixed-with-hemp buzz), and the rich stew of a foreign language. For recreation we played tennis at the U.S. embassy compound (where an American cook served warm chocolate chip cookies and juicy cheeseburgers). Our funds were so lean, however, we made a pact as we moved about town: we would use only the local buses, which charged 7 cents a ride. The 25-cent fixed-price taxi fare was just too steep for our budget.

One day, as Lew and I were sharing a street-roasted ear of corn, about as cheap a meal as we could find, the usual city din was muffled by the sudden appearance of an entourage, headlights blinking, sirens wailing. First a jeep, then Land Rovers and trucks bristling like porcupines with solder's rifles, then, slowly, a long black Rolls-Royce. It was the great high forehead himself, Emperor Haile Selassie, the two hundred and twenty-fifth direct-line descendant of Menelik I, son of the Queen of

Sheba and King Solomon. He was handing out birr as he passed by. We needed every birr we could get to pull off our adventures, so I shouldered forward into the crowd to see if I might receive some royal beneficence . . . but Lew grabbed my shoulder and piped me back. "It's not fair money . . . they need it more than us. We can do without." The car passed, and the emperor's metallic eyes locked with mine. Then he was gone, and the pedestrians went about their business, or lack of, moving with the skittish walk of silent movie actors.

The night before departure for the Awash, Lew, John, Tom, and I went to the Three Tukuls disco just off Bole Road, a club equal parts African and ex-pat. After a couple beers, Lew pulled from his jacket a 45-rpm record and took it to the DJ. It was Elton John's "Crocodile Rock," and it had us all hoppin' and boppin', and Lew was extending his hands as though they were the jaws of a snapping crocodile in a kind of handshake dance. Lew's spontaneous dance-floor contrivance would become the official SOBEK handshake. When we sank back in our chairs after the sweaty jig, a woman, glassy and gorgeous, her spectral face hanging like a lantern in the dark room, slid down next to me. Ethiopian women are legendary for their beauty, with coffee and cream skin, Levantine lips, fine bones, distinctive high cheekbones, and thin noses, but this woman, who called herself Diamond, had a beauty beyond any I had ever imagined. I couldn't believe it when she agreed to dance with me. I didn't deserve such company and had never been this close to perfection. We danced for hours, and with every song she writhed closer to me, touched me in intimate ways, and smiled white embers of desire. Somehow in the scrum of our wild dancing I noticed it was midnight. I panicked and said I had to go, as we had a 5:00 A.M. lorry to catch, and some packing yet to do. She tugged at my sleeve, flashed an imploring, smoldering look that knocked me back. I had an idea. "Why don't you join us on the expedition?" I asked. "We have extra gear, everything you need. All you need is a toilet kit, your personal effects. I'll take care of the rest." She nodded approval, and I wrote on a napkin directions as to where to meet us. She took the napkin, stuffed it in her breast, and said she would be there. She winked, and blew a kiss.

I couldn't sleep at all that night, restless with the upcoming adventure, but perhaps more with the prospect of rafting with the most beautiful woman I had ever encountered. There was enough sublimation that night to power a motorboat. It was the ultimate wet dream.

We had hired a sugar-agro lorry from the Ethiopian Distribution Company to tote our gear and ourselves down to the Awash River. A young administrator, who was sympathetic to our wild scheme, arranged for a driver at a deep discount. I asked the driver to wait a few more minutes, then a few more. Diamond hadn't appeared. I had no contact for her, only her word she would be here. Finally, the driver said he couldn't hold back any longer, and he revved up the diesel engine and steered the old Mercedes out into the road. I sulked in the back, until George came back to comfort me. "You realize, don't you, she was a hooker? It never would have worked." In the naivete of youth, I hadn't made that connection, but with recognition of George's truth, I grinned. "You're right, it wouldn't have worked . . . but it would have been fun trying."

CHAPTER 6

# THE RIVER AWASH

"The world is a rose; smell it and pass it on to your friends."

—Persian proverb

B esides our core crew of five Americans, we had also recruited Ifru Gabreyes, who spoke Amharic, the agglutinative national language, as well as Saho, the language of the Danakil, whose depression we would be passing through. But Ifru spoke no English. To communicate with Ifru we brought along Lemma Tessema, who spoke Amharic and English, our translator for our translator. Both were former imperial bodyguards, and qualified wildlife guides.

The rafts were crafted with revolutionary design for the times: both ends spooned up at a 20-degree angle to cut the splash factor, and they were quite light, weighing in at 130 pounds, excellent for portaging. The rest of our gear was a mixture of army surplus and donated gear from sponsors.

It was Saturday, March 10, when we pumped our two rafts along the banks of the Awash. Stepping into the rafts there was that first sensation of rushing water beneath us, a sound like compression brakes. Then we pushed off into the African unknown.

First we rowed upstream to the seven veils of the sixty-foot-high Awash Falls, and took an early morning shower in its cool spray. Life jackets secured, we turned downstream.

Though I had secured a classified set of maps from the CIA, I quickly found they had little basis in reality. In fact, because the maps were created from satellite pictures of the Awash in August, when it was in flood, there was practically no cartographic information of any accuracy. We really did not know what to expect.

I had read of Wilfred Thesiger's explorations of the Awash, in which he walked to its mouth between October 1933 and May 1934. He was twenty-three years old, a year older than me, and had written words that beaded up and rolled into my soul: "I had felt the lure of the unknown, the urge to go where no white man had been before, and I was determined, as soon as I had taken my degree, to return to Abyssinia." He did not leave any usable maps, only strong words of warning about several expeditions ahead of him that had been wiped out by fierce Danakil tribesmen, or Afar, as they call themselves, the Hamitic people, linked by legend to the biblical sons of Ham. The Danakil occupied the blistering Awash valley and the surrounding moonscape deserts, wastelands with phantasmagoric rock outcroppings and treacherous craters filled with melted chloride. If ever a people matched the personality of a landscape, these were they. "If you went down into Danakil country, you'd be unlikely to come back, and if you come back, you would probably be missing some of your vital organs," Thesiger wrote.

We had talked to a few pilots who had flown over sections, but they had little to offer, except that much of the winding course was hidden from aerial view by thick vegetation that canopied the water. All we really knew was that we would start the trip right below Awash Falls in the national park. The only other point of accessibility to the river was a small agricultural school near the desert town of Gewani, and this was one hundred miles farther from our starting point by road, certainly much more by river, perhaps double or more. The Gewani Peace Corps School was our target take-out, and from there we would call our friend Bob Denton, a communications expert at the embassy, who would then pick us up in his Land Rover. What lay between Awash Falls and Gewani was anybody's guess. We estimated six days traveling time, purchased food for eight days, and told the embassy chargé d'affaires not to worry if he hadn't heard from us by ten days.

~~~

The first morning the boats leapt, turned, and tipped down cataracts in rapid fire. It was a great beginning; spirits crackled with excitement.

Being first to travel this river we tried to stop and scout each rapid. We would tie up the rafts and make our way along the cliffs until we found a vantage point where we could best determine how to make the run. Then we'd cross fingers, make the SOBEK handshake that Lew invented, and go for it.

After fifteen miles of white-jacketed water, we spun into a tranquil pool, and I shipped my oars. Frowning basalt cliffs, some four hundred feet high, framed a bright blue sky. Silently we drifted around a bend and caught sight of a small herd of lesser kudus drinking at river's edge. The antelope spotted us, hesitated, then trotted off to the protection of a vegetation-choked flat. On the other bank I spied a black and white masked beisa oryx, his back jeweled with a red-billed oxpecker, his head adorned with distinctive straight horns, each like the horn of a unicorn.

Shortly downstream we saw a strange dull blue and white object bobbing through the water. We fell into silence as I pulled closer. A few feet from the object Lew shattered the silence: "It's a dead fish!"

It was huge, the size of a small dog. I poked its hard skin, and over it slowly rolled. The entire bottom section was missing . . . it had been bitten in half. For a beat nobody spoke a word, but we could all hear the common thought echoing—crocodiles. Up at the falls where we launched we had met a Danish tourist who told us that just two years earlier a couple of Germans had constructed a makeshift raft and headed downstream. They were forced to abandon their trip after two days when their paddles were bitten to pieces by hungry crocs.

Believing crocodiles would be a problem, I had smuggled in, through diplomatic pouch, a collapsible .30-06 rifle. I now pulled it from its case, assembled it, and positioned it next to my leg, within easy reaching distance. Minutes later we spotted the pebbled skin of our first crocodile. As we rounded a bend it splashed into the water, the speed of a rat. We guessed its length as about five feet. Nervously we all bunched toward the center of the boat, though I couldn't help but feel it was like rearranging deck chairs on the *Titanic*. If the crocodile wanted to sink our craft, he could do so with a snap. But the crocodile never resurfaced, perhaps more scared of us than we of him. We wondered. I asked Lemma how we should deal with a crocodile about to clamp down on a body part. His useful reply was that I should stick a knife into the croc's mouth and cut its jaw muscles. "But you must be fast," he warned. I had also read that because the reptile's jaw muscles are basically one-directional, a quick-thinking person could actually hold the snappers closed with bare hands. A third method was explained in a book I was carrying in my ammo box, *Animal Kitabu* by Jean-Pierre Hallet. He said that crocodiles cannot turn heads sideways because their cervical vertebrae bear bony ribs that stiffen and immobilize the neck. Crocodile jaws are forced to operate in a strictly horizontal plane, and thus if a man can remain in a vertical po-sition, he is, theoretically, in no danger. Jean-Pierre said he tested this the-ory once on Lake Tanganyika when a misfired dynamite blast threw him out of his boat, taking off his hand, and severely lacerating his face. Not one to panic, Jean-Pierre—when he saw seven giant crocodiles speeding toward him—assumed a vertical position and did a one-handed dog pad-dle one hundred feet to shore. All the thwarted crocodiles could do was snap in vain, and occasionally sample bits of Hallet's shirt.

As we continued down the Awash we sighted about one hundred crocodiles, some measuring up to twelve feet long, but all reacting in the same swift, nervous manner, without attacking or even charging us. Per-haps naming our exercise SOBEK worked.

Under the ruddy light of pre-evening we strained oars to pull into an eddy halfway down a rocky rapid where stretched some small, shale ledges. The ancestral fear of wild animals had us seek a safeguarded place to camp. The rapid, we figured, would offer protection from crocodiles, and with boulders walling in much of the camp, we had only to defend one side. But once the gear was unloaded, Ifru pointed out we were ad-jacent to a game trail. With that information, Ifru and Lemma began building a witchburner fire, but one strategically placed so as not to illu-mine any sleeping figures on whom a Danakil could draw a bead. "They are bad people," Lemma explained, "who shoot first and use their knives afterwards."

Because we were just 9 degrees north of the equator, the night fell like a guillotine at six. The stars had a diamond quality, undimmed by clouds or city lights. There was a rattle of breezes in the thorn trees. The crack-ling howls of hyenas, the eerie yelps of jackals, and the grumbling of other animals came out of the surrounding forests at disturbing intervals. Lions and other cats have been known to attack campers at night, but hyenas are the only animals that attack fairly regularly. At park headquarters we had been told of some recent tourists who slept out in the open without a fire, and they were found the following morning, faces chewed off.

Just as we slipped into our sleeping bags, we heard a rustling just beyond the camp perimeter. I turned on my flashlight, swept the beam around, and caught the reflection of a spotted hyena's eyes thirty feet away. His was a loping, ghostly form, and his insane, windblown laughter sounded like some demoniac convocation of witches, and sent a shiver down my spine. His marble eyes, chuckling and cunning, were devoid of innocence—no innocent creature survives along this river. I suggested we alternate vigils, volunteered for the first watch, and stoked the fire. The smoke of doom seemed to drift like a deadly gas all night.

I awoke at the crack of noon. Actually, it was 6:00 A.M. on my watch, but Ethiopia uses a clock that is six hours later than our own, which makes sense because hour one begins at dawn, rather than after one goes to bed.

Faces intact, we made breakfast, and each popped our once-a-week-on-Sunday malaria pill, a 200-mg prophylaxis tablet that would keep the sporozoan parasites from the bites of anopheline mosquitoes inactive. Then we loaded the rafts and spun downstream. We were scarcely an hour out of camp when we spied on the bank a young man leading a camel. A thin strip of leather was tied across his forehead and back into his bushy hair. On his narrow hips rested a curved, double-edged knife as broad as a hand and almost long as a sword. Over his shoulders rested a long, ancient rifle, supporting both hands. He was a Danakil.

From all the varied information and misinformation we received in Addis Ababa, one fact emerged without dispute: we would be traveling through the cruel heart of Danakil country. Ethiopia is a land of many nations, some of which have paid no more than token allegiance to the government. We were in one of those places. The Danakils are traditionally a warrior people and place a different value on human life than most—especially a stranger's. In fact, for centuries, to have killed a man was a prerequisite for social status.

Particularly disturbing was the manhood rite we were told was still practiced. When a man reaches marriageable age, he must leave his village on a quest to prove his worthiness. He cannot return until he brings with him the testicles of a member of an enemy tribe, or a *ferenji*. We, like all foreigners, were ferenjis.

Wilfred Thesiger wrote of the cult of murder among the Danakil: "A Danakil man's prowess is rated by the number of 'kills' of other men. Naturally, proof of these kills is required, so the hunter castrates his victims, sometimes while they are still alive."

What was even more alarming was that we had been told this was the marrying season, and that those on the hunt wore headbands, such as the one sported by the man on shore. We had few options as the current swung us closer to the fuzzy-haired nomad. We could posture aggression, position my rifle with its plastic stock, but his was a more powerful-looking weapon, and he looked more experienced. We could ignore him, looking the other way. Instead, we all pulled out our harmonicas and began playing a lively rendition of the Marlboro theme song, slapping thighs in rhythm, trying to look happy and carefree. With insolent eyes he watched our antics. Then, just as we slid past his perch he broke into a smile white as bleached bone, and raised his hand to wave.

For lunch we stopped at a grove of tamarind and sycamore fig trees crowded with silky-furred colobus, barking like frogs, and making acrobatic leaps among the bearded branches. The spot smelled strongly of sulfur, and back from the river there was a sharp-edged wall, broken by scooped-out cavities and curves, down which a small waterfall trickled. The rock around the falls was dull red, like burnt brick, splotched with sulfurous yellow and faded, weathered brown. The wall looked unfinished, like an interrupted explosion. We walked back into the woods above the cliff to investigate. There we found a small mineral hot springs. An acacia spread across its dark pool. Its rough foliage, structured in horizontal layers, was unlike that of any tree I had seen in America. Its formation gave it a heroic air, like a full-rigged ship with sails clewed up.

The acacia seemed so ancient it would have been easy to believe it had stood there for hundreds, perhaps thousands of years. Around the springs were various offerings—a jar of oil, a heap of millet, a white plastic button, curls of wire, small piles of roasted coffee beans. In their own way these oblations contributed to the peculiar character of the place: eerie, but by no means menacing. I shivered, feeling goose bumps for the first time in Africa.

What multiplied this otherworldly effect, however, was the fact that every branch of the tree to a height of about six feet had been festooned with woven strips of varicolored cloth and string. Rustling in the wind, these waving pennants and ribbons seemed to whisper and murmur, as though seeking to impart a message. We touched the living wood, sensed its age, and then, even though it was over 100 degrees in the shade, we stripped and slipped into the hot springs for some sort of sanctification bath.

After lunch the sun unleashed its full power. It felt as if we were rowing wrapped in hot towels. The air burned our throats. It felt like hell. The effect was heightened by the presence of rows of marabou storks, some hooked around dead branches that looked like gibbets. With their bald red heads, dandy gray feathers edged in white, fleshy pink necks, rattling bills, and wings folded to an oval, they looked like undertakers in morning coats. They evoked an air of irredeemable depravity as a group gravely pecked at an unidentifiable carcass. But our infernal passage was forgotten with the next attraction.

We heard the splashing and shouting long before we saw "Maytag" beach. The town of Awash Station was nearby and this was the municipal watering and washing hole. Awash Station was the contact point between the desert nomads, Afars and Issas, and the Amhara highlanders, between Muhammadism and Christianity. This was a border few crossed with impunity. When the desert dwellers ventured to higher ground their camels would die and they would soon lose heart in the fearful cold. When the Amharas came down into the desert their mules collapsed in the appalling heat, and they were soon driven back into the hills for lack of water. It is a conflict point between two absolutely different ways of life. Only the river bound these opposing worlds together. And only the raft bound our two guides, Lemma and Ifru. Lemma—thin, lively, and good-looking, with light coffee skin—was a Christian Amharic, and he exuded a certain hubris that came with his highland blood and a religious tradition that dated back well over two thousand years. Ifru came from the desert; he was a Muslim with skin so dark it absorbed my camera flash. Yet, while working together to get our boats downstream, their differences disappeared, and the common goal erased all borders.

We couldn't have guessed at the reception, or at the numbers of people, clothes, fishing lines, camels, goats, cows, and donkeys we would pass. At least three hundred people were working, milling, playing along the shore. Bare-breasted women were slapping brightly colored cotton clothes on the rocks; others were filling goatskin waterbags and then carrying them on their heads with perfect posture back to the village. Swart, butter-groomed men with rifles slung across shoulders surveyed the scene like room proctors from the upper beach. Children were bathing, splashing, giggling. Teenage girls were dressing one another's hair in multitudinous tiny plaits.

The boys spotted us first, and hit the water from every direction and began swimming our way, yelling, "*Carmella! Carmella!*" (candy). I cranked my rowing into a higher gear as we watched the armada of thrashing, naked swimmers get closer. "This ain't no Disneyland," Lew observed with a crinkly smile.

Fortunately, a Class III rapid intervened, and kept the swimmers at bay as we rounded a bend and left the human chaos behind.

Now all we heard was the rush of the river. We turned another corner and surprised the stateliest of antelope, the greater kudu, with its long spiral horns and distinctive white body stripes. Another turn and we spilled into a curvy, narrow, steep-walled canyon, which we dubbed the Labyrinth. The river branched and brachiated, boiled into dusty eddies and side currents. Right-angle turns in the tight main channel caused us to collide with walls, glance off, and gyre down the maze. It formed a plexus of waterways so confusing it could never be mapped. Like billiard balls on a ten-cushion shot, we bounced through.

After the mitotic expansion of the Labyrinth, the river began to flow easily for some time, which was fine with us, as we were approaching the Awash Station Bridge and hoped to slip beneath it as unobtrusively as possible. It was here the young Wilfred Thesiger in 1930 did some spying for the British government, and a letter to his mother let the cat from the bag: "I am rather busy at the minute finding out about possible landing grounds, food, etc. for the air force. I have got to be rather discreet as the Abyssinians are not to know." Five years later the Italians invaded Abyssinia and blew up the Awash Station Bridge.

So it was with some justification there was a certain paranoia that existed around this reconstructed bridge. The reign of Emperor Haile Selassie I, King of Kings, the Negus Negesti, Elect of God, Conquering Lion of the Tribe of Judah, had not been without incident. Rebel groups had formed, attempted assassinations, and had tried to take strategic sectors of the empire, including bridges. Haile Selassie was a strong-armed ruler, though, and had successfully snuffed out all insurgent attempts to this point. One way he had done this was by stationing armed guards at all bridges, at all times. We did not want to incur the wrath, or even provoke the curiosity, of the guards on the Awash Station Bridge.

So, our goal was to glide silently beneath the girders and slip around the bend unnoticed. Just above the bridge, however, Tom's oar caught a rock in a trifling rapid. The rope holding the oar to the lock snapped, and he struggled to negotiate the boat with the single oar. There was no time to stop and try and fix the oar; he had to keep going. But the single-oar maneuver put the raft into a spin, and it struck several rocks, sending noisy splashes into the air, and the commotion caught the attention of two armed guards on the bridge. They waved their rifles wildly at us and shouted abruptly, clearly wanting us to stop. Instead, we picked up the pace, spun beneath the bridge, and began a dash for the next turn of the canyon. The guards ran across the bridge and then along the canyon rim, chasing us, making threatening gestures. The swift water and tight rocky channels were making it tough for Tom to maneuver, but he kept his head low and kept pulling his one oar, bouncing off the big rocks at just the right angles so the raft would miss the smaller ones that could catch and hold it, which would give our pursuers the extra minutes needed to overtake us.

Finally, we outdistanced them and rounded a bend that put them out of sight. The water was calmer now. We had entered what we would name Warthog Canyon. As we drifted along, Tom repairing the oarlock, we surprised a convocation of warthogs. They seemed to be sniffing something on the north shore, but when they saw us, they shot their fly-swatter tails straight into the air and scrabbled away in line with neat small steps. We pulled over to see what had brought them to the bank, and there found the carcass of the warthog, dried to a veiled vellum, that had taken the fall off the canyon rim a week before during our scout. Its ten-inch tusks curled into the gravel, and bouquets of flies buzzed around its rotting flesh, and maggots negotiated its sticky, dried blood. Were the other hogs grieving, scavenging, poking about in curiosity, or engaged in some unidentified behavior? Unlike the big-eyed primates that attract researchers and funding, the warthogs, so ugly by our standards, have never had a Jane Goodall or Dian Fossey to devote long-term study and analyze behavior, so what they do and how they act in the wild is still a mystery.

A few hours later the walls tapered back, the valley through which we sailed wrinkled into dry ridges, like a badly healed cicatrix, and we entered a zone we would call the Doldrums. The landscape became monotonous: mud banks, hard red termite mounds, trees with finger-sized thorns, a sun-fried furnace under a bleached sky. Dust devils whirled up like great columns of smoke. The river became sluggish, and the boats seemed to hang motionless on the water like junks in a Chinese painting. We could shut our eyes for an hour and when we opened them again see exactly what we saw before. Not only were there no signs of life or current, there was the smell of death in the air. Spaced along fairly regular intervals were the carcasses of dozens of wild and domesticated animals, several impaled in the broken branches of the countless logjams that clogged this section of the river. The hot sun scooped up the smell and spread it like a thin mist.

We were seeing the results of a drought that had been gripping parts of Ethiopia for years, one the outside world knew little about, as Haile Selassie had done his best to conceal it for fear of international repercussions. He was a wealthy emperor, with huge land ownings and Swiss bank accounts, and the world might not understand if he continued to wrap himself in opulence while thousands of his subjects were dying in drought.

For days we were never able to get our backs into the oars before we had to stop for a tree blocking the way. Most of these, we could see, had been chopped down, likely by local herders to bring the buds and green tree stems to their hungry livestock and camels to feed. This was one obstacle even our perfervid imaginations never anticipated.

While negotiating the Doldrums the chief excitement was listening to the soft lament of the emerald-spotted wood dove, and watching black kites float, without moving their wings, in the currents above. Even the crocodiles didn't oblige us with a scare. The river's dry banks jeered at us, grinning through mustaches of driftwood left from long-ago high water. We prayed for the long-overdue short rains. We couldn't go for a swim to cool off for two very good reasons: it took just one crocodile sneaking up from below; and there was the distinct possibility of schistosomiasis, or bilharzia, a fatal snail-borne disease found in slow-moving tropical waters. George Fuller, who in his capacity as a pathobiologist was studying schistosomiasis distribution for Haile Selassie I University, had brought collecting nets on the trip, and had in fact scooped up some vector-carrying mollusks in this section, and he accordingly announced we should avoid even the briefest contact with the water (it only takes a few seconds of exposure to contract the disease).

For four days we strained bodies and oars through this snaking trench, the river surface flat as a griddle, hoping each bend would be the last, watching the right bank like hawks to be sure we wouldn't miss the little stone school house that meant we had reached our destination— Gewani. Yet all we ever found was another bend, and more camel flies. Then the current died completely, petered out in a haze of heat, as though dammed or confined in some way farther down, and we were deprived the luxury of drift. Dead leaves bobbed motionless on the water as oars clumped against the frames, rhythmic and dull. Something seemed wrong. Did the river just dead-end? I knew the river eventually emptied into the briny waters of endorheic Lake Abbe in the Danakil Depression, at 380 feet below sea level, the lowest point in Africa, at the border with Djibouti. Even though our maps had lost their grip, they showed this lake to be two hundred miles away. Wherever we were, the river here certainly wasn't going anywhere; it had simply stopped running.

CHAPTER 7

# CAPSIZE

"The face of the water, in time, became a wonderful book—a book that was a dead language to the uneducated passenger, but which told its mind to me without reserve, delivering its most cherished secrets as clearly as if it uttered them with a voice. And it was not a book to be read once and thrown aside, for it had a new story to tell every day."

—Mark Twain, 1883

We all sensed an intangible atmosphere of imminence, as though a huge charge of lightning was building up within a thundercloud. Suddenly we heard a soft roar and scanned the distant river line for the telltale signs of a cataract—smooth approach water, the occasional tossed spume, and the perceptible fall in the tree line on either side. The water beneath our boats began to agitate almost imperceptibly; delicate swirls appeared on the surface as if traced by a feather. Then they multiplied, and cut deeper, and the sound came on. This was more than a rapid. This was the deep-throated thunder of a waterfall. We moored at the top of the falls and ran ahead to see what we could hear. Starved for excitement over the past days of "Sargasso River," there was a flickering of hope in all our minds that we would be able to run it. The falls took a sheer fifteen-foot drop across the entire river, except for a rock-scattered ledge that descended diagonally down the escarpment on the right side.

If we attempted it, it would be the biggest falls any of us had ever run, with a likely capsize outcome. But the botfly of boredom had been buzzing our boats, so we were ready to try anything.

We would have to enter dead-on, going as fast as possible, with all our weight in the back. We wanted to shoot the bow out into the air as far as possible to avoid an end-over-end flip. The approach, unfortunately, was narrow and rocky. We decided to ship the oars and use the paddles to get through, as a bad oar stroke could catch a crab and turn us sideways on the brink.

We lined up above the target channel when a precious moment was lost to indecision.

"To the left of that round one?" Kramer asked, pointing at a nubbin rock near the lip.

"No, to the right," George answered.

"To the left!" I screamed.

My paddle cracked against a rock; we started to pivot sideways. "Straighten us out!" I cried.

Too late. The raft hung sideways on the brink of the falls for a long instant, and then very slowly started to tilt. We were capsizing, sideways. I looked below and tried to scout the rapids into which we were about to tumble. I thought of holding on in hopes my weight might right the boat. But it was futile. In a flash we were over the edge. George Fuller, on the other side of the boat, directly below me, was framed in the foam at the foot of the falls, his face with the look of a puzzled sheep. We landed softly enough as the boat plowed underwater on one side, and folded lengthwise to absorb the shock. I pushed myself off the raft while it was still falling, but it was directly above me now. I was suddenly underwater. A muffled explosion echoed above me.

I've got to get clear, I thought to myself, recalling tales of drowned boatmen on the Colorado caught beneath rafts.

$$\sim\!\sim\!\sim$$

I felt the blow of tons of water thudding down on my head. The river went into my ear like an icepick. I thrashed a few desperate strokes toward the direction I hoped was up, and suddenly found myself gasping those first precious breaths of air. Looking back, I saw the slamming cascades of the falls not ten feet behind me. But I saw no sign of Kramer and George. Were they knocked out? Swept downstream? Caught beneath the raft? First George broke the surface, sucked in air, breathing like a bus. Then Kramer was vomited up in a whirl of whitewater. We each struggled to shore. The upside-down raft spun into an eddy, and there, with the entire crew, we righted it. Nothing lost; just a layer of grit, and pride.

There was no time to rehash the run over the falls. The sun was setting, and we had to find a campsite. As fast as we could, we carried the other raft around the falls, then relaunched. Below us were three smaller falls, which we maneuvered uneventfully, and then we pulled into a pleasant-looking spot for camp. We had just begun to unload the first of our gear when I glanced up. What I saw made me drop the bag I had just been handed. It was a graveyard silhouette of two men with rifles and long knives. They were unmistakably Danakils, and they were wearing the telltale headbands, indicating they were out to prove their manhood by stealing someone else's. We quickly reloaded the boats and pushed back into the current. The tribesmen followed us along the shore, ululating and waving their weapons. After a couple miles we lost sight of them and came to a booming rapid we didn't want to run in the fading light. So, we pulled over, with intent to camp, but first we scouted the long, steep rapid with flashlights, trying to memorize the run, just in case we might have to abandon the site in the middle of the night.

That night, we did our cooking on a GAZ stove, ignoring the abundant firewood on the shingle beach. While other nights we built huge fires to keep the wildlife at bay, here we figured it might act as a beacon to Danakil testicular trophy hunters. This time I volunteered for the last shift, so I quickly slipped into my bag after our dinner of fried tuna and cheese and tried to force sleep. But the music of the African night was too loud. Insects, birds, and monkeys screeching in the most bloodcurdling manner kept me awake, or so I thought. Kramer shook me awake as the gibbous moon began to set. I wrapped my sleeping bag over my shoulders, sat cross-legged with the .30-06 across my lap, and hummed Beatles songs to keep me awake. I was aware of the faint effulgence shed by the clusters of stars and the moon, and I could just make out the silhouettes of wild animals at our perimeter. But I would blink, and see they were bushes and trees. The long, lonely hours with the barrel barely glinting in the bright starlight gave me time to reflect on what I would do if actually attacked. I had gone on a white-tailed deer hunt once, but never saw one of the antelopes, just a pair of antlers on a trail, which I brought home as my trophy. Now I wondered if I could pull the trigger on a human.

The shuttles of dawn nudged me awake. I had fallen asleep on the job, but we were no worse for my failing, and nobody seemed to hold it against me, if they even knew, and I didn't volunteer. We didn't dally, though, especially when Ifru noticed a deeply rutted camel track to the river adjacent to camp; he figured this was a watering hole, and drivers and guards would be here with the sun.

We didn't float far before encountering a small boy, perhaps ten years old, with a camel on the bank. He waved us over with a frantic gesture. "Don't go," George said sternly, "it could be a trap." But as we hied by it looked as though the boy was in pain, and he pointed at his eye. "Let's take a look," Lew suggested. "He's just a boy." So, I turned my raft in and beached at the feet of the boy. We all got out and the boy pointed to a suppurating right eye, which had the beginnings of a yellow film and gobs of mucus dripping down his cheek. George was our trip doctor, and we asked what we might do, and George looked at the eye and pronounced it beyond saving. "Can't we do anything?" I implored.

"No . . . and what's the use? If we give him something it will run out and he'll be back where he was. And the others who are sick in the village will give him an unfounded higher status if he gets medicine from ferenjis. It's akin to begging; it will encourage all of them. In Calcutta some parents cut off the limbs of their children because they make better beggars. It's a slippery slope if we give out medicine randomly. I say we just keep going."

It all seemed well articulated to me, and I began to wrap up the bowline. But as I was readying to push off Lew snapped open his ammo box, pulled out a small tube of infection medicine, and handed it to the boy, who bowed deeply several times in gratitude. "I don't care about George's rationalizations. If I see someone who needs help, I will help." With that George and Lew climbed on different rafts, and we pulled into the current.

By this time the drudgery of slogging through the blazing "Sargasso" stretch was forgotten, and we welcomed the rest a short section of flat water afforded. We didn't relax long, though, before discovering the cause of the laggard water: immense strands of lava, twisted like cordage, wrapped around a tremendous blob of basalt, damming the river. A nearby volcano had erupted millions of years ago, and a molten hunk the size of a city block landed in this spot, causing the river to go mad, and making our passage a bit of a dilemma. Here the water entered a dark warren of waterways, honeycombs of falls, secret passages, and channels that went in circles. Half the water escaped into hidden catacombs; we could get a boat into this mess without much problem, but we would never be able to get it back out again. A Hotel California: we could check out, but we could never leave.

We had reached the beginning of the most hated task of all river runners: the long portage. This was to be a hot, joyless, backbreaking task. As we lugged our equipment the half mile around the grotesque formation there was no smiling as we passed one another coming and going. We began by hauling the lighter stuff, the fifty-pound food bags and water-saturated clothing duffels, dragging them over unavoidable barriers and down the steep final drop that stepped to the river. Then we hoisted the boats onto our raw, sweat-soaked shoulders and stumbled through the scoriae, balancing precariously as we alternately dropped into dry sink-holes and stepped over crusty crags. There were moments when each of us stepped into a hollow, and the weight was momentarily carried by the others; worse was when one of us stepped up while everyone else went down, and the entire two hundred pounds was suddenly on a single neck. One slip would be a broken neck or leg, or crushed skull. Six hours after we began we had the boats back in the water, fully dressed. We had been lucky; our only casualties were one severe headache (Lemma's) and one badly wrenched neck (Kramer's).

We had traveled less than a mile on this, the eighth day, and wanted to take advantage of the smooth water ahead to make up lost time. Our friends in Addis were expecting us two days ago, and we had no idea how much longer it would take, not that we ever really did.

We had barely stoked the oars to cruising speed when we once again heard the liquid thunder. Just downstream the river went roaring over another fifteen-foot waterfall and landed in a pile of sharp rocks before falling twice more and coming to rest in a swirling pool. For a moment I thought there was a slim chance of making it, and I might have tried it, but for Lew, who in his unschooled wisdom looked at the maelstrom and interposed, "Jesus, a guy could get killed in there." The words were a re-ality check, and I backed down. I recognized that besides the objective dangers, after a day of grueling portage in the desert heat our reflexes were sluggish, there was a sort of woolliness in our minds. Judgment was probably not at peak levels.

My body felt like it had been used for batting practice, my mind was numb, and my consuming desire was to finish our journey. So, I called camp at the most dangerous spot yet—a watering hole right above the falls. There was no escaping downstream if we were visited in the night. So, we readied the rifle, axes, and knives, prepared a soul-strengthening dinner of lentils, chicken soup cubes, canned fruit, and hot peppers with at least 200,000 BTUs, and we built a zareba of thorn bushes and hedges around the perimeter of the camp with various used food cans hanging from branches at intervals. Lemma and Ifru volunteered for an all-night vigil, despite Lemma's bad headache, and what must have been exhaustion as severe as mine.

With the rifle neatly tucked into the bilge, I pillowed my head on my hands and tried to sleep in the boat, thinking I might protect our only means of transportation in a last-ditch effort. But just as I was drifting off, I heard the sound of crocodiles splashing, and moved my feet closer to the middle of the raft. Knowing that just twenty-one inches of plastic tube was all that separated me from the water, I couldn't bring sleep, despite utter fatigue. In the middle of the night I looked over to see Ifru and Lemma both fast asleep. I considered getting up, but exhaustion overcame anxiety, and I at last slipped into sleep. A sharp pain in my neck jolted me upright—I had bent a muscle trying to use the raft tube as a pillow. I looked to shore. Lew was reheating the lentils; Lemma was stuffing a wetpack. The sky was purpling with the first thin streak of dawn.

"Lining" the boats, or lowering them down the falls on ropes, is easier than portaging. We decided we would line the boats at this juncture. The only question was how?

We considered a Tyrolean traverse that would extend diagonally from the island over the falls to the left-hand bank. The British Army team had tried this on the one-hundred-foot Tissisat Falls on the Blue Nile, only to have one of the boats get caught in the thrashing maelstrom for twenty-four hours. We considered belaying the boat from certain rock or tree anchor points. We finally decided that all plans had the same likelihood of failure as the simplest one of all: kick the boats over the falls (with ropes tied to the bows) and pull them in below.

And that's what we did. We emptied the boats and carried the gear and provisions around the falls. We tied our goldline to one end of the first boat and uncoiled it out to Lew and Lemma, waiting below the falls. Then Tom and I, with the bowline, positioned the boat atop the falls, anchored by a chrome-moly piton we had hammered into a crack. Then we pushed the first raft into the current. It hung up on a nubbin at the edge of the falls, at a nasty spot we didn't particularly want to broach. While arguing options, a Danakil suddenly appeared, hair daubed with ghee, his snow-white teeth filed into points so they looked like fangs. He waded into the fast current to his waist and pushed our boat off the rock, over the falls. Lew and Lemma were able to pull the raft in like a big fish at just the right moment, and paid the boat into a tiny chute free of rocks. The Danakil assisted with the second raft as well, then waded over to Lew, took his hand, and kissed the back of it. Lew bent over and returned the gesture. Then the Lone Danakil stepped up the bank, strode across the hard-packed bank, and disappeared into a portable brushwood hut the size of an igloo. "He may be a murderer," Lew laughed, "but no one could call him inhospitable."

In the sweet liquid light of the African morning, we loaded the boats and off again we sailed. The rapids encountered were all easy to run, and consisted mostly of sharp fin waves with few rocks. These were the most pleasurable rapids run so far, and we were as giddy as the needle of a cheap compass. Lew suggested this would be a fitting end for the trip.

By midday, however, the current quickened, and around one bend we were ripped into another pipeline. Dry wind in our faces, a buckle of noise in the air, mist kicking over the bow, down the Awash we sped. We dodged a small rock to the left, then a promontory on the right, and scraped a boulder in the center as the channel narrowed.

The river was now less than ten yards wide. The current roared down a funnel between two boulders turning the air between them white. We were headed for something terrible. At the touch of the left bank, Lew leapt out into the air with bowline in hand. I pulled back on the oars as hard as I could to try and slow us down. The only way we could stop before being hurled into the explorer's lacunae, that space between the known and imagination, would be if Lew could arrest us from shore. But first Lew had to get past the slick and slimy moss coating the rocks at waterline. Lew slapped down one foot after another, running at full speed but losing ground to the frictionless surface beneath his feet. I could see him running even while his head disappeared into the muddy water. His dunking, though, didn't last but an instant. Propelled by fear, he lurched from the water, draped his whole body around a boulder, and used the added traction of pants and life jacket to embrace the shore. Lew established a beachhead and tied us in. The rope went taut. We stopped, at the edge of oblivion: a thirty-foot waterfall that crashed into a rack of sharp rocks.

The portage around the falls took several hours, but we launched again late afternoon. The rest of the day was spent charging down a river writ with lightning. Below one cataract, we spilled over to a rock patch, and I dipped my oar into a crack to hold the boat while I waited for Tom's raft to catch up. And while watching upstream, I felt the blade of my oar move in an unnatural way. I turned and jumped back at the sight: a rock python, maybe eight feet long, was slithering across the blade of my oar, up toward me, like a train coming into a station. I grabbed the oar with both hands and shook it violently. The snake fell off, plopped into the water, and swam away.

As the hot red sunset burnt out the remnants of the day, we pulled the boats over to stop and bed down for a well-deserved night's sleep. As the rest of us were rolling out sleeping bags, George, ever-energetic, donned a headlamp, slipped on his rubber collecting gloves, set out the castor oil plates, took out a mist net and aspirator, and began his nightly search for exotic insects and ectoparasites. Whenever he found something he liked, he would drop it into a tube filled with formalin solution, or display it volant in a collection book. He alone was fulfilling our obligation to Smithsonian, and it was his favorite part of the trip.

A pale dawn swallowed the ink of night. It was our tenth day on the river. Since we had expected to be out only six, we hadn't packed an excess of food, and now were running short. However, there was no reason to fear going hungry. The fish in the Awash apparently had little experience with fishermen (who could ever get into these gorges?), and the only problem was that so many were breaking our six-pound test line as we hauled them up the cliff, we were losing most of our hooks. One large fish I pulled in flopped about camp, whiskers spitting water, and I reached down to prevent it from flipping back in the river, and was knocked back several feet, my hat flying off, as though I'd put my hand in an electric socket. It was an electric catfish. Nobody intervened as the fish wriggled itself to the edge of the cliff and plopped back into the river. But the other fish, mostly Nile perch and tilapia (a breamlike fish), made for good eating.

We didn't have to go far before the next obstacle presented itself. Protruding rocks, like giant, black, crooked shark teeth, shielded the entrance to a five-hundred-foot gorge. By the simple expedient of standing still these rocks dashed hopes of easy navigation. Beyond the rock jaws, we couldn't see a thing. Tying the boats to a crack in the wall, Tom, Kramer, and I scaled the cliff to a ledge from where we could see what needed to be done. The only way through was to turn the rafts on their sides and squeeze them through like toothpaste. With four of us standing on one entrance rock, three on the other, we tugged, nudged, yanked, dragged, crammed, and pinched the boats through.

Another mile and the canyon walls began to retreat. Lew ventured, "This looks like the end of the gorge." The last rapid was an easy pitch, and then the Awash took its foot off the accelerator, never to speed again.

The following afternoon we drifted to our destination, the Gewani Peace Corps School. Lew, in best Al Jolsen imitation, broke into song: "Gewani, how I love ya; how I love ya, my dear old Gewani." We pulled in and were greeted by two men from the nearby Trapp Construction

Company, who had flown over us that morning and calculated our arrival time. They took some photos and treated us to an ice cooler full of beer, Fanta, and Ambo, Ethiopia's own sparkling mineral water.

As we posed for a final shot, holding an oar between us, Lew smiled expansively and said, "We made it! Two hundred and forty virgin river miles in eleven days. That's history, man!" It was a full hundred years after Stanley had found Livingstone, and I felt like a pioneer. I reached over and held the heels of my hands together; the fingertips yawed wide like the open rictus of a crocodile. Lew looked at my gesture, then winked and slipped his hands between mine to work the SOBEK handshake. We each then went to the others and performed our ritual. We'd done it.

Back in Addis, we reveled in our success. I gave a slide show to a packed house at the USIA center, and the embassy threw a party in our honor. I appeared on Ethiopian TV, my first time on camera, and I felt like Henry Morton Stanley as a guest on Johnny Carson. I traded in my torn cutoffs for a new pair of khaki shorts and strutted like an explorer.

# CHAPTER 8

# THE RIVER OMO

"Of the gladdest moments in human life, methinks, is the departure upon a distant journey into unknown lands. Shaking off with one mighty effort the fetters of Habit, the leaden weight of Routine, the cloak of many Cares and the slavery of Home, man feels once more happy. The blood flows with the fast circulation of childhood. . . . Afresh dawns the morn of life. . . ."

—Richard Burton, journal entry, December 2, 1856

F our weeks later, still basking in the shine of our successful Awash expedition, it was time to get back on a river. As we went over the list of possibilities, we decided on the Omo, as we felt emboldened and a bit competitive. Why not beat the *National Geographic* expedition to the River Trip of the Century?

On April 24 we piled into the back of a long-bed pickup and bounced four hours down a rough gravel road south to the Jimma Bridge at the village of Abelti, the put-in for our Omo expedition. At noon we were unceremoniously deposited along with our two rafts and nine wetbags at the upstream side of the bridge. And without so much as a farewell honk, the truck drove off. Kramer was no longer with us; he had had enough of the company of men and was anxious to get back to his girlfriend. Ifru was no longer part of our party either, as nobody spoke his languages where we were going. That left Tom Cromer, Lew Greenwald,

Lemma, George Fuller, and myself. To the group we added Diane Fuller and Tadessa Wolde Gossa, who had been on the British Blue Nile expedition, and was much lauded as a team member.

Late April was just after the "little rains," and the water swirling between two steep hillsides was more creek than river. A couple of herders drove a dozen dusky lyre-horned cattle to the water's edge as we pumped our rafts. By late afternoon the rafts were rigged and loaded, and we shoved off into the swift current, three months ahead of the scheduled Ron Smith–*National Geographic* "first descent." The river here, called the Gibe, caught and sped us along beneath the arching spans of the bridge, where a dozen spectators stared as though watching the condemned on the way to an execution. In a couple minutes we passed around a sharp bend marked by a molar-shaped volcanic plug, looking like a big thumbs-up. The bridge and people disappeared from sight. We were committed, to a bigger, longer river than the Awash, one that truly flowed into a heart of darkness.

Three miles downriver the Gibe merged with the Omo and the combined stream took on the latter name. The hills rose steeply on either side and soon became cliffs, the cliffs formed themselves into precipitous gorges of columnar basalt, and we were dropping deeper and deeper into the Omo canyon. In a few days we found ourselves at the bottom of a magnificent four-thousand-foot gorge, and the river was littered with boulders, so much so we spent much of our time wrestling the rafts through rock gardens. Radiating out from the main canyon, though, were an increasing number of tributary streams, and each one added a little bit of water to the mother river, and made floating easier. Much of our time was given over to exploring these smaller canyons, hiking back through tangled undergrowth, along well-trodden hippo trails, up rushing streams. There were waterfalls of seeming infinite variety, some plunging more than a thousand feet, the wind catching the flow and blowing great billows of mist over the forest below. One such falls I climbed to its lip alone and gazed down on a landscape that might have been seen from an airplane. The river slipped illimitably between narrow cliffs. Some of the plains looked almost manicured, so meticulously had they been mowed by the mouths of munching hippos. And the dreamy green hills rolled like surf into a distance where they turned purple. I felt fairly certain no human had ever gazed upon this scene. I couldn't resist the moment and sat down on the lip, legs dangling over a thousand-foot drop, and broke out into song: "I'm sittin' on top of the world . . ." The off-key performance echoed up the canyon, warbling back and forth across the boundary between fettered human and feral beast.

As we explored we found emerald grottos dripping with velvet mosses and delicate ferns, still, deep pools perfect for swimming, with rocky perches to one side for diving, and ideal chutes for watersliding like otters. Hours were spent in steamy hot springs, body-sized basins carved from the rock, and polished smooth as bathtubs. At one point I shared an unsuppressed feeling with Lew, one of superiority that comes from moving fast through a pristine wilderness. Because the river appeared so devoid of people, it was easy to imagine that whatever I saw belonged to me. Who else would want it? Simply by traveling so far, did I not have some special claim? Lew let out a great gout of laughter. "You don't own the river; it owns us. It decides what we see and feel, whether we're in awe or dread, whether we live or die. For now, it likes us."

The first few days our most constant companions were the brown-haired Anubis baboons. Frequently troops of thirty to fifty baboons would race ahead along the river's edge. Some were mothers with tiny babies clinging precariously to their backs. At a specific call, they would all dart into the security of the trees while their pack leader assumed an exposed position atop a rock, barking fearlessly at us as we glided by.

The bushbucks, duikers, and dik-diks were all new notches in a burgeoning career of wildlife encounters. One day I swung the boat beneath some overhanging tamarinds, and a three-foot monitor lizard dropped into my bilge. At first I thought it was a crocodile, and made quick-time for the gunwale, ready to dive into the river, but the lizard beat me to it.

But the biggest kicks, literally, were the hippos. Our first encounter with the ponderous quadruped was innocuous: we spotted a pair of beady eyes and wiggling ears sticking out of the water. A few miles later we watched one stroll along the far shore. He walked with elevated deportment, shifting his weight as though he had weak ankles, a great pig with an enormous head and a long, upturned smile. Seeing our rafts, he slipped into the river, opening his mouth to an incredible 45 degrees, the angle of his jaw starting just behind his eye. Then, on the fourth day, I was sawing my oars through a rocky rapid, when my left blade struck a gray rounded boulder . . . and to my shock, it stood up, and with a crooked grin and pink tail spinning, it waddled downstream.

About five feet tall, weighing in at about five tons, about the same as two Land Rovers, hippos are proportionately the fattest animals on earth. And the hippopotamuses were far and away the most abundant form of wildlife along the Omo. In the cooler hours of the day we often surprised them ashore, feeding on the greensward or simply sunning on the beach, and they would react to our sight by stampeding into the river, creating a small tidal wave that would rock the boats. During the heat of the day they wallowed at the bottom of the river, and would constantly bob up out of the water, catch a fast breath and snort at our passing fleet, then dive back under the river's dark lid. Because the river was so silt-laden and murky, the hippos could not see well when submerged, and never really knew where they would surface. More than once the clouds got closer and my stomach sank deeper as an unsuspecting hippo surfaced under my boat and temporarily changed my altitude by several inches. Bolder ones would often stay above water and perform for us— aquatic prima donnas, bulky ballerinas, diving and leaping like the frilly pink-tutued dancers in Disney's *Fantasia*.

As we sank deeper into the Omo canyons the hippo population increased to the point where crowds constituted a real navigational hazard. Sometimes a score would pave the Omo like giant pink stones. One lardy lady rose from the waters about two feet from my gunwale, clacking jaws like an industrial steam shovel. I reacted by stabbing my oar down her throat, a giant tongue depressor, and she plopped back underwater, leaving a thundering silence. On the day of our greatest count— we dodged 375 hippos in a twenty-mile stretch and collided with four—it was like maneuvering through a sea of land mines. Cries of "Hippos right!" or "Hippo left!" rang out every few minutes all day long. From then on we learned to run the gauntlet, carefully hugging first one bank, then the other, always keeping to the shallowest water, where best to see a submerged river horse.

On shore the hippos had a nasty habit of spinning their tails while scattering dung to stake out private territory. On a couple occasions we watched two hippos in disagreement dueling with each other, back to back, using the same far-flung technique. Often there was dung sowed around our campsites, and sometimes we would stake out our own territory as a disincentive to midnight contentions.

Afternoons on the river were hot affairs. Sunlight, reflecting off the water, skip-bombed our eyes. We all wore long pants and shirts, not because of fear of too much sun, but fear of the tsetse flies. Tsetse flies, with their sinister whizzing, dive-bombed into their human targets, hypodermic snouts boring through shirts, pants, even sneakers, sucking our blood with no regard for insect repellent. Though no humans lived in this part of the gorge, it was not because of sleeping sickness, it was that these flies carried disease fatal to cattle. "The tsetse fly," George proclaimed, "is the savior of the African wilderness."

"But this is a rich valley. People are starving in the north. Wouldn't it make sense to eradicate the tsetse and let people move here?"

"No way," George countered. "There are too many people already, and not enough wilderness," and he pulled his raft away.

Halfway down the river we came to a place where the hills jostled one another to the water's edge, and spanning the river was a Bailey bridge, a bizarre edifice as the road on the western side wound up to the village of Soddu, while there was nothing but a cul-de-sac on the eastern side. Here Tom, Tadessa, and Lemma decided to leave the trip. It was the last marked exit point on the river, and the hippos, the heat, the rapids, the portages had taken their toll. We gave them a compass, a Chinese flashlight, some first aid, and money, and made our adieux as they clattered across the wooden planks and headed up the hill. That left four of us: George and Diane Fuller in one raft, Lew Greenwald and myself in the other. We were heading down the vein of darkness. We weren't even certain of the take-out. We had food for two more weeks, and a map that showed the Mui Game Reserve off the eastern bank near the Kenyan border.

Below the Soddu Bridge the crocodile population increased to frightful numbers, but they generally proved elusive and difficult to photograph. Sometimes we'd catch a blur as one scrambled down a bank, its long jaw slightly agape as it vanished into the water. Usually we spotted them floating in the brown waters, pairs of turreted eyes and long nubbined noses, armored backs showing, looking like harmless water-logged pieces of driftwood. Most were leery of our little flotilla, and as soon as they'd sense our presence they would dive underwater, where they could hold breaths for up to an hour. Some bolder ones would resurface for a second glimpse, checking out dinner possibilities, and, of course, these gourmands were the biggest, with the beadiest eyes and the yellowest teeth. Their diet consisted mainly of catfish and Nile perch, but they loved the occasional antelope or bird, and a human was a special treat. Since most of their catches occurred at the eddy line below rapids, they hung out there in big numbers, making the incentive to stay in the raft during a rapid all that much greater. Often when we spilled into the eddy below a rapid, a croc or two would charge the boat with motorboat speed. To deter the charging crocs we used the modern method tried and tested by the British Army on the Blue Nile: we shouted obscenities and threw rocks at the approaching heads.

On day fifteen we were feeling pretty seasoned, accustomed to sharing the river with the crocodiles. There was a subtlety in the predators that defied description and eluded cameras, a capacity to move without exciting attention, a wraithlike quality of unobtrusiveness. Most crocs dove as soon as we'd make a peep, and as we wanted to get some photo documentation of the crocs, we decided to withhold shouts and croc rocks until the last second so we could get some movie footage.

George was our cinematographer with his Super-8 camera, and he was grinding happily away as a fifteen-foot croc slipped off the bank and started steaming toward George's hippo-gray raft. Water skimmed off the croc's snout like spray off the bow of a speedboat. George desperately tried to focus. Twenty feet. George steadied himself in the raft, tightened the grip on his camera. Ten feet. George could see the beady eyes and the acid-yellow teeth. Five feet.

George saw the fleshy yellow lining of a crocodile's throat filling the entire viewfinder. WHAM! George came back to reality to find the thirty-six sharp teeth on each jaw wrapping around the deflating tube of his boat. Cursing, George jumped to the oars and started rowing downstream fast as he could to prevent a half ton of carnivorous vengeance from climbing on board.

Lew and I were upstream and turned when we heard George shouting. I started rowing as hard as I could to catch up, but George was practically hydroplaning, dragging the leviathan as if it were a water-skier, and I couldn't make any headway. Over my shoulder I watched as Diane leapt to the bow of the boat and started beating the bewildered croc on the head with a metal bailing bucket. Crocodiles have unidirectional jaws; they can slam their jaws shut like an iron trap, but almost any pressure can prevent their opening them. The croc's teeth were stuck in the fabric of the boat, so it couldn't release, and it began shaking the raft back and forth like a dog with a rag. George rowed faster, and even though he was dragging several hundred pounds of crocodile, I believe he set a new world rowing speed record, and left me in his wake. After a seeming eternity, perhaps ten long minutes, the dragon finally broke free and disappeared into the river's Cimmerian depths, still hungry, and shedding perhaps crocodile tears. The front section of George's boat was reduced to a shriveled blob. When Lew and I caught up, George was still cursing. Not because of the close call or the punctured raft. George was livid because he missed the shot.

〰〰

Although baboons, hippos, and crocs were our most constant companions, they were not the only ones. We passed vervet and colobus monkeys, rock hyraxes, defessa waterbuck, wild dogs, hyenas, warthogs, and klipspringers. May was a good time for game viewing, dry in the highlands, and animals sought the water of the river. There are about 830 different species of birds in Ethiopia, a couple dozen unique to the country, and we identified a good number. We saw sacred and hadada ibises (with their hilarious mocking cries), snowy egrets, yellow-billed storks, herons, bee-eaters as vivid blue as sapphires, bataleur eagles, malachite and giant kingfishers, a covey of plump blue and gray guinea fowl, masked weavers, and the African fish eagles, with their regal white breasts, tails, and heads. Egyptian geese were everywhere, and at every alarm, imagined or real, they would take flight, hissing and honking about the rafts with a proprietary air. We caught catfish, Blue Nile perch, and when one unidentifiable silver fish jumped into Lew's raft as he was negotiating a ripple, we had the tastiest dinner of the trip.

On the eighteenth day of the expedition we sighted tidy fields of corn and sorghum on the west bank, nodding in a breeze, and a large, needlelike dugout canoe hollowed from a tree moored at the bank. Then we sighted a half dozen hemispherical huts, dotted aimlessly like molehills on the bank— our first village. Several women who were winnowing grain stopped mid-toss, dropped their huge wicker trays, grabbed their children, and ran into their windowless beehives. The men cautiously stepped down to greet us. Regal in simple robes of beaten bark and ivory bracelets, they stood quietly, leaning on the butt end of seven-foot leaf-bladed spears, waiting. They were evidently Nilotic, with their tall, lithe bodies and features much finer than the Bantu tribes to the south. Each man had plucked out all the hairs on his head, save little weaved tufts on the frontal lobe, braided and tied with colored beads and pointing upward like antennae. All of them had their share of decorative scar tissue (keloids) on their shoulders, stomachs, arms, and faces. All were uncircumcised, and we envied them the size of their genitalia. A few had smeared their skins with ashes, a natural sunscreen. It was, perhaps, a first contact, as these people had lived in the geographical and cultural formaldehyde of seclusion for centuries, and had no connection with a country called Ethiopia, and as we later learned from anthropologist David Turton, there were no previous recorded encounters with outsiders. We smiled, made friendly hand gestures, and offered gifts of salt, soap, sugar, cigarettes, and fishhooks, and they warily accepted all. When I offered an Ethiopian coin with Haile Selassie's visage stamped on the front, the leader looked at it for a long time, rubbed his thumb over the face, turned it over, and then gave it back to me. He had no idea what money was and could think of no use. Lew and George made attempts to try and record their unrecorded language, by pointing to familiar things, such as rocks and trees, and eliciting words.

This was, indeed, a primitive place. The year before, a hundred and fifty miles downstream, near the Kenyan border, paleontologists discovered a group of hominid fossils about three million years old, almost double the earliest dated fossils to that point. It was easy to imagine here the Garden of Eden, the Cradle of Man, the Font of Life . . .

Our crude maps showed only two ways to exit the Omo: floating all the way into Kenya, to the soda waters of Africa's second largest lake, named for Prince Rudolf of Austria, where the river flows in and nothing flows out; or by hiking twenty-five miles up a tributary called the Mui River until reaching an airstrip that served a C-47 that brought supplies in once a week to a primitive game park in development. The former option would require an extra two weeks, as the Omo goosenecked for two hundred torpid miles, with upstream winds, before effluing into Lake Rudolf, and we were down to our last couple days of food. Even if we could make it to Rudolf, there was nothing there, save the biggest single population of Nile crocs in the world, some fourteen thousand by recent estimates. Eight years earlier a palm-log "hotel" was built one hundred miles down the lake from the Ethiopian border. But bandits attacked it one night, killing the manager and a Catholic priest who was the sole guest. They captured a third man, an Italian driver named Tony, and forced him to drive the hotel Land Rover until it ran out of gas. Rumor had it that after killing Tony they skinned him, and members of the gang were reputed to be wearing pieces of his skin to this day. The hotel never reopened.

So, we had to find the Mui River. The canyon had opened to valley, and the river had taken a sharp turn to the south past the Maji Mountains and was littered with islands. Matching compass bearings with our map we knew we were in the general area, across from a region cryptically marked as the "Plain of Death." At every tributary on the eastern bank we would stop and hike up a ways to see if it might fit the tracings on the topos. But every tributary turned the wrong way, or didn't seem to carry enough water to qualify as the Mui "River." Some came close, and we debated if we should commit to an extended survey, which would cost days when we were down to hours of food supply. But we always voted to continue. If we missed the Mui, we figured we could starve to death. The stakes were suddenly high.

On day twenty-three Lew was rowing. I was crouched in the bow, lethargic from the heat, calluses burning, given up swatting tsetse flies. I glanced over to the eastern bank and saw, beneath the shiny dark leaves of a spreading fig tree, a clear creek spilling into the Omo, but we were past it. "Lew . . . pull in!" I yelled. He turned the raft and bent his back to fight the current and get the boat to shore. George and Diane were upstream, saw our maneuver, and followed suit. Lew pulled in several yards down from the confluence. A missed glance, another few minutes, and we would have passed it.

This must be it, we all agreed, though none was certain. We agreed George and Diane would camp at the confluence and wait with the gear, while Lew and I would hike up the tributary and hopefully find the Mui River camp and airstrip. We had two cans of tuna left and split them between our two parties, and Lew and I set out. For hours we splashed up the clear river, finding no sign of any human presence. Strawy elephant dung, electric with flies, littered the banks. At one point we turned at a bend in the river and found ourselves face-to-face with a Nilotic buffalo, a mean-spirited beast, heavy of hoof and horn, that usually charges first and never asks questions. He glowered with almost tangible menace, pawed the ground, and snorted short Hemingway sentences, resonant with ill will. We beat a quick retreat to the woods and wandered among the ficus and tamarinds. We wandered for hours. Still no sign of a camp or trail or strip. At sunset, we decided to climb trees, and we each shimmied up as far as we could go on separate trunks. But we could see nothing, just the midnight green of endless primary forest. The ultimate in hopelessness is to be lost, and we were.

We set up our tiny $30 Sears A-frame tent in a tight clump of nettles and bamboo, thinking it would prevent buffalo or other large wildlife from making unwanted visits. We crawled in and opened the last can of tuna. As we shared it we reflected on the adventures we had shared since being in Ethiopia, and wondered aloud if they might be our last. Then we talked about how if we made it out of the Omo we would work hard to make our little enterprise, SOBEK Expeditions, a viable one, one that would take us around the world exploring and adventuring. We admitted we would never get wealthy or well known doing this, but we would have fun. "Wait a minute, Rich," Lew injected. "I have an idea. When we get back, I'll change my name to "Famous." Then we can be Rich and Famous, and have fun, too." We laughed ourselves to sleep.

〜〜〜

Next morning I awoke to rustling and pulled back the tent flap. There, not ten feet away, was a white-buttocksed waterbuck, noshing on breakfast leaves. The delicate animal turned and stared at me, twitching its pointed ears, but continued chewing, showing no signs of fear. "Look, look, look!" I nudged Lew awake. The waterbuck saw Lew's face emerge, and he softly strode toward the tent. Somehow motion seemed frozen as he strolled toward us, pausing a few feet from our portal. Lew gently pulled back the mosquito netting and extended his hand. Instead of running away, as I expected, the waterbuck walked closer. Lew and the antelope exchanged looks, and touched each other for a second, the black nose nuzzling Lew's big hand. Then the waterbuck quietly stepped back into a stand with leafy branches that hung like waterfalls and disappeared.

For a few thaumaturgic moments I didn't harbor any regrets for being lost, didn't begrudge our predicament. I only thought about the unpredictability of nature, and how accepting that can open the mind to surprise and wonder and the delight of serendipity in body Africana.

My stomach growled and the moment broke. We needed to get going if we were to emerge alive from the Omo Valley. We decided to hike inland from the tributary, as we might be able to see farther from the savanna than from within the dense riparian vegetation. But as I made my first steps, arrows of pain shot up my legs. In high school I had been on the track team, and occasionally would suffer from shinsplints. Now, perhaps because I had spent so much time in a raft over the previous weeks, my shins were splinting. It was terribly painful to walk, and I could do so only with a slow limp. To make matters worse, we had to hike through a fence of sharp spicules that lacerated our legs. Lew offered to help me along and carry my pack, the tent, and my canteen. Still, it was tough going.

All day I limped across the savanna, one hand on Lew's shoulder, hunger and exhaustion welling. At one point I stepped on something, and it slithered out into the open—it was a giant rock python, we guessed about seventeen feet long. I was in too much pain and too exhausted to react. It vanished in the undergrowth, and we continued. Late in the day Lew insisted we climb a small hill to see if we might see something. He practically dragged me to the top, and once there I scanned the horizon to all points, and saw herds of Burchell's zebra, bouncing gazelle, a couple of eland and hartebeest, even a running ostrich . . . but no airstrip, just endless wilderness and wildlife. I was ready to lie down and admit defeat, and I told Lew so. "No, we're gonna be rich and famous . . . hang in there," he soothed as he continued to look. Then he stopped and grabbed me. "Look . . . out there." I strained but saw nothing. "Look, beyond those trees." And, yes, I saw it—a tiny metallic glint. The sun had lowered enough to send back a flash of reflecting light. It was something manmade. A renewed energy charged through me.

We practically ran down the hill and made in the direction of the glint. An hour later we summited a small rise, and there in front of us was a thing of phantasmal beauty—a small mud shed with an aluminum roof. Next to it was a hand-painted sign, "Mui International Airport," and beyond, a rough airstrip cleared from the elephant grass. In the shade of the hut was a sleeping teenage boy, and when we woke him up, he stared as though in the midst of his worse nightmare. But he gathered his senses and led us down a path to a small-tented camp beside the Mui River. There we met the park ranger, Mesfin, an Amhara with a Land Rover, and he pulled us into his canvas tent and fed us mountains of millet. Our faces creased as we remembered how good it felt to scratch the elemental itch of hunger. Then, because my leg was still on fire, Mesfin tucked me into my sleeping bag and drove back with Lew to fetch George and Diane Fuller, who had given us up for lost and were preparing to relaunch to cast their fates to the river. For three days we lounged in relative luxury. Mesfin had an old copy of *Reader's Digest* featuring a piece on 101 ways to make hamburgers, and Lew and I drooled over the pictures, vowing to make every recipe with our return to the U.S. Two days later, the Ethiopian Airlines C-47 flew in, and we made the noisy three-hour flight back to Addis, back up over the magic medley of ravines and valleys that made up the Omo catchment, another exploratory expedition under our belts. River water was now my plasma.

Back in Addis, the dynamics were changing. Up to this point, aside from my time on the Colorado, nobody had ever seriously asked my opinion, had ever entertained consulting with me. Now people sought me out, especially the ethno-ists. A man named Leo Sarkesian, calling himself an ethnomusicologist, cornered me at the embassy and wanted my recommendations for Ethiopian instruments. "Listen to the Krar tunes," I proffered, but he misinterpreted and thought I was talking about animation. A young Harvard Medical School graduate, Andrew Weil, found me in the Mercato, and introduced himself as an ethnopharmacologist. He asked if I could recommend any natural drugs found in Ethiopia. "Try chat," I said. "It can put you in an altered state." Lisa Conte, an ethnobotanist, asked if I knew any shaman native medicinal cures. If the tag line meant looking for something in the nonwhite world, I guessed I was an ethnoadventurer.

The Colorado River season had started, so it was time to get back home, to replenish my pockets and start developing our enterprise, which Lew and I now vowed to turn into a business. But just as I was leaving we got caught up in the final scenes of a Hollywood film being made in Ethiopia, *Shaft in Africa,* with Richard Roundtree. Several of my friends in the embassy had walk-ons, and I stood in the wings starstruck as I watched the workings of a big-budget film. For hours Richard Roundtree as John Shaft did takes on an entrance into the Addis Hilton, past an uncooperative lion and a consular officer with whom I had shared several cheeseburgers at the embassy. It was a thrill to be this close to Hollywood, here in Africa, and I had never watched anyone in the process of making a film before. I had met Candice Bergen, but this was different—this was celebrity in action.

CHAPTER 9

# CAPITAL
# PUNISHMENTS

"Usually speaking, the worst-bred person in company is a young traveller just returned from abroad."

—Jonathan Swift

L ew and I flew back to Bethesda together in May 1973, where we
planned to spend a few days before heading in different directions
for a couple of months. I planned to head west and guide a few Colorado
trips, and look for clients and more guides so we could start a commercial SOBEK season in September in Ethiopia. We wanted to make an exploratory descent of the Baro, a commercial Omo expedition, and then
exploratories on the Blue Nile and the Tekeze. Lew was going to head to
Connecticut to sell his car, close up his practice, put his marriage on
hold, and then meet me in Ethiopia for our first real season as a company.

After a couple days of decompression, we picked up my film of the
Omo from the drugstore and made our way to downtown Washington,
D.C., to Seventeenth and M streets, where the venerable National Geo-
graphic building stood. We went inside and I asked the receptionist for
Joseph Judge, assistant editor. She called, cited my name, and he said he
had never heard of me, didn't have time to meet. I asked the receptionist

to call back and say we had just returned from the Omo River and brought our slides. In minutes Joe Judge was escorting us into the inner chambers of *National Geographic* magazine and sitting us down in a conference room. He called in Gilbert Grosvenor, the editor, as well as senior assistant editor Bill Garrett and senior editorial staff member Bill Graves, and he put my slides in a carousel and projected them onto a screen at the head of the conference table. I knew well that in a few months' time Ron Smith's team, heavily funded by *National Geographic,* was headed for what was proclaimed in his published brochure as "The River Trip of the Century," and that we would deflate sails that had been billowing for months. The expedition Ron Smith's literature was billing as "The First Descent of the Omo," we had just successfully completed. But I still hoped that perhaps there was a way Lew and I might be involved, perhaps as guides on the historic trip. If nothing else, I hoped *National Geographic* might want to publish some of my pictures.

I carefully narrated the slides, and a funereal silence gripped the room. At the end, Joe Judge asked me how much our expedition cost. I mentally broke it down, calculating shared costs for food and transport, as well as time in Addis. "About fourteen hundred dollars for the whole expedition," I replied. "You mean fourteen hundred dollars per person?" Joe asked. "No, for the whole thing. For the four of us who went the whole way it was about three hundred dollars per person. Tom Cromer, who left halfway, made up the difference." It was apparent the editors were upset. We had heard they had joined with Britain's Survival Anglea television, and some wealthy clients, and in all committed upwards of $60,000 for the privilege of exclusive coverage of the great first descent. I asked if they might want to publish any of my slides. They declined, and Joe accompanied Lew and myself downstairs and to the door. As we shook hands good-bye, I offered Joe some information I hoped might be of use: "You know, August is not the best time to run the Omo—it will be in flood." Without acknowledging my notice, he turned and stepped back into Explorers Hall.

In August 1973 the Ron Smith–*National Geographic* team, with famous wildlife photographer Alan Root, made the second descent of the Omo River. It was indeed in spate, and as such it was impossible to hike up the flooding tributaries to the spectacular waterfalls; the wildlife stayed in the highlands, and little was seen at river level. And, in a rapid that had become ferocious with the high water, one of their rafts flipped, losing Alan Root's cameras and exposed film. The Omo article never ran in *National Geographic.*

I spent the summer trying to find an additional partner for SOBEK Expeditions, as we needed more boats, gear, and boatmen if we were going to make a business. Lew and I were broke. John Yost promised to buy a raft with the monies he expected to make in his import business over the summer, but we needed more. I wrote to the largest Grand Canyon rowing outfitters, ARTA, Wilderness World, and O.A.R.S. ARTA never answered; Ron Hayes, the actor who played the father in the TV series *Lassie* and part owner of Wilderness World, called me and asked how much I would pay to have his company join as a partner. George Wendt, owner of O.A.R.S., called and said he thought it was a neat idea and arranged a meeting.

A week later I was on an old school bus at Lees Ferry meeting with George. I proposed he supply a brand-new raft, life jackets, and other essential gear, and two guides for the upcoming season; that he use his mailing list to solicit clients, and that he advance a little money to take an ad out in *The New York Times,* for a quarter of SOBEK Expeditions; the other shares would be divided equally between Lew, John, and myself. We shook hands, and George went out to fetch his first candidate for a guide: Sam Street. Sam was somewhat of a mystic character in the realm of macho Grand Canyon guides. He brought his own macrobiotic menu on trips, meditated whenever possible, wore loose-fitting long paisley pants in a culture of cut-offs, issued crunchy environmental wisdom, and spoke Zen bumper-stickerese. He often said he didn't use his muscles in rapids, that he would find the flow and go with it. When he came into the bus to interview to join me on African rivers in the fall, I told him about the crocodiles, and how they had almost done us in. He listened respectfully, paused, and with a shake of his waist-long blond hair replied crocodiles were not a concern for him, that he would commune with the crocodiles, connect with their psychic center, and intone them to leave us alone. I thanked Sam and said I would get back to him.

When he left the bus I told George the partnership was off to a shaky start, that we had to do better. Meat-eating crocodiles were not going to stand down for Sam Street, or anyone. George said he had a couple other candidates, Robbie Paul and Jim Slade, and as they were on the river, he would have them call me in a week. They did, and I liked their take on river running and signed them both on. Slade in particular seemed to have a formidable intelligence, and he was ready for the job. We talked for a long time, and he gave me his background: a degree in economics from Williams College, a slew of athletic awards, an acceptance at Columbia Law School that was on hold while he explored adventure, including a recent climb up Orizaba, an eighteen thousand-foot Mexican volcano, and a raft run down the Rio Grande de Santiago that was interrupted with bandit fire. The fact that Jim wanted to go to Africa after the experience of running rapids with bullets whizzing by his head impressed me; he was just crazy enough to fit in. I gave Slade the date to rendezvous in Addis, and a phone number to call on arrival, and suggested he cut his hair before arriving. Our first trip would be the Baro in September.

I also spent time with Bart Henderson that summer (we competed for favor from a lovely Swedish girl named Sunshine, and I lost), and I invited him to join me in Ethiopia. He said sure, and promised to be there early so he could make the scout of the Baro with me.

With George Wendt's advance, I sent a check for my last $300 to *The New York Times,* and in the September 2, 1973, Sunday edition the following appeared:

### THE ADVENTURE OF 10 LIFETIMES!

Be among the first to run the Omo, Blue Nile and Tekeze Rivers—through the high mountains of Ethiopia. More than 350 miles of just-discovered river . . . rapids as rousing as the Colorado's . . . through mountains, desert and jungle. Many truly wild (but unhostile) tribes. Big game and birds for photography by the hundreds. All it takes is 2 to 4 weeks. Trips are scheduled between September and February—with prices ranging from $665 to $1500 plus airfare and a touch of the pioneer. Write right away!

To my amazement, the ad actually generated response . . . about a dozen inquiries. The only takers, though, were four Americans posted in Asmara (Clyde and Betsy Selner, Mary Ann Straton, and Rich Miller), who called and said they would go if I offered a 50 percent discount. I had no choice, but at least we had a trip.

Just before leaving for my second season in Africa I stopped in Bethesda to visit my family. My mother, little sister, and brother met me at the airport. My father was at home, having just returned from a mental hospital; he had suffered a series of nervous breakdowns, and was on medication and practicing meditation under the guidance of a psychiatrist. When I talked with my mother about the breakdowns, she said it was common among CIA employees; the secrets, the isolation, the bureaucracy got to a lot of people.

For the first twelve years of my life I had no idea what my father did for a living. When required in school to fill in the blank "Father's Occupation," he had instructed me to put "State Department executive," and it seemed sufficiently innocuous that I never questioned further. Things changed in October 1962. My father came home one day visibly distressed and had us haul cans of food and water to the basement. He put his hands on my arms and locked my eyes to explain something. He said he worked for a sector of the government that was involved in spying, and that something had gone very wrong. A terrible thing might happen, a big bomb might be dropped, and if the air raid siren went off, I was to rush to the basement and wait for him to come home. A few days later, on October 22, he insisted the family sit in front of the television set as President Kennedy announced a naval blockade around Cuba, and demanded the USSR dismantle and remove ballistic missiles and other weapons it had assembled on the island ninety miles south of Florida. I didn't really understand what was going on, but sensed it was serious, and I could see the fear in my father's eyes. He hugged me hard that night. Four days later Khrushchev blinked, agreeing to Kennedy's demands. I remember my father saying at dinner, "You'll never know how really close we came to a nuclear war."

My father's career was not satisfying to him. He sometimes talked of how he was recruited from Yale, just short of his Ph.D. in psychology, to go work for this young intelligence agency that suggested he might become a real-life James Bond. He admitted he was attracted to the adventurous career, and the romantic notion of a globe-trotting spy protecting freedom for the Free World. The reality was nothing like that. Long before the CIA became a popular whipping post for all that was wrong with the Vietnam War, my father was troubled with his employer and with his own choices. Occasionally he lamented about how he might have gone into theater, or broadcasting, or teaching. And then one day he went berserk, crashing around the house, breaking things, toppling his beloved piano. He was taken away in a straitjacket.

As my mother drove me to the drugstore to pick up some medication for my father, she blurted something I had never heard before, that he hadn't really ever been the same since he got back from Iran. "When was that?" I asked. "Nineteen fifty-six. He made a movie there for the company." I tried to remember 1956. I was six years old. Only one memory remained, of a camping trip he took me on, when a tent he set up collapsed, and I found a river.

The day before departure I noticed in the paper that *Shaft in Africa* had premiered. I thought it would be a good idea to take my father to see a movie that showcased the country I had fallen in love with, and that had scenes (less than seven seconds long) with people I actually knew. But the film wasn't playing anywhere in the suburbs. Its only showcase was the Howard theater, in southeast Washington, D.C., a predominantly black neighborhood with not the best of reputations. My dad was resistant— the neighborhood was just not the place for us suburbanites to visit, and though a movie buff, he really didn't have much interest in films of this genre. Still, I exhorted and pleaded. I so wanted to share this piece of my life with him. At last he relented, and we agreed we would take in the early show, so as to be back to the Oldsmobile while still light.

So, we trekked down to a part of town we didn't know and eased into the theater. We noticed immediately we were the only whites in the crowd, and when the film came on I found the theme a bit uncomfortable, that whites were orchestrating a slave ring that Shaft was sent to bust up. Every time Shaft beat up or killed a white man, the crowd went wild, yelling, "Kill the honkie" at the screen. And every time they yelled, I slouched deeper in my chair, trying to become invisible . . . and I watched my father do the same. With the movie's end, we hustled out to the street and made our way to the car. Once there I noticed I was missing my wallet, and so I asked if my father would go back in the theater with me to find it. He insisted he stay with the car, and so I mustered the courage and walked back in. It was filling with a new crowd, and a large man who looked like Isaac Hayes with chains dripping from his sleeves was in my seat. I meekly asked if he would look underneath, and he obliged, found my wallet, passed it to me, and I bolted to the door.

Two days later I was back in Addis, preparing for the Baro River expedition with Jim Slade, John Yost, George and Diane Fuller, Bart Henderson, another Hatch guide I had recruited, Gary Mercado, and Lew Greenwald and his wife, Karen, who was here on a mission of marital therapy. Ever since Lew had thrown his hat into my ring, things had become strained between him and his wife. Lew now called his relationship "estranged," and talked of a life beyond Karen. Now, she was here to see if she might become a part of this new passion in Lew's life, exploratory rafting. In addition to our core few we were joined by a couple of newcomers to river running. It would be a trip that would change us all forever.

# CHAPTER 10

# LOST ON THE BARO

"If we could be twice young and twice old, we could correct all our mistakes."
—Euripides

Above, the jungle was a brawl of flora and vines and roots. Colobus monkeys sailed between treetops, issuing washboard cries.

Below, three specially designed inflatable whitewater rafts bobbed in a back eddy, looking, from the ridge, like restless water bugs. There were eleven of us, all whitewater veterans, save Angus. He was in the raft with me, Karen Greenwald, and John Yost, who at last was joining a SOBEK Expedition, the concept we had hatched together the year before. As the leader and the most experienced river runner, I was at the oars.

Our raft would go first. At the correct moment we cast off—Angus coiled the painter and gripped for the ride. I adjusted the oars and pulled a deep stroke. For a prolonged instant the boat hung in a current between the eddy and the fast water. Then it snapped into motion with a list that knocked me off my seat.

"This water's faster than I thought," I yelled. Regaining the seat, I straightened the raft, its bow downstream. The banks were a blur of green; water shot into the boat from all sides.

Just minutes after the start of the ride, we approached the rapid. Though we'd been unable to scout it earlier—its convex edge was clad in thick vegetation, preventing a full view of the river—I had a hunch it would be best to enter the rapid on its right side. But the river had different notions. Despite frantic pulls on the oars, we were falling over the lip on the far left.

"Oh my God!" someone screamed. The boat was almost vertical, falling free. This wasn't a rapid—this was a waterfall. I dropped the oars and braced against the frame. The raft crashed into a spout, folded in half, and spun. Then, as though reprieved, we straightened and flumped onward. I almost gasped with relief, when a lateral wave pealed into an explosion on my left, picking up the raft, slamming it against the nearby cliff wall like a toy, then dumping it and us upside down into the millrace. Everything turned to bubbles.

I tumbled, as if falling down an underwater staircase. Seconds later, I surfaced in the quick water below the rapid, a few feet from the overturned raft. My glasses were gone, but through the billows I could make out another rapid two hundred yards downstream, closing in fast. I clutched at a rope and tried to tow the raft toward shore. Behind I heard Karen: "Angus. Go help Angus. He's caught in a rope!"

He was trailing ten feet behind the raft, a snarl of bowline tight across his shoulder, tangled and being pulled through the turbulence. Like the rest of us, he was wearing a sheathed knife on his belt for this very moment—to cut loose from entangling ropes. His arms looked free, yet he didn't reach for his knife. He was paralyzed with fear.

I swam back to Angus, and with my left hand seized the rope at his sternum; with my right I groped for my own Buck knife. In the roiling water it was a task to slip the blade between Angus's chest and the taut rope. Then, with a jerk, he was free.

"Swim to shore," I yelled.

"Swim to shore, Angus," Karen cried from the edge of the river.

He seemed to respond. He turned and took a stroke toward Karen. I swam back to the runaway raft with the hope of once again trying to pull it in. It was futile: the instant I hooked my hand to the raft it fell into the pit of the next rapid, with me in tow. My heart, already shaking at the cage of my chest, seemed to explode.

I was buffeted and beaten by the underwater currents, then spat to the surface. For the first time, I was really scared. Even though I was swashed in water, my mouth was dry as a thorn tree. I stretched my arms to swim to shore, but my strength was sapped. This time I was shot into an abyss. I was in a whirlpool, and looking up I could see the surface light fade as I was sucked deeper. At first I struggled wildly, but it had no effect, except to further drain my small reserves. My throat began to burn. I became disassociated from the river and all physical environments. Then I became aware of a strange thing. The part of me that wanted to panic began to draw apart, and then flew away. There no longer seemed any but the flimsiest connection between life and death. I went limp and resigned myself to fate. I seemed to witness it all as an onlooker.

In the last hazy seconds I felt a blow from beneath, and my body was propelled upward. I was swept into a spouting current, and at the last possible instant I broke the surface and gasped. I tried to lift my arms; they felt like barbells. My vision was fuzzy, but I could make out another rapid approaching, and I knew I could never survive it. But neither could I swim a stroke. The fear of death was no longer an issue, for that seemed already decided. But I kept moving my arms automatically, for no better reason than that there was nothing else to do. It felt like an age passed like this, my mind stuck in the realization of my fate.

Then, somehow, a current pitched me by the right bank. Suddenly branches and leaves were swatting my face as I was borne around a bend. I reached up, caught a thin branch, and held tight. I crawled to a rock slab and sprawled out. My gut seized, and I retched. A wave of darkness washed through my head, and I passed out.

When my eyes finally focused, I saw figures foraging through the gluey vegetation on the opposite bank. John Yost was one, Lew Greenwald another. Lew had been in the third boat, and seeing him reminded me that there were two boats and seven people behind me. How had they fared?

John paced the bank until he found the calmest stretch of river, then dived in; the water was so swift that he reached my shore fifty yards below his mark. He brought the news: the second raft, piloted by Robbie Paul, had somehow made it through the falls upright. In fact, Robbie was thrown from his seat into the bilge during the first seconds of the plunge, and the raft had continued through captainless. The third boat, handled by Bart Henderson, had flipped. Bart was almost swept under a fallen log, but was snatched from the water by the crew of Robbie's boat.

All were accounted for—except Angus Macleod.

〜〜〜

The date was Friday, October 5, 1973. The place was Ilubabor Province, Ethiopia, and our goal had been to make the first raft descent of the Baro River, a major tributary of the White Nile.

I felt I understood the reasons for everyone's involvement in the expedition, except Angus's. He was the odd man out. I met him in Clifton, New Jersey, a few weeks before our departure. We were introduced by a neighbor of his, Joel Fogel. Joel liked to tell people that he was a "professional adventurer." He'd had a brochure printed up describing himself as "Writer, Scientist, Adventurer, Ecologist." Something about him seemed less than genuine, a legend in his own lunchtime, but he had hinted that he might invest in our Baro expedition, and we desperately needed money. I agreed to hear him out. In August, Joel flew me from Arizona to New Jersey. I was impressed—no one had ever offered to pay airfare to hear my plans. In fact, I decided Joel was suffering from affluenza; coming from a wealthy family, he apparently never really worked in his life, and spent his time trying to make himself famous. In exchange for what seemed like a sizable contribution to our cause, Joel had two requests: that he be allowed to join the expedition, and that I consider letting his friend, Angus Macleod, come along as well.

I was leery of bringing along anyone outside my tight-knit, experienced coterie on an exploratory, but the lure of capital was too strong. Joel, however, would never make it out onto the Baro. He traveled with us to the put-in, took one look at the angry, heaving river, and caught the next bus back to Addis Ababa. He may have been the smartest of the lot.

Angus was altogether different. While Joel smacked of presentation and flamboyance, Angus was taciturn and modest. He confessed immediately to having never run a rapid, yet he exuded an almost irresistible eagerness and carried himself with the fluid bounce of a natural athlete. It had struck me that Angus had the same surname as the British fatality on the 1968 Blue Nile Expedition, Ian Macleod, and I even mentioned it to Angus, but neither of us was superstitious.

He was ruggedly handsome and had played professional soccer, and though he had never been on a river, he had spent time sea kayaking the Jersey shore. After spending a short time with him I could see his quiet intensity, and I believed that, despite his lack of experience, he could handle the trip, even though there would be no chance for training or special conditioning before the actual expedition.

Once in Ethiopia, Angus worked on the preparations for the expedition with a lightheartedness that masked his determination. On the eve of our trip to Ilubabor Province—a seventeen-hour bus ride on slippery, corrugated mountain roads—I told Angus to make sure he was at the bus station at 7:00 A.M. for the 11:00 A.M. departure. That way we would all be sure of getting seats in the front of the bus, where the ride wasn't as bumpy or unbearably stuffy. But, come the next morning, Angus didn't show until 10:45. He got the last seat on the bus and endured.

Later, after the accident, standing on the bank of the river with John Yost, I wondered if I'd made the right decision about Angus. We searched the side of the river where I'd washed ashore; across the rumble of the rapids we could hear the others searching. "Angus! Are you all right? Where are you?" There was no answer. Just downriver from where I'd last seen him, John found an eight-foot length of rope—the piece I'd cut away from Angus's shoulders.

After an hour John and I gave up and swam back across the river. We gathered the group at the one remaining raft, just below the falls.

"He could be downstream, lying with a broken leg," someone said.

"He could be hanging on to a log in the river."

"He could be wandering in a daze through the jungle."

Nobody suggested he could be dead, though we all knew it a possibility. All of us had a very basic, and very difficult, decision to make, the kind of decision you never want to have to make on an expedition: should we stay and look for Angus, or should we get out while there was still light? Robbie, Bart, and George and Diane Fuller didn't hesitate—they wanted out. Karen Greenwald wanted to continue searching, but she seemed hysterical. Against her protests, we sent her out with the others.

That left five of us—Lew Greenwald, Gary Mercado, Jim Slade, John Yost, and me. We decided to continue rafting downstream in search of Angus on the one remaining raft. I had mixed feelings about it—suddenly I was scared to death of the river; it had almost killed me. The ambient sentiment was that we could very well die. Yet I felt obligated to look for a man missing from a boat I had capsized, on an expedition I had organized. And there was more: I felt I had to prove to myself that I had the right stuff, that I could honor the code, and do the right thing.

But the river wasn't through with us. When we were ready to go, I climbed into the seat of the raft and yelled for Jim to push off. Immediately we were cascading down the course I'd swum earlier. In the rapid that had nearly drowned me, the raft jolted and reeled, kicking Gary and me into the brawling water.

"Shit—not again" was my only thought as I spilled out of the raft into another whirlpool. But this time I had the bowline in hand, and I managed to pull myself quickly to the surface. I emerged beside the raft, and Lew grabbed the back of my life jacket and pulled me in. My right forearm was lacerated and bleeding. Jim jumped to the oars and rowed us to shore.

My injury wasn't bad—a shallow cut. But Gary had dislocated his shoulder; he'd flipped backward over the gunwale while still holding on to the raft. He was in a load of pain, and it was clear he couldn't go on. Lew—thankful for the opportunity—volunteered to hike him out.

John, Jim, and I relaunched and cautiously rowed down a calmer stretch of the river, periodically calling out for Angus. It was almost 6:00 P.M., so the sun was about to set. We had to stop and make camp. It was a bad, uncomfortable night. Between us, we had a two-man A-frame tent, one sleeping bag, and a lunch bag of food. Everything else had been washed into the Baro.

〰〰〰

The rude bark of a baboon shook us awake the next morning. The inside of the tent was dripping from condensation, and we lay in a kind of human puddle. I crawled outside and looked to the eastern sky, which was beginning to blush. My body ached from the previous day's ordeal. I wanted to be back in Bethesda, at my folks' home, warm, dry, and eating a fine breakfast. Instead, we huddled around a wisp of fire, sipping weak tea and chewing wet bread.

That morning we eased downriver, stopping every few minutes to scout, hugging the banks, avoiding rapids we wouldn't have hesitated to run were they back in the States. At intervals we called into the rain forest for Angus, but now we didn't expect an answer.

Late in the afternoon we came to another intimidating rapid, one that galloped around a bend and sunk from sight. We took out the one duffel bag containing the tent and sleeping bag and began lining, using ropes to lower the boat along the edge of the rapid. Fifty yards into the rapid, the raft broached perpendicular to the current, and water swarmed in. Slade and I, on the stern line, pulled hard, the rope searing our palms, but the boat ignored us. With the snap of its D-ring (the stern line attachment), it dismissed us to a crumple on the bank and sailed around the corner and out of sight.

There was no way to continue the search. The terrain made impossible demands, and we were out of food, the last scraps having been lost with the raft. We struck up into the jungle, thrashing through wet, waist-high foliage at a slug's pace. My wound was becoming infected. Finally, at sunset the light folded up on itself and we had to stop. We cleared a near-level spot, set up the tent, squeezed in, and collapsed. Twice I awoke to the sounds of trucks grumbling past, but dismissed it as jungle fever, or Jim's snoring.

In the morning, however, we soon stumbled onto a road. There we sat, as mist coiled up the tree trunks, waiting. In the distance we could hear the thunder roll of a rapid, but inexplicably the sound became louder and louder. Then we saw what it was: two hundred machete-wielding natives marched into sight over the hill. General Goitom, the police commissioner of nearby Motu, hearing of the accident, had organized a search for Angus. Their effort consisted of tramping up and down the highway—the locals, it turned out, were more fearful of the jungle canyon than we were.

I remember very little of the next week. We discovered that Angus held a United Kingdom passport, and I spent a fair amount of time at the British embassy in Addis Ababa filling out reports, accounting for personal effects, and communicating with his relatives. John and Jim stayed in Motu with General Goitom and led a series of searches back into the jungle along the river. We posted a $100 reward—more than double what the villagers earned in a year—for information on Angus's whereabouts. With financial assistance from Angus's parents, I secured a Canadian helicopter a few days after the accident and took several passes over the river. Even with the pilot skimming the treetops, it was difficult to see into the river corridor. The canopy seemed like a moldy, moth-eaten army tarpaulin. On one flight, however, I glimpsed a smudge of orange just beneath the surface of the river. We made several passes, but it was impossible to make out what it was. Perhaps, I thought, it was Angus, snagged underwater. We picked as many landmarks as possible, flew in a direct line to the road, landed, cut a marker on a tatty dohm palm, and headed to Motu.

A day later John, Jim, and I cut a path back into the tangle and found the smudge—a collection of leaves trapped by a submerged branch. We abandoned the search.

CHAPTER 11

# HIPPO ALLEY

"Life is short, the art long, opportunity fleeting, experiment treacherous, judgment difficult."

—Hippocrates

After the disastrous Baro, we retreated to Addis to lick our wounds and contemplate next moves. Lew thought perhaps we should pack it in and head home; the death of Angus seemed to spook him the most. But the rest of the group wanted to move forward and make our planned commercial Omo expedition, and Lew agreed to come along. So, the second week of November we piled onto a local bus, caromed down the rough road, and camped under a full moon at the Jimma Bridge. There were sixteen this time, including the four Americans working in Asmara who had seen the ad in *The New York Times;* Jerry Shea, a filmmaker and ex-boyfriend of George Wendt's wife; Karen Greenwald; Jim Slade's girlfriend, Cherry Jensen; and one full-paying client, Anne Mulqueen, a single Pan Am stewardess whom I had met on the Colorado on the last trip of the season, and who ponied up $1,500 for the privilege of joining our expedition full of single guides.

Shortly after sunrise we were up and patching the rafts. As per agreement, John Yost had paid for a fourth boat for his quarter stake in SOBEK, and it had arrived via diplomatic pouch two days before the

Omo departure. But the other three rafts we had salvaged from the Baro, and they were riddled with holes and rips. One was still scarred and leaking from the crocodile bite on the Omo in May. Since the special vinyl glue required for our Holcombe Industries Havasu rafts had only arrived from the States with the new raft, this was our first chance to patch, and we weren't certain the rafts would ever float again. But after two and a half days of mending, we had four well-nigh-usable rafts. Bart's raft had leaks bow and stern, and needed new air every half hour, but my boat leaked the most, and the front section had to be pumped every fifteen minutes. Since we had lost several oars on the Baro, I had commissioned a woodworker in the Mercato to fashion a half dozen with a wood he called *wonza*. When we finally cast off, Bart was pulling on a pair of "wonza wonders," and a few strokes into the first rapid an oar snapped in two. Was it Bart or the oars? we all wondered. An hour later another wonza oar snapped, this time under my scripting, so we knew it was the wood, not strength, that was busting them. We only had sixteen oars for the three-week expedition, twelve made of wonza wood, and the future didn't look promising at the moment.

The water was much higher in November than on our May exploratory, and on the fourth day we entered a gateway where jets of water danced like tongues of white flame on the surface. We pulled over at the entrance to the black canyon to scout the rapid, which was a quarter-mile long, full of holes, hydraulics, and roostertails. Bart wanted to portage, but despite my failures on the Baro, I thought it runnable, and jumped in the raft with Lew as my passenger and bounced safely through. Bart went next and got caught in a hydraulic for a churning five minutes, during which another wonza oar washed from the raft, floated some one hundred feet downstream, and promptly sank. Next, Robbie Paul tried the route with George on board. Halfway through, they washed up on a steep rock and Robbie flew out of the boat, into the crocodiled waters. George turned around to find Robbie gone. Face frozen in panic, he grabbed the oars and managed to maneuver through the rest of the rapid and into the eddy. Robbie, though, still hadn't surfaced. Seconds dragged by—he could have drowned, been pinned underwater by a rock or snag, or grabbed by a croc, then, finally, he popped up from under the boat, where he'd been snared. He had come within a few breaths of drowning.

Early on John Yost took the title of chief cook, as it was clear he had a talent and passion for creative outdoor cooking. One day, after a filling breakfast of Yost toast (bread dipped in egg batter, then fried to a crisp over the campfire), we were lounging naked in the cool spray of a large falls, enjoying a respite from the aggressive tsetse flies who turned entire days on the river into long swatting sessions. The spot was an Eden of butterflies, some big as pie tins and colored like Shanghai silk, others yellow as buttercup petals. There were rainbows, and waterslides, but our attention turned to the unexplored canyon above the falls. Unable to resist the allure, Jim Slade, Cherry Jensen, and I set off up the steep gorge. We forged through vegetable matter that resembled barbed wire, sometimes swinging across gullies on creeper vines like Tarzans. Our bodies glistened with sweat, hair netted with cobwebs, as upward we scrambled. Finally, the canyon walls began to echo with a growing roar, until we turned a corner and faced the most spectacular waterfall any of us had ever witnessed. As is the privilege, and burden, of explorers, we needed to name the natural wonder, and in the long tradition of naming discoveries after the discoverers, we agreed to name the high cascade "Slade-Bangs-Jensen" Falls, and it was true.

One afternoon I started to hiccup incessantly, something my father occasionally did. It went on for hours, all through the night, into the following day, each time feeling like I'd been kicked in the stomach. I tried all the tricks, swallowing water upside down, thinking of ten bald men, but nothing would stop the hiccuping. I asked George Fuller for help, but he just said, "You'll be fine." That was George's prescription for practically everything. George refused to attend to the normal cuts and bruises that were the daily doses of an expedition. "You'll be fine," he'd scoff whenever someone complained of an abrasion or a loose stool. And, more often than not, whenever an expedition member sought George out for medical advice, or a fresh Band-Aid, the doctor was out—nowhere to be found. In fact, he was usually off photographing or collecting bugs.

When, at last, on the afternoon of my second day of hiccuping a hippo, with the biggest open mouth I'd ever seen, clamped its jaws down on Bart's boat in a short-but-damaging display, my hiccuping went away. It took a day to repair Bart's boat and we used up the last of our glue. And, we were getting low on spare fabric to use as patching material. When a coffee smuggler from Kaffa Province crossed the river while balancing on a tightly inflated goatskin, we eyed his craft with envy, and impure thoughts.

Dinner was often after dark, as the sun set so early, and instead of candlelight, there were hundreds of blinking fireflies creating that special ambiance. In the distance, on the upper slopes of the canyon, we would sometimes see the eerie spectacle of wildfires, looking like a faraway city in the desert at midnight. They were fires set by Galla tribesmen, burning the forest to enhance the soil with nutrients to fertilize their crop seedlings. Under the necklace of these lights, John would do his best to metamorphose another macaroni and cheese dinner into a gourmand's delight and, with a deft ladle turn, a pinch of spice here and there, he often succeeded. Afterward, Bart would sometimes cook up a batch of Jiffy Pop, a snack he carried over from the States for my benefit, as he knew I was addicted to the stuff. Then we would retire to the tents, lie in our bags, and listen to the symphony: tympanies played by an assortment of cicadas, the tenor band saw of flapping bats, the soft clarinet of the Cape turtle dove, the soprano whine of mosquitoes, and the basso profundo of hippos bellowing in protest that we were in their seats. Hippos exit the river when the last smudges of light blot away to wander the grasslands and graze, cropping a couple hundred pounds of grass a night. In most cases, when we chose a wide beach to pitch our tiny town of tents, it was also a hippo passageway. One evening I crawled into the pup tent I was sharing with John Yost on a beach pockmarked with hoof prints across from a bloat of hippos blowing their tubas. In the morning, we awoke to an earthquake. We looked at each other and simultaneously yelled, "Hippos!!" We knew they were rampaging through camp on the way back to the river before sunrise. The zipper was jammed, so we ripped the fly apart, and jumped out to see several tons of river horses thundering through camp, tripping over guy lines, and diving into the Omo.

〜〜〜

A few days later John Yost was rowing my boat, while I lounged in the bow. We saw a pair of baby hippos and rowed over to admire the cute, pink creatures. With a whoosh of thick air, the mother popped up three feet from my face, grabbed the inflatable in her jaws, and shook so hard I almost fell out. John's high voice shot an octave. A hiss, like a punctured lung, discharged from the raft, and the cow submerged. A pause. The whole canyon inhaled and held its breath. Overhead, a black cormorant silently rode an updraft, for a second blotting the sun. Then with a snort, mother torpedoed to the surface, a great, gray hulk, water washing from her head as though off a whale's back. I looked directly into a pair of angry, flashing eyes, and an awesome mouth stretched to its limits. They were huge, old jaws, pitted and scored like corroded chunks of cast iron, studded with short, sharp carrot-sized teeth, wielded by bulging neck muscles, displaying enough ivory to cover the keys of a Steinway. John pulled his oars with everything he had, but the mad mother porpoised to keep up, and then the fleshy, saliva-rimmed cavern closed. The raft exploded. I scrambled to the frame as the fabric beneath my feet sank into the river. Her points made, oral reprimand delivered, she swam off triumphant, leaving us sinking in her wake. Other hippos in the river seemed to blow a uniform Bronx cheer. When John got the boat to shore we surveyed the damage—three sections and a seam were badly torn. The raft was Yost toast. We folded it up, stashed it in the stern of Bart's boat, and then fitted Bart's raft with the extra two-by-six frame and extra people for the rest of the trip. We called the raft that then carried all the extra gear and people the *African Pig*.

At the Soddu Bridge, Karen Greenwald left the expedition—she just wasn't getting along with Lew—and a primate researcher who had worked at Gombe with Jane Goodall, Anne Pierce, joined, bringing a fresh supply of food and drinks. It was a good thing, too, as the following day was Thanksgiving. Thursday night John pulled out all the stops, and even though we were in the wild heart of Africa, we sat down to a feast of baked ham, sweet potatoes, haricot beans in creamed mushroom sauce, sautéed zucchinis, coleslaw, fruit salad, rum cake, and spiced tea; and Lew led us in grace, thanking God for allowing us to share friendship and bounty in such a special place.

In the months between the two Omo expeditions I had contacted David Turton, an anthropologist at the London School of Economics who was studying the tribes of the lower Omo. He told me the two main tribes above the Mui River were the Bodi and Mursi. Though he had never met them, he was planning to hike in early the next year and spend time there researching for his doctorate. He couldn't offer more than rumors he'd heard of their existence and was keenly interested in our observations.

So it was with a more appreciative eye that we rounded a bend on the lower Omo and saw a group of naked hunters gathered around a freshly speared hippo. They were just starting to skin the mammoth ham as we pulled to shore to watch. At first they were aloof and distrustful, but once they realized we wouldn't steal their meat, they became friendly and curious. We laughed and talked in sign language, showed them our boats, and they proudly showed us their dug-outs. They wondered about the black boxes we held to our eyes, and they giggled as we let them look through the viewfinders. They got a bigger kick wearing our sunglasses. After a while the headman had one of the younger men build a fire and roast strips of meat, which they then offered graciously to us. Though little more than chunks of pig fat, this was the first fresh meat in weeks, and we shnorked it down, even as it made my tongue curl like a millipede. Jean-Pierre Hallet had written that "the smoked flank of a hippo is the most delicious treat that Africa can offer," further eroding his credibility in my young mind. However, when the bladder and stomach of the dead hippo were cut open and spread along the beach, a nauseating stench rose and hung like a fog about the carcass. It was time to leave. While boarding my raft, and holding my nose, I asked if the people were Bodi, and the chief nodded as if to say yes. We then waved good-bye so vigorously our armpits threatened to crack and hurried to fresher winds.

A bit farther downstream we came to a Mursi village, and this time, with Cherry leading the way, we were able to meet the women. Several were in front of their huts grinding guinea corn and sorghum with stones, and they stood up excitedly to greet Cherry. They tugged in disbelief at her golden hair, rubbed her breasts, and touched her pale skin. They'd never seen such a specimen before and couldn't seem to land a feeling, a response—aloof or astonished or amused. An elder man approached me and gestured to several of the village women, then to Cherry, over and over—he seemed to be offering a trade. I was tempted, but Cherry wouldn't hear of it, despite the royal possibilities of fulfilling an H. Rider Haggard role.

Unlike the men, the women weren't naked, but wore crude tan bark-cloth skirts from their narrow hips to knees. No hair at all anointed their heads, and the earlobes had big loops for earplugs. About half the women wore lip plates, a holdover from slave-trading days when the desirable East African women made themselves and their children as ugly as possible to discourage slavers from dragging them off. The lower lip was pierced and stretched out slowly until it fit around a clay disk several inches in diameter. While the women looked bizarre wearing the plates, when they removed them, the loop of the lower lip hung down around their chins and dangled like a rubber band that had lost its snap. It seemed unlikely they did much kissing.

Several in our group wanted to trade for their tightly woven baskets, the three-legged stools the men carried as pillows on hunting treks, and some of the women's bone and feather finery. T-shirts and shorts were pulled from wetbags to start the bargaining. George spoke up and said, sotto voce, he thought trading was a bad idea, that it would accelerate the inevitable process of Westernization that one day would have the Mursi looking like second-class Western citizens instead of the regal tribesmen they were born to be. Lew argued that we should let the Mursi decide their fate. He called George's benign-neglect proposal specious and elitist, imperialist and anti-evolutionist. We were all aware of Lew's real career as a sociologist, and his liberal leanings for the betterment of the common man, but we weren't prepared for such a loaded reaction. He cited sentiments from those who live in the rain forests of the Amazon reacting to khaki-wearing Americans and Europeans who showed up proclaiming they were there to save the planet. "Who are we to think we have a right to impose strictures on these people? Look around you, George—these people are in a better space than we are. We've already cut down most of our trees, killed our greatest herds, polluted our cities, dammed our rivers. These people should decide their future, not us. I say if they want to trade with us, let them."

After the lively debate, the group sided with George, and agreed to forgo trading this passage. But, a few days later, as we pulled out into the current at the final village, I looked back upstream at a waving Mursi, and he was grinning beneath a pair of sunglasses. Simultaneously, one of the clients from Asmara proudly held up a stool he had traded for the glasses.

Just five months previous, on the first Omo expedition, we had met the Bodi and Mursi peoples, and spent hours exploring one another's effects and sharing food and drink, but we didn't take anything from them, nor leave behind anything that wouldn't be gone in a short while, such as soap and spices. Then we disappeared around the bend, leaving them in the Stone Age.

Streaked with guilt, thinking we may have introduced something to a culture that would upset its value and more systems (à la the Coke bottle in *The Gods Must Be Crazy*), perhaps alter its cosmology (the cross in *The Mission*), even elevate the status of the man who randomly received the glasses (like winning the lottery), Lew and I decided to seek out the right thing to do. So, upon returning to the States, we wrote up an account of the incident, and concluded by stating we hoped to return again and again to the Omo with more clients, but we hoped for some guidance as to how to handle this intercultural exchange. We then sent the query to the head of every college anthropology department in the U.S., and some overseas. Within a couple weeks replies began to fill my mailbox. A month later I received a call from my little sister, Cindy, an undergraduate at the University of Wisconsin, who said my query had ended up as the final in her anthropology class, and wondered if I had insights as to how to write the essay. I didn't, but had a pile of wildly differing opinions from the experts.

Maybe a third of the respondents chastised our fledgling business for venturing into a pure environment, a rare field laboratory circumstance, in which an untainted culture could be examined by trained social scientists. With nary a Ph.D. among us, we were contaminating a petri dish, and we were advised to cease and desist.

Another third wrote back and commented that progress was inevitable, that freeways would soon be passing through these villages, and we need not concern ourselves with adversely affecting a culture doomed to dilution anyway, so raft and enjoy.

Then there was a middle ground. Several professors advised that change is destined, and the wise course is the one that attempts a sensitive, responsible, softly stepping approach. They suggested we trade with the people we met on the river, but we do so in a judicious way, trading simple things they could use (fishhooks) and biodegradable items (soap, spices), rather than Hawaiian shirts and yo-yos, or icons that could radically revise a system. And that became our policy.

SOBEK still runs the Omo River, and has done so almost annually since that first expedition in 1973. A lot has changed. Anthropologists from around the world have dropped in on the Mursi and Bodi and come out with Ph.D. theses. There is now a money economy and an awareness of a world beyond the banks of the Omo. Not far away there is a clinic to which the Omo people take their ill, and a few have left the valley for schooling. There is talk of a road coming in.

At least one Mursi still has a pair of sunglasses. Change has occurred, as it always does, always will, and is the desire of the locals. There are downsides to change, to cultural evolution, but from the point of view of those in the midst, it is better than being damned as a museum piece to serve the romantic or academic notions of tourists.

CHAPTER 12

# THE BLUE NILE

"He who has not seen the Blue Nile will praise a stream."

—ancient Ethiopian proverb

B ack in Addis Ababa after the second Omo trip I was wandering through the recesses of the spice market when a vendor I knew approached me. "Mr. Richard, did you hear about Mr. Angus? They say he is alive. He was found by villagers on the river, and he is living with them now. It is the talk everywhere. I do not know from where the story comes."

I went to the British and U.S. embassies. People there, too, had heard the rumor. One consul said he'd heard a fanciful embellishment to the story—that Angus was living fine and well as king of a tribe of Amazonlike women. As the story went, Angus had been visited by outside villagers and invited to leave with them, but he declined. He was in paradise.

Hearing the rumors was hard. I wanted to squelch the sensationalistic gossip, to finish business left undone, to determine beyond all doubt what really happened to Angus. And to cleanse my conscience. So in January of 1974, I made another trip to the upper reaches of the Baro. This time the river was ten vertical feet lower than on our last trip: it was dry season in a drought year. What was before a swollen rampage was now a slow, thin trickle, the bones of the river poking through what had once been the flesh of great rapids. This time there were four of us in a single raft: Lew Greenwald, Gary Mercado, Professor Conrad Hirsh of Haile Selassie I University, and me. John Yost left to float the Zaire River and collect art for his store, the clients had gone back to work, Jerry Shea returned to L.A. to edit his film, the Fullers didn't want to have anything to do with another Baro attempt, and Jim Slade and Cherry Jensen decided to take some time to climb the mountains of Kenya, but hoped to return for another river descent in a couple months.

As with the initial Baro attempt, we reached the first rapid within minutes. This time, though, it was a jumble of bus-sized basalt boulders, the bedrock that fashioned the falls during times of flooding. It was unnavigable, so we stood in chest-deep water and wrenched the inflatable boat over and down the rocks, turning it on its side to push it through the tighter passages. A similar configuration constituted the next rapid, and the next, and the next. The routine was quickly established. It was a constant battle against rocks, water, heat, fatigue, and insects. We had naively hoped to run the raft some 150 miles to Gambella, near the Sudanese border, where the river flows wide and flat. We had rations for a week. With all the portaging, we were making less than five miles a day.

Scattered along our course, sometimes in branches high above us where the water once swirled, we found vestiges of the first expedition: five oars, Jim Slade's sleeping bag, a torn poncho, a pack of the insect-collecting equipment donated by the Smithsonian, crushed pots and pans, and a ripped sweater that had belonged to Angus, one he had packed in his duffel. But no sign of Angus.

After six days we had made only thirty miles; our bodies were pocked with insect bites, and we had exhausted our food and strength. A trail up the steep slope put an end to our ordeal. We returned to Addis Ababa with no new answers.

At this point I had achieved a small measure of infamy among the expat community in Addis. Some thought my explorations were worthwhile endeavors; others thought them stupid and dangerous and cited the death of Angus Macleod as proof. Kathy Chang, the exotic-looking owner of the China Bar and Restaurant, rumored spy, and part-time journalist, did a profile on my adventures for the Ethiopian *Herald,* the government-owned English-language newspaper. She made the classic mistake of new journalists, though, and allowed me to look at the story before it was published. I read it, thought it was lacking, and called Kathy to ask if I could noodle with the piece. She said sure, and I ended up completely rewriting the story. It ran the following Sunday, to much praise, under Kathy's byline. A week later she came to me with a story on hippos and asked if I would help her, as I knew the subject. Again, I rewrote the piece, this time so that every word was my own. It ran under her byline and again was praised. This happened a few more times before Kathy came to me with a proposition. Would I like to move in with her, free room and board, in exchange for writing her weekly features? I accepted, more out of lust than economics, and began a period of blissful indentured servantry.

Kathy was well connected, and I found myself attending fashion shows at the Hilton, sipping G&Ts under Cinzano umbrellas, schmoozing at embassy parties. Through her contacts I was even asked to photograph the crown jewels at the Jubilee Palace.

Kathy drove me through the palace gates, past some of the forty black-maned lions kept as pets, as well as several long-necked swans and peacocks. In a bedroom full of brilliant chandeliers, an attendant laid out the jewels on a shiny inlaid desk, and stood back to watch as I set up my flimsy tripod and began to click away. Then there was a phone call, and the attendant gathered up the jewels and told me to stay put— he'd be back. I was left alone in this regal bedroom, and as I looked around it dawned on me that this was where the emperor slept. An opened closet showed off dozens of crisp uniforms, and photographs around the room showed the emperor with various heads of state and celebrities. The canopied bed was old and short, and a thought struck. I turned the camera toward the bed, put it on self-timer, and raced to the perfectly made bed and lay upon it. A click, and I was immortalized on Haile Selassie's bed.

After a few weeks of living with and writing for Kathy, I had to change. I felt guilty. Lew was staying at the Itege Hotel, the country's first government hotel, founded by Empress Taytu in 1907, and seemingly untouched since. And I had written a story I was particularly proud of about crocodiles. I had asked Kathy for a byline, or even a co-byline, but she refused. So, I moved back with Lew, and we spent our time running one- and two-day Awash trips for the ex-pat community, and we were pretty happy.

∿∿∿

With the river season approaching in North America, we decided we had time for one more Ethiopian River expedition before heading back.

Of the Grand Slam river expeditions we had originally targeted (Omo, Awash, Baro, Blue Nile, and Tekeze), two remained on our list: the Blue Nile and the Tekeze. But it was March, and with the continued drought we figured the Tekeze too low, and would have to wait until the following fall. The last unrun section of the Blue Nile, from below Tissisat Falls to the Second Portuguese Bridge, was also too low, so we would postpone that as well. Instead, we would close out the season in Ethiopia running the 140-mile stretch of the Northern Gorge of the Blue Nile, the section the British had hailed as the Grand Canyon of Africa when they passed through in 1968. Jim Slade and Cherry Jensen had successfully climbed Mount Kenya and Kilimanjaro, and telegraphed that they wanted to join the Blue Nile expedition, so we awaited their return before heading to the northern tablelands. While waiting, I met a young American, Scott Johnson, who had been inspired by Colin Fletcher's book, *The Man Who Walked Through Time,* an account of the author's traverse by foot of the entire Grand Canyon. He decided he wanted to make a similar traverse through the Grand Canyon of Africa, the Blue Nile gorge, and write a book and become famous. He asked if he might set up an arrangement wherein we would bring him a resupply of food about halfway down the Northern Gorge. We rolled out a map and agreed to tributaries where he would leave notes about his progress tied around the closest tree. He would leave a week before us, and we would catch up about seventy miles downstream. I agreed to the plan, shook his hand, and wished him luck.

〰〰〰

When Jim and Cherry arrived we took the once-a-week flight to Mota on the edge of the Blue Nile gorge, hired donkeys, strapped our rafts and oars and gear on to the wooden saddles, and whacked their hindquarters to begin the twelve-and-a-half-mile trek into the canyon. It was a path that curled and scrambled like a lizard, and kept the Blue Nile hidden from us until we reached the lip of the last gorge. There, suddenly, was the river, and spanning it, this unlikely structure—*Sabera Dildi,* or the Second Portuguese Bridge. A stone structure built originally by the Portuguese in the seventeenth century, it had two arches over the river and three increasingly smaller ones on each side. There were two quite impressive approach ramps with low walls. But the setting of the bridge was bizarre, for both the Gojjam and Begemdir banks rose up almost sheer above the bridge, and there was nowhere for the approach ramps to go;

they ended abruptly at the foot of a daunting rock scramble some three hundred feet to the cliff top.

The bridge had collapsed at some earlier stage, and Emperor Menelik II in 1908 ordered its reconstruction. Menelik added an imposing gateway on the Gojjam side, on which there was a cement panel commemorative of this work. At low water, as it was when we arrived, the bridge loomed high over a deep cleft like some Victorian railway viaduct. But we could see the high-water marks when the river swirled at the tops of the ancient legs.

More recently it had suffered another grave blow. In the late 1930s the Ethiopian Resistance was trying to stop Italians in Begemdir from joining up with those in Gojjam. A local squireen with a band of forty men dug up the central arch. Unfortunately, while they were digging, it collapsed into the river, and all forty drowned. The Italians shot six men in Mota as a reprisal.

Since then the bridge was never permanently repaired. It was made usable by a rickety balk of logs, saplings, and gravel, across which herdsmen unconcernedly drove their tan and white goats. Rather than cross this precipitous arch, we turned down a tortuous trail and emerged at river's edge, where we supped on a freshly slaughtered goat purchased from a passerby. That night I sat by the river and marveled at its hoary currents, a bewildering skein of contradictory forces. So much water rippling along at different speeds, displaying a glittering richness of surface texture, gave the Blue Nile a dangerous, vibrant look. I couldn't sleep, as the stringy goat meat hung all night in my belly like a stone.

The next morning we inflated our two rafts, rigged and loaded, and then set off down East Africa's most famous waterway. The stream pulled at our oars as it churned down between rocky banks. The rapids were modest by our standards, Class II and III, and the gorge was nowhere near as stunning as that of the Grand Canyon of the Colorado. And we saw no wildlife or village life. After a couple days of rafting we began to wonder if the river had been oversold. At least we found the notes left by Scott Johnson at the appointed tributaries, and that added a dimension to the adventure.

On the third day we turned into a region of natural grandeur. Across the line of the river from the Gojjam bank a great vertical slab of basalt reared up. It was fifty feet high and relatively smooth, with here and there trees sprouting the spherical nests of busy, black-headed, yellow-bodied weaver birds.

The cliff went on for miles, increasing in height as we passed along it, first to sixty feet, then eighty, and finally after some miles to a cathedral-like scale of about 120 feet. At water level the amygdaloidal basaltic lava was constantly washed, so that it shone like a black sculpture.

Around one long corner we encountered two huge, isolated pillars, slices of cliff cut off by the river. They soared, narrow and sheer, to about 120 feet, beautifully shaped and crowned with mossy trees and shrubs. Beyond was another cliff, this one lined with a restless nation of black vervet monkeys, all with their long tails hanging down.

In all this wildness it was a shock suddenly to see in the cliff face a man-made wall, and doorways to two caves, one triangular, the other semicircular. There were no signs of steps from the river to the grottos, twenty-five feet up, or from the top of the cliff downward. How did people get there? We had a climbing rope and some pitons and were able to make our way to the caves, which were filled with pottery and old basketwork. The triangular cave curved inward, upward, and to the left for about twenty-five yards. It seemed to be a natural excavation by river erosion. The only human modification had been a platform of dressed stone at the mouth. There was no sign of any permanent or even temporary arrangements for getting in and out of the cave. Yet its umber floor, liberally heaped with evil-smelling bat dung, showed traces of human use: broken shards, arrowheads, strips of rattan, fragments of old wickerwork, and, in the farthermost corner on a constructed stone platform, the bases and lower parts of two terra-cotta storage jars. It was possible to move around and up to the semicircular entrance of the other cave, which was shallower in depth, but which was divided between two levels. On the upper one we found a complete black canopic pot, and more fragments, some of which clearly fit together. We had no idea how old these finds were, but they looked ancient. I decided to take the black jar and bring it back to the Institute of Ethiopian Studies in Addis Ababa, so experts there could determine if we had stumbled onto anything of significance.

Back on the river, we floated a few miles when from the top of the cliffs we heard a number of whooping cries, the sort often heard exchanged between travelers in the quiet of the Ethiopian countryside—but here, they were excited and in concert. We were all slow to appreciate the significance of the whoops echoing back and forth across the gorge. Suddenly, our reverie was disturbed by a fusillade of rocks. We looked up and about seventy-five yards away, along the rim of the cliff, among the fringe of gnarled trees and scrub, appeared a motley crowd of about a dozen men shouting angrily and gesticulating. As the ragtag warlord of the group gave a signal, a rock was fired down into the river, then another, and another. Spurts of water danced up in the stream about us.

We were dumbfounded. We knew the British Army had been attacked by shifta gunfire in this section of the Blue Nile, but up to this point all our encounters with Ethiopians had been friendly, even among the famously fierce Danakil. However, it didn't take long to react. I leaned into my oars and started rowing as hard as I could, and Jim Slade piloting the other raft did the same. Still, angry men were picking up jagged pieces of basalt and flinging them down at us. At the next bend we were pulled into the magnetic field of a rapid and whipped out of sight of the shiftas. For whatever reasons, they didn't use their rifles (the bullets are expensive and hard to replace), and we suffered no scars from the attack.

We camped by a tributary where Scott Johnson was supposed to leave another note, but we could find none. We checked every side canyon for the remainder of the trip and never saw another note.

Beyond here the gorge opened out and the cliffs were replaced by sloping hillsides. These were dotted here and there with plantations of maize, guarded by ramshackle watchtowers on which small boys were set to protect the corncobs from baboons. There were some truly beautiful hikes up tributary side canyons, and occasionally a natural arch or basalt monolith would wow us, but it didn't make up for the extreme heat that left us breathless and weak. Even the flies were torpid, unable to muster enough energy to bite. On the final days of the trip we were showered with a heat so terrifying and unbearable, we decided to alter our routine. Before the dawn was whole we would get up and float in the relative cool until midmorning. Then we would find shade beneath an acacia or cliff and rest until around four-thirty, playing endless games of Botticelli. Then we'd float until dark. It was the only way to beat the truly brutal midday heat.

We took turns standing guard at night, knowing shifta were around. It was downstream that the Franco-Swiss Expedition of 1962 met grim disaster. The six expedition members were sound asleep on an islet when, at about 1:30 A.M., under a full moon, the shifta opened fire. Two men were killed instantly; another was wounded as he and the survivors took to their boats and launched downstream in the darkness. Another hail and the boat was holed and a paddle smashed. But the remaining four survived.

With great relief, after nine days and 140 miles, we reached the steel supports of the Shafartak Bridge, the only modern span that arches over the length of the Blue Nile in Ethiopia. Moving slowly in the breathless heat, we exchanged the SOBEK handshake, took the obligatory take-out photograph, and headed up the hill to flag a passing bus. We asked all who passed if they had seen another ferenji walking solo down the river, a man called Scott Johnson, and nobody responded. Scott Johnson was never heard from again. For the first time, I wondered if I wanted to return to a river to run its undone section.

Departing for the Awash River expedition. Top of Land Rover, *left to right:* Lew Greenwald, Richard Bangs, John Kramer. On ground: two drivers, Tom Cromer, Dr. George Fuller.
JOHN KRAMER

Rafting the world's toughest rivers inevitably entails dangers, as on this SOBEK trip on the Franklin River in Tasmania. RICHARD BANGS

Lew Greenwald on the first descent of the Awash River in 1973, the beginning of his transformation to river guide. JOHN KRAMER

Richard Bangs rowing Lew Greenwald down the Awash River in 1973.
JOHN KRAMER AND RICHARD BANGS

Richard Bangs in the royal bed of Emperor Haile Selassie. There to photograph the royal jewels, when alone for a moment, he set his camera on a tripod, jumped on the bed, and snapped
the picture. RICHARD BANGS

The core Tekeze team. Back row, *left to right:* Jim Slade, John Yost, Richard Bangs, George Fuller, Bart Henderson, Pasquale Scaturro. Front row, *left to right:* Eric Magneson, Greg Findley, Daniel Mehari, Brian Stevenson, Mike Speaks. LEWIS WHEELER, COURTESY TURNER ORIGINAL PRODUCTIONS

Rafts at campsite on the Tekeze, at the bottom of the deepest gorge in Africa. Here the crew found an array of inscrutable rock art. BART HENDERSON

Sliding down the Fountain of Youth, a waterslide on the lower Tekeze. *Left to right:* Bart Henderson, John Yost, Jim Slade, George Fuller, Richard Bangs. JONATHAN CHESTER/EXTREME IMAGES

Richard Bangs rowing the mighty rapids of the Tekeze on the exploratory expedition. In front of raft: Jim Slade, Bart Henderson, and George Fuller. LEWIS WHEELER, COURTESY TURNER ORIGINAL PRODUCTIONS

During a funeral in the highlands above the Tekeze Gorge, a priest reads Ge'ez scriptures from a huge goatskin parchment book. BART HENDERSON

The marketplace at Lalibela. Here the expedition stocked up on final supplies before trekking into the Tekeze Gorge. JONATHAN CHESTER/EXTREME IMAGES

A Coptic Christian priest in front of an underground church hewn from stone. BART HENDERSON

Beta Gioghis (Church of Saint George) in Lalibela. Standing more than forty feet high in the center of a deep, well-like pit, the church has been shaped to resemble a cross. JONATHAN CHESTER/EXTREME IMAGES

Photographer Jonathan Chester squaring off a $24,000 Kodak digital camera with a shooter of a different kind, a Tekeze villager who thought the expedition might be filled with bandits.

JONATHAN CHESTER/EXTREME IMAGES AND RICHARD BANGS

"The Call of the Wired." Uplinking from the bottom of the Tekeze Gorge, team members send and receive e-mail, and relay expedition news and multimedia to the wired world.

JONATHAN CHESTER/EXTREME IMAGES

# CHAPTER 13

# THE EMPIRE STRIKES BACK

"Africa, amongst the continents, will teach it to you: that God and the Devil are one."

—Karen Blixen

After a Filowa bath and some time in the cool breezes of Addis I was feeling pretty trick that late spring of 1974: square, decent, fit, living up to a code, as when walking into a cold evening after leaving a gym with hair seriously combed and wet. I had several river expeditions under my belt, I was writing under my own name for the Ethiopian *Herald,* and SOBEK's Awash program was bringing in a little money. But while things were going well for SOBEK, the rest of Ethiopia was breaking apart, revealing its natural fault lines like a gem under a jeweler's hammer.

Haile Selassie had run the country as a private fiefdom, as a firm and uncompromising imperial leader. There were stories of entire villages razed at his command with the whiff of rebellion. While still a world hero, and the inspiration for the growing Rastafarianism movement, at home he had led a brutal campaign to squelch any resistance to his absolute power. But the emperor was now an octogenarian, and his grip was loosening.

Haile Selassie was born Ras Tafari Makonen (hence Rastafarianism) in 1892, and was crowned emperor under the name of Haile Selassie in November 1930. He was credited with creating the first unambiguously unified Ethiopian state, and equally unambiguous was the fact that this state gave no meaningful constitutional protection or power to the overwhelming majority of its citizens.

The first serious challenge to Haile Selassie's rule came not from within the country, but from Italy. The immediate effect of the Battle of Adwa in 1896 had been the abandonment of Italian colonial aspirations south of the Eritrean border, but the humiliation afforded to the Italian Army still rankled, particularly in the nationalistic fervor that accompanied the rise of power of Mussolini's fascists in 1922. Mussolini's initial attempts to gain economic control of Ethiopia were disguised behind diplomacy, but by the time Haile Selassie had gained power, the Italians abandoned this approach in favor of subterfuge and force. The former tactic was most effective in Tigre, through which the Tekeze runs, and which has close historical and cultural links to neighboring Eritrea. Italy charmed the Tigrean nobility, whose response when war broke out in 1935 varied from lukewarm resistance to taking the Italian side against Ethiopia.

The Italian Army crossed from Eritrea in October 1935. The Ethiopian Army entered Tigre in January 1936, just as Haile Selassie appeared as the *Time* magazine Man of the Year. After a couple minor Ethiopian victories, Italy's superior air power, and its use of prohibited mustard gas, proved decisive. Haile Selassie went into exile, and the streets erupted into anarchy and violence.

Throughout the Italian occupation, the Ethiopian nobility combined time-buying diplomacy and well-organized guerrilla warfare to undermine the foreign regime. The fascists' response was characteristically brutal, and they used tactics Haile Selassie would later incorporate as his own. When, in 1937, an unsuccessful attempt was made on the life of the Italian viceroy, the Italian Blackshirts ran riot in the capital, burning down houses and decapitating and disemboweling Ethiopians, mostly at random, though the intelligentsia were particularly targeted. The Ethiopian Resistance won few battles of note, but its role in demoralizing the occupiers laid the foundation for the easy British victory over the Italian troops in the Allied liberation campaign of January 1941.

Lieutenant Colonel Orde Wingate led the emperor back from exile at the head of "Gideon Force," which marched from Khartoum with fifteen thousand camels (only fifty camels reached Addis Ababa; an officer reported that "a compass was not needed, one could orient the column by the stink of dead camels"). Haile Selassie was returned to his throne immediately after the Allied troops drove Italy back into Eritrea, and once there he asked the UN for Eritrea to be folded into his imperial government to allow access to the Red Sea. Both Britain and the U.S. had a vested interest in keeping a Red Sea territory in friendly hands, and they lobbied other member states to grant Haile Selassie's request. After no meaningful consultation with Eritreans, the UN forced Eritrea into a highly ambiguous federation with Ethiopia.

As the oil-rich Middle East, just across the Red Sea from Eritrea, came to play an increasingly important role in international affairs, so did Ethiopia and its Red Sea harbors in U.S. foreign policy. In 1962 Ethiopia formally annexed Eritrea with hardly a squeak from the international community, but Eritrea launched a war for self-determination that lasted almost thirty years, and cost the lives of more than 100,000 Eritreans, and which never once figured on the UN's agenda. The U.S. did more than look the other way. In exchange for using Asmara as a spy communications center and a military base, the U.S. developed a military training program for Ethiopia that, by 1970, absorbed more than half the U.S. budget for military aid to Africa.

Few modern leaders became so deeply associated with a country's image for so long as Haile Selassie. He ruled almost unchallenged, except for the brief Italian interlude, between 1930 and 1974. But for all the mystique surrounding him, Haile Selassie did very little to develop his country, and there were endless rumors of vast wealth ciphered into Swiss bank accounts while thousands in remote villages starved. In essence, the Ethiopia of the early 1970s, when I was exploring its rivers, was no less feudal than the Ethiopia of 1930.

Over the years Haile Selassie had suppressed coup attempts, resistance movements, and any challenges to his absolute authority with the same brutal techniques employed by the occupying Italians. Few lived to incur his wrath a second time. But by the time of my arrival in 1973, the aging Haile Selassie was losing control. The cries for land reform (most peasants were still subject to the whims of local landlords) came to a head over the 1973 famine in Wolo in Tigre, during which an estimated 200,000 people died. But it was the oil crisis that kicked him in the gut. Haile Selassie had declared that taxi drivers in Addis Ababa could charge only a fixed price of 25 cents wherever they took passengers in the city. This worked fine when oil prices were low, but when the embargo of 1974 sent oil prices rocketing, the drivers found themselves losing money with every fare. Attempted strikes in the past had met with quick and repressive measures by the government, but the cabbies felt they had little choice, so en masse they went on strike, and braced for the worst . . . but to everyone's surprise, Haile Selassie acquiesced, and agreed to a subsidy for gas prices. This was such a huge victory that within a few days the bus drivers went on strike. A creeping revolution had begun. I remember wandering about the Mercato and seeing the carcasses of burned-out buses, dismembered trucks, and pockets of loot-ing and rioting. Again, the emperor capitulated to the strikers' demands. Next came students, trade unions, air traffic controllers; even 200,000 Coptic Christian priests threatened to go on strike for more pay. The emperor began to go along with reforms that dismantled centuries of feudalism. This didn't go unnoticed by the military, whose members also felt underpaid. They too went on strike for better pay conditions. And they got it. All the while there were demonstrations, local peasant revolts, rebel groups fighting in the north and south, food and fuel riots, and mu-tinies within the military.

⌁⌁

The oil crisis also affected me. As we packed our gear for storage after our Blue Nile expedition I was looking forward to heading back to an-other season guiding the Grand Canyon. I now had five seasons under my belt guiding for Hatch River Expeditions and loved it. But as I got back to our rented house near Arat Kilo, I saw an envelope with the fa-miliar Hatch logo of a boat with long oars rafting the globe. I ripped open the letter, and it was a short message from Ted Hatch himself: "Due to the oil crisis, we find we have to cut back on our personnel this sea-son. As such, we won't be needing your services. I hope you have a good summer. Regards, Ted Hatch." I was crushed. I was fired. And the oil cri-sis was such a bad absolution. I had heard rumors that Ted wasn't pleased with my founding of SOBEK, and that he considered my enterprise competition. But I couldn't help but wonder if there was more to it. If I had somehow not done the best I could; if I had fallen below the mark.

But good things come out of bad situations. Instead I called George Wendt at O.A.R.S., and asked if Lew and I might come to Angels Camp, California, and work there for the summer. George said fine, and Lew and I flew back to the United States in April after having spent eight months in Africa. Before heading to the Gold Country, though, Lew and I drove to Los Angeles to help edit and write the Omo film that had been shot by Jerry Shea. We moved into the tiny Hermosa Beach apartment of Anne Mulqueen, who had been on the expedition, and for the following month we dutifully drove over to Jerry's house on Centinela Avenue every morning, and edited and wrote all day long. Finally, in late May the film was completed, and we somehow recruited Marshall Thompson, the B-movie star of such film classics as *Clarence, the Cross-eyed Lion* (1965) and *East of Kilimanjaro* (1957), and the lead in the sixties television series *Daktari,* to narrate the film. It was a highlight of my life at that point to go into a real Hollywood sound studio and direct a real actor in how to read our script.

In late May, Lew and I hitched up to Angels Camp, and settled in an old bunkhouse for a fabulous summer. During the weekdays we would trek over to George Wendt's basement, where with a single manual typewriter and a single bare lightbulb hanging from the ceiling, we would tap out letters of invitation to join us in rafting the Omo. We would divide up and personally call every lead. On the weekends we went rafting, down the Stanislaus, the South Fork of the American, the Tuolumne, and the Merced. Lew became a full-fledged rafting guide and was loved by all who rowed with him.

One summer weekend Jim Slade, who was out between Grand Canyon trips for a few California runs with us, got suddenly sick. He had a steep fever, then wild chills, and a croupy cough. Lew and I piled Jim into his light blue 1966 Ford Econoline Supervan and drove him to the Mark Twain Hospital in San Andreas. We checked Jim in and waited in the emergency room for an answer. An hour later the doctor walked in and threw up his hands. He said it was vivax malaria, not a typically fatal variety, but a nasty one nonetheless. And while there had been, he said, the occasional bout of malaria in the San Joaquin Valley, the San Andreas hospital didn't carry any quinine, at least not any that could be accessed on a weekend when the pharmacy was closed. "You might try Stockton," the doctor suggested. So, Lew drove the Supervan the ninety minutes to Stockton while I stayed with Jim, and was back by late afternoon with the medicine. The doctor gave Jim strong doses of quinine and warned a relapse could come at any time. Jim took it all in stride and left for the Grand Canyon again, promising he would see us in the fall back in Ethiopia. A similar bout of tropical malady hit Robbie Paul that summer, and as he rolled around in pain he begged out loud for the doctor to put him out of his misery. When finally released, he vowed he would never do another overseas raft trip, and he disappeared from the scene.

By summer's end Lew was as trim and tan as any nineteen-year-old guide, and happier than a puppy. And with summer's end we had some decisions to make.

Our small company was making a little money, but its future wasn't something anyone would bet on. The writing bug had bitten me. Having published several pieces now about our adventures in Africa, I had dreams of becoming an author. After so much time on water, in the social vertex of rafting, I liked the notion of the desert of lonely creation. As such, I had applied to graduate school at USC in journalism and was accepted for the fall term, beginning late September 1974. We had managed to sell an October commercial Omo trip, and we had talked all summer of attempting the last two major exploratories, the unrun section of the Blue Nile, and the grand prize of African river exploratories, the Tekeze.

After much soul-searching, and not a small amount of angst, I decided to forgo the commercial Omo expedition, as well as the Blue Nile exploratory, in favor of graduate school, and a job as a waiter at a Bob's Big Boy outlet. My experience with the Blue Nile, despite its great name and history, had not been overwhelming. And, I was still haunted by the drowning of Angus. Missing the next Blue Nile exploratory was an act of self-abnegation I immediately regretted. But, I reminded myself and all who would listen, I would definitely be there for the Tekeze, which we were now scheduling for the fall of 1975. With all the trouble in Ethiopia of late, most of it in the north, we would need permits for both the Blue Nile and the Tekeze. We agreed that I would go over to Ethiopia in early September, before starting J school, and work to get the necessary permits, and then Lew, John Yost, and Jim Slade would head over to Ethiopia in October to run the Omo. In January they would attempt the unrun upper section of the Blue Nile.

I had fallen in love with O.A.R.S. guide Candy Unenyo over the summer, and she moved into the Playa del Rey apartment I had taken for school, just underneath a landing path at LAX. She would oversee the place while I made a quick trip to Addis Ababa to try and nail down the permits.

~~~~~

I arrived in Addis Ababa the second week of September, just after the rains. The day was cool, washed in a flat, white light. As I drove down the Bole Road I looked through a spiderweb of cracks running from a bullet hole in the taxi's windshield to the sight of buses overturned, charred, and cannibalized. Anger soaked the air. I checked into the YMCA for my short stay, and all night long heard the crack of rifle shot, and the howling of dogs. The next day, after a soak at the Filowa baths, I visited geologist John Kalb, who was exploring the Awash for fossils of the "missing link," and who was storing our rafts in exchange for occasional use. He had bad news. The government had nationalized our rafts and confiscated them. We'd have to bring over another set. In the afternoon I visited my friends at the embassy, who expressed great concern over the deteriorating situation and who had heightened security around the compound. They talked of the U.S. ambassador who was assassinated in Khartoum, and didn't end their sentences, but the train was clear. Trouble was brewing. I missed curfew, so an embassy van took me back through the near-deserted streets, peopled only with whores, who scissored their legs and kissed the air at my passing.

The following day I awoke to the prayer call of a muezzin, something I hadn't remembered from earlier visits. I got up and walked over to the offices of ETO, the Ethiopian Tourist Organization, run by a smart, fast-talking Columbia University–educated Ethiopian named Hapte Selassie (no relation to the emperor). Director General H. E. Hapte Selassie had helped me in the past, and was intrigued with my introduction of adventure travel to Ethiopia. I had given him many slides from our previous expeditions, and he had already made some into posters and postcards, and was planning a government brochure on the rafting and adventure opportunities in the country.

Dark-suited, with pointed shoes and an Italian cigarette, he greeted me graciously. With the distant manner of an aristocrat, he gestured for me to sit in an oak chair in front of his ornately carved desk beneath an Italian oleograph. Everything about Hapte Selassie spoke breeding and money and a lifetime of privilege. Yet, he was drawn to the rough and raw adventure I represented. I had written him well in advance of the meeting requesting the permits. As I laid out my plans, he reminded me things were not so stable in the north. I said I knew that, but that my team was willing to assume the risks if we could secure the permits. After a pause of consideration, he clasped his hands together in front of him, and then rested them, like a completed sentence. He said he would issue the permits, and he pulled from his desk two pretyped letters of authorization for us to make our rafting exploratories on the Blue Nile and Tekeze. He placed them neatly on his desk, and proceeded with a flourish to sign the first one, the one for the Blue Nile. He then pulled out a government seal, and stamped the paper with a thud, and handed it to me.

Then as he looked to the second paper, the permit for the Tekeze, the door burst open with a crash. A file of army soldiers in combat fatigues, olive drab garrison belts, and spit-shined jump boots stormed into the room and surrounded us. There was the harsh metallic clunk of rifles being cocked. One man yelled in Amharic, and guns were raised and leveled at Hapte Selassie. More commands were issued, and Hapte defiantly sat in his chair, his hand tightened angrily around the stamp. Again the same words were yelled, but this time four soldiers went to the back of Hapte's chair and lifted him to a standing position. Then the officer in charge marched over to Hapte Selassie and undid his tie. He pulled it off in a burst, picked up the papers on the desk, then barked more orders, at which the soldiers shuffled His Excellency out the door, slamming it behind them. I was left alone with the single permit. It was September 12, 1974.

Little did I know that at that same moment around the city various ministers were being rounded up by a cabal of junior army officers leading the coup d'état. As each was arrested, his tie, a symbol to the revolutionaries of neocolonialistic hierocracy, was ripped off, and he was taken to jail, or to a wall and shot dead. Just a few blocks away another set of soldiers burst into the Imperial Palace and arrested its eighty-two-year-old occupant. He was ordered to take off his regal robes and change into commoner's clothes. And he was told he could not bring his beloved Chihuahua, Lulu, with him as he was escorted out the door, his last African walk. Three thousand years of Solomonic rule ended with His Imperial Majesty Haile Selassie I being driven unceremoniously from his palace in a Volkswagen Beetle.

After Hapte Selassie's arrest, I walked out to the street, and Addis Ababa felt ugly, out-of-joint in a way that was entirely new to me. I wanted out and headed home.

On the way home I routed through Washington, D.C., and stopped by the Ethiopian embassy to assess the situation. The new government, a socialist-inspired military coordinating committee, known as the Dergue ("committee" in Amharic) assured me we would be allowed to run the Omo, and they would honor the permit for the Blue Nile, but certainly there was no way to run the Tekeze. Back in California I consulted with Lew, Jim, and John, and our eight clients, and they all agreed to go forward with the Omo expedition. Even Candy was willing to make the trip, and seemed thrilled with the added edge of rafting a river in the midst of a revolution.

I drove Candy to the airport, kissed her good-bye, and went back to bury myself in my studies. I wondered endlessly if I made the right decision. And then a month later she returned, tan and happy, with tales of how wonderful Lew had been—a bit of my own spirit sailed with her through him. Over Christmas I got a call from Ethiopia. It was Lew, who asked if I might change my mind and jump on the upcoming Blue Nile exploratory. I hesitated, but then said no. I had to follow this course for a while. "Then promise me we'll do the Tekeze," he said through the scratchy phone connection. I did. I promised I would be back. We would get the permit for the Tekeze, and we would share that exploratory together. Of that I was certain.

CHAPTER 14

# A DEATH TOO SOON

"Even at the height of the dry season it tears and boils along too fast for any boat to live upon its surface."

—Alan Moorehead, *The Blue Nile*

Things were going fine. I was enjoying my studies, working toward a master's in journalism. After school and on weekends I attended to the business of SOBEK, answering the letters and phone calls, mailing out our fliers. But it didn't take a lot of time, as we didn't have much product to offer, and we didn't have many customers. Ethiopia wasn't suffering from an overabundance of good press, and we had yet to explore a river beyond its boundaries. So, the job of president of SOBEK Expeditions was not a taxing one, and I even had time to start an adventure travel magazine, *Bush League*, which promptly went bankrupt after publishing its one and only issue.

January 1975 rolled around, and I wondered how my pards were doing on the Blue Nile without me. When neighbors came over, Candy often showed slides from her recent Omo trip, and I felt a tinge of regret well up.

The morning of January 21, I got a call. I recognized the sonar voice of an overseas operator. She had me hold for a long minute, and then I heard the voice of John Yost, phoning from Addis Ababa. It was a scratchy connection. "Lew drowned," John said matter-of-factly. "Can you repeat that?" I spoke back into the receiver, my lip quivering, hoping I heard it wrong. "Lew is dead. He drowned on the Blue Nile," John said in slow, measured tones. He continued to speak, but the whole world seemed to balance on a point of silence. I hung up the phone. My temples began to throb. I buckled to the floor, and cried.

They had launched just below the First Portuguese Bridge, Agam Dildi, the entrance to the Northern Gorge, and immediately found themselves in a series of tight, twisting black basalt gorges, packed with Class V and VI rapids. Much of the trip they spent portaging or lining. The second day, January 17, Jim Slade awoke and wrote in his diary: "Dreamed my brother had died, and that Lew was my brother. Hope it was not an ill-omen or presentiment of things to come on this trip." It was the first time Jim had ever dreamed about death. Downstream later that day they came to a rapid not as bad as what they had battled. The river split, then reunited. They took the right channel. Then it split again, and the boat got caught in a small recirculating eddy on the right side where the water piled up against a blue-black wall. It didn't seem too dangerous, and they were tired of portaging. It was January, the water was fairly low, and they felt the current was forgiving enough that they could actually push the boat down the side of the wall and back into the main current.

Nobody was rowing. The oars were shipped. John Yost, Conrad Hirsh, Lew, and Jim Slade were standing on the tube and pushing the boat, working the boat, along the wall. They were making good progress. But a section of the wall stuck out a few inches, and the boat got lodged at the strongest intersection of the main river current and the back current of the eddy. With the powerful main current pushing against the outer tube, the boat slowly started to rise up the wall. The four tried to push the raft back down, but the current was far too strong, and it continued to rise. It became clear the boat was going to capsize. John was closest to shore, and he made a flying curvet and landed on solid ground. The boat continued to rise to a near tube-stand. Conrad was next, and he jumped as far as he could and landed waist-deep in water. The raft was now starting its roll over, and Lew jumped next into water over his head right where the stern line was trailing. He went under, and surfaced with a frightened look, and then in an agonal effort screamed that his life jacket had clipped to the stern line. Slade jumped last, but by then the raft was over. Jim and the boat sailed out into the main current and over a steep drop-off rapid. Jim was out front, and a couple hundred yards downstream he managed to make his way to the left shore. He then saw the raft charging toward him, and he swam back out, grabbed a D-ring, and with all his remaining strength he dragged it to a gravel bar.

John was on the opposite shore, and as Jim was catching his breath he watched John jump into the raging current and swim the entire width of the Blue Nile. He splashed to the boat, and between gulps told Jim that Lew was missing and before disappearing had yelled he was caught on the stern line. They immediately checked the stern and bow lines, and found a nick in the former where it looked like something had snagged. They checked under the boat, where people often get caught in a capsize. And then they searched the banks, howling Lew's name, sweeping the river, fearing the worst. At nightfall they collapsed in exhaustion.

With daybreak they could think of nothing to do but head downstream. A few turns downriver they found Lew, floating in an eddy, his orange Mae West life jacket pulled halfway up his head. Like Shorty Burton on the Colorado, who died when his life jacket clipped to a gas can during a capsize, it seemed Lew had jumped into the water and his jacket had clipped to the stern line. He was then dragged over the next falls, and downstream until he drowned, and then somehow came loose.

The surviving crew pulled Lew to shore and weighed options. They had an unknown distance yet to run, and in all likelihood, many dangerous rapids yet to face before reaching the Second Portuguese Bridge. And from there it was a full day's hike to the village of Mota, where they could catch the once-a-week plane to Addis Ababa. Lew had loved rivers, and they had changed him for the better. So, they decided to lay him to rest by the Blue Nile. The ground was too hard to bury him, so they found a small hollow and covered him with stones. Then they built a small fire, a funeral pyre on top, and performed a simple ceremony. They had no idea they were being watched, but a year later Karen Greenwald hiked into the gorge and met villagers who said they witnessed the funeral, and they took her to the spot. She removed Lew's remains, and brought them to a Jewish cemetery in Addis Ababa, where he was laid to rest in consecrated ground.

The news of Lew's death sent me into a tailspin. Up to that point, I saw river rafting as the finest expression of freedom and self-validation that existed, and the death fifteen months earlier of Angus Macleod a rare aberration. I believed that the American idea of freedom was Huck rafting the Mississippi, or Thoreau going up the Merrimac. I had seen firsthand the transformational power of river journeys, and Lew was living testimony: he had trimmed down, found a confidence and a lightness that had been hidden, and let it be known that his life was full of joy. But with his drowning, I saw the dark side of adventure. How could anything be celebrated that snatched away lives so full of promise, charity, and happiness? What sort of Faustian bargain had I struck? I had spent six years challenging wild rivers around the country and two in East Africa, and had amassed more than my share of thrills and spills. Now, not only did the guilt of Angus's fate resurface, but the shock that my close friend was dead numbed my world. Shame ran through me like a sword. The life jacket in my closet hung like an accusation beside my winter coat. Suddenly the thought of rafting down a river seemed evil, a frivolous exercise that had such an insidious downside that I couldn't imagine why people would risk it. I saw it all as a photographic negative of the way I had seen it before; everything white was black. The thought of laughing while paddling through the raised fist of a wave, a slap of whitewater that could knock a person unconscious and suck the life from a precious body, was abhorrent, pornographic, insane. I wanted to call all my past passengers and tell them the truth about river running and urge them to stay away from rafts and rivers.

My attitude about rivers bent like a gooseneck. Rivers didn't assert life; they took it away. They weren't innocent; they were dissolute. Rivers were acid baths. I didn't ever want to go near one again, didn't want one to come within my compass. I hung up my paddle.

I was in such a sulfurous funk I was a monster to live with. I carved out my own little meat department of metaphysical angst, and it stunk. Candy moved out; moved to Montana and not long after married a doctor. I never saw her again. I buried myself in studies and tried to forget the pain. My life became bland and vapid, a world behind glass. But, as the months wore I began to soften. Friends would stop by my apartment on their way to run a river, and when I tried to explain my hostility for what they were doing, their eyes looked over my shoulder. And, at social functions, I couldn't ignore the palpable excitement across the room when talk finally steered to rivers run and yet to be. That spring my most exciting endeavor was watching the tomatoes grow.

CHAPTER 15

# DELIVERANCE

"In the midst of winter, I finally learned that there was in me an invincible summer."

—Albert Camus

I n late summer of 1975 I headed east with John Yost for a visit with our families. While there we went to River Bowl, the high school haunt where we had met, for a game of ten pins, a nice, safe activity. Steve Jovanovich, another high school buddy, and Rick Szabo, a college fraternity brother and former Colorado river guide, joined us. In the midst of the fourth game John turned to the group and suggested we should run the Chattooga down on the South Carolina/Georgia border while we were all back east. Rick and Steve loved the idea; I hated it. I had sworn off rivers, and wanted nothing to do with them—especially the Chattooga, which evoked thoughts of death and memories of Lew. Resistance rose in me like marble.

But John, Rick, and Steve persisted, saying it would be fun and perhaps therapeutic. It was supposed to be an especially beautiful river, and the rapids, though challenging, were nothing like those of the Blue Nile. In fact, in the wake of *Deliverance,* the river had become one of the most popular in the country, with some 50,000 boaters running its rapids each year, up from the 800 who had floated it in 1971, the year before the film

was released, and the 100 who had run the river in 1967. In the end I capitulated. It did sound like fun, a break from the flat pitch my life had become, and maybe a chance to lift out of the bad mood that had plagued
me for months.

I screwed up my courage and asked my dad for the car for our little
adventure, and he handed over the keys without so much as a query as to
our destination. My dad's bitterness toward his work and employer had
intensified, his nervous breakdowns had continued, and with each he
seemed to retreat deeper into an inner space. He had been several times
hospitalized, had attempted suicide, had undergone more violent
episodes. He was still in therapy, trying different meditations and new
medications, and seemed increasingly disconnected to his family. He
really had no idea how rivers had affected my life, and never asked, never
probed. He was exploring another current.

So, on a sultry August Sunday we piled into my dad's Oldsmobile and
headed south to run the *Deliverance* river. We got out of the car at Bryson
City, North Carolina, home of the Nantahala Outdoor Center, the southeastern river runners' salt lick. The air was so thick with humidity you
could pick it up and throw it. It was a major relief just to step inside the
log cabin hut. There we met owner Payson Kennedy, who had been the
stunt double for Burt Reynolds playing Lewis, and he looked eerily like
Lew. Over salt pork and sow belly, Payson told us about something he
called the *Deliverance* Syndrome, a phenomenon that the film and book
incited. Despite its message of ill-conceived adventures and death, thousands of viewers and readers had been inspired to come and boat the
Chattooga. Many had no whitewater experience and were improperly
outfitted when they headed downriver. There had been too many drown-
ings in the past few years attributed to boating under the *Deliverance* influence, and Payson saw no end in sight. Then he invited us to share a few
beers before we headed down to the river. We drank, and all but one of
us laughed as he told stories of the fools who headed down the river sans
life jackets or spare paddles and never came back. Even the moon looked
a little ill that night.

The next morning we headed for our encounter with the Chattooga.
The river begins its life as a clear trickle near Cashiers, North Carolina,
adjacent to Whiteside Mountain. It hooks and cramps for fifty miles
through the blue-hazed Appalachians, dropping a vertical half mile in the
process, until it succumbs to the static waters of Lake Tugaloo.

Through the years, few have enjoyed the river's beauty. The Chero-
kees had a large settlement on its banks prior to 1700 and they gave the

river its name, Chattooga, meaning "place of the white rocks." The first white settlers did not come to the river until the 1800s, and because the land was so rugged, there were not many of them. Loggers worked the river in the early part of this century. Towns grew nearby in later years. But still the Chattooga stayed wild. The local people fished for trout and redeye bass, camped, and swam in the cold water.

But as the 1960s drew to a close, something new arrived. Young out-landers, usually from the city, began showing up with canoes, kayaks, and rafts strapped to their car roofs. At first, they trickled in, but each year their numbers grew. The locals didn't quite know what to make of them. And then, to further complicate matters, *Deliverance* came along.

For most of its course, the Chattooga divides South Carolina and Georgia, creating the boundary between the Sumter and Chattahoochee national forests. The Chattooga remains one of the last free-flowing streams in the southeast. In 1974 it qualified for federal protection under Wild and Scenic status.★

The Chattooga is divided into four sections, each more difficult than the one before. Against my wishes, the group set sights on section IV, dropping thirty feet per mile. The one concession I got was a warm-up at the last rapid on section III before we committed to the final run. We carried our raft three hundred yards upstream to a rapid called Bull Sluice, one that I had read Jimmy Carter had pioneered.

The undulant valley of the river sloped gently, covered with white pine and hemlock, dogwood and sourwood, rhododendron and laurel. Beyond, a mountain loomed, high, broad, and blue, the color of concen-trated wood smoke. I looked out over the white caps of the rapid and ex-pected to see bursting knives lashing at the sky; but instead the rapid looked inviting, more like cream on cappuccino.

I took my position in the raft, the right stern, where I would act as paddle captain, and we pushed off into the river. The current entered my muscles and body as though I were carrying it; it came up through the paddle. We dropped ten feet in two successive waterfalls, and practically shot through the curling central hydraulic at the bottom. It was a rousing ride, one that had John, Steve, and Rick whooping at conclusion. I let a

---

★In 1968 the U.S. government created a Wild and Scenic Rivers System to provide federal protec-tion for rivers in much the same way that parklands are protected. Certain criteria—scenic, recre-ational, geologic, historic, and cultural value, as well as fish and wildlife populations—are evaluated in selecting the rivers. Once chosen, the rivers are protected from dams, diversion projects, and river-side development that would alter their character.

smile steal across my face. I looked skyward, and quoted from the film the words that Bobby (Ned Beatty) spritzed after running their first major section of rapids: "I tell you, Lewis, that's the best—the second best—sensation I ever felt."

We paddled under a silver bridge and were immediately surfing through more rapids. There was no sensation of the water's raging, but rather of its alertness and resourcefulness as it split apart at rocks, frothed lightly, corkscrewed, fluted, fell, recovered, jostled over smoothed stones, and then pattered out of sight along garden-staircase steps around an-other turn. Usually softspoken, I was screaming as we worked to the right and blasted through Screaming Left Turn. We hopped from eddy to eddy in a jumble of rocks, where I called out a bad command, and we paddled smack into a boulder, which spun us around and sent us falling backward into a great vortex. Then we tumbled into a quiet cover, where we pulled in our paddles and I bent to catch my breath. The thrill of running rapids coursed through me, but I was out of practice, out of shape. And the most dangerous rapid was next.

We pulled over to scout Woodall Shoals, rated VI, which the guide-book said was suitable only for a "crazed team of experts." All others were supposed to portage. A granite ledge jutted from the left bank, forc-ing the current into a narrow channel. The river dropped over the ledge with a roar, sending up a perpetual spindrift. I stared into the infamous hole at the bottom of these falls. It didn't look that bad, though a tightly coiled, powerful wave was recirculating at its lower end. This was the killer hole that had, since the movie's debut, refused to release so many bodies. But as I scrutinized the water dynamics, I knew we could get through it if we just kept the raft dead-on straight. The same requirement I needed when I ran the waterfall on the Awash, only there I blew it, and we flipped, with no bodily consequences. Here the downside was a bit dearer.

I was repulsed and ineluctably drawn at the same time, desperately frightened, but also calm. A part of me, a cerebral side, told me that portaging was the judicious thing to do. If I had portaged the first rapid on the Baro, Angus would be alive today. If my friends had portaged on the Blue Nile, Lew would be here paddling with us. This was high-risk water, the kind of water that has killed scores over the years.

But another side, an emotional, irrational, adrenaline-fueled side, wanted to run Woodall Shoals. I felt we could do it, and I wanted to do it.

"Let's run it," I said.

〜〜〜

Yost and Rick were psyched. Steve, who was new to the sport, wasn't so sure. But he climbed in and assumed his position in the bow.

As we approached the tongue, I pointed the raft like an arrow directly downstream and instructed that nobody paddle until I gave the command. I had to keep the boat straight, and would do it by letting the current propel our craft while I ruddered in the rear. Just before we dropped into the hole, Steve inexplicably shot his paddle into the current for a quick stroke, reminiscent of John Kramer's and George Fuller's last-minute move atop the falls on the Awash. I could feel my body tense like a drawn bow. I watched in horror as the water broke around his paddle like glass, and the boat turned slightly. I couldn't correct it, and we washed into the hole at an angle, just what we didn't want. The raft buckled and kicked and rose to ride the hydraulic, then it stalled. I slammed my blade like a beaver tail into the curl. If the raft slipped back, we would be caught in the death trap. We hung at the rounded crest of the hydraulic for an eternity—the raft and the wave like two wrestlers locked in a trembling stalemate, waiting for one to give. The fabric beneath us seemed to shudder as though about to explode, and then suddenly we shot to the other side, safe and sound. We erupted in frothy cheer.

Below Woodall Shoals we passed a Forest Service road, a place I had seen on the map and considered as an exit opportunity if things weren't going well. But we passed it by, and the banks grew steeper and the river began to narrow to less than half its upstream width. The canyon walls were gray, limestoneish, pitted and scabby. We were committed now. There was no way out except downstream. We bounced through Double Dip, careened over Seven Foot Falls, and had a close encounter with Alligator Rock, which took a snap at us, grazed the side of the raft, but left no scars.

A broad beach on the right offered the ideal lunch stop, and we pulled out sandwiches, trail mix, and pork rinds and sat back, paddling our feet in the water. I hadn't enjoyed a meal outdoors since Lew's accident, and as the river whispered at my feet and the warmth of the sun caressed my naked back, I felt flushed with good feelings—for nature, for life, and for pork rinds, which I usually hated. The river was good, I remembered.

Soon afterward we were flying over ledges, punching through holes, sliding down sluices. We paddled past a dark rock that looked like a mountain gorilla. We picked our way through labyrinthine Stekoa Creek rapids the wrong way, ending up in a raft trap on the right, where the boulders closed in on us like a vault door. Rather than attempting to paddle back upstream to the correct route, we used a system I had perfected in Ethiopia: we simply jumped out into the waist-high water, wrestled the raft over the boulders, and continued on our merry way.

On the South Carolina side we passed Long Creek Falls, which made a cameo appearance in the film. Now it splashed its load into intense needles of light, almost solid enough to pick up like nails from the surface. A turtle was sunning himself on a dark rock just below the spray, a crooked smile on his tiny face.

Not long afterward we reached Deliverance Rock, a medium-sized rapid where many of the scenes from the movie had been shot. Although a technical rapid with several maneuvers along the cross-grain of the current, it presented no problems, and we were soon at Raven's Shoot, named for the beaklike river-wide ledge, which we launched over as though in flight. The boulders were covered with moss and green lichens and contained a large amount of mica, causing them to glitter in the sunlight. In the quieter pools the mica hung suspended like gold flakes. We sneaked next through the Tunnel of Love, where two boulders leaning against each other formed a small arch just wide enough for our raft.

We slopped over Last Supper, so named because it is the final rapid before the Five Falls section, a quintuplet of class IV and higher rapids, the worst section on the river. We paused in a pool known as Calm Before the Storm. The air shook from the sound of the rapids ahead—low-throated, massively frantic, and authoritative. We all exchanged looks and nods, then dug the paddles deep.

We plunged down a long stubble field into Entrance Rapid, peeling from one side of the river to the other, crashing over a four-foot drop to the right of VW Rock. The hydrotechnics had begun. We corkscrewed through the rapid of the same name, pitched over a pour-over, and bumped smack into the boulder barricade at Crack-in-the-Rock. We took the middle crack and fell over a five-foot falls into the beginning of Jawbone. The rapid growled at us, snapped its white fangs, and filled us with water as we slid past Decapitation Rock out of control. We had hoped to stop and scout the last pitch, Sock-Em-Dog, but we were too full of water to maneuver to shore, and the next rapid jumped at us almost immediately. It was the last rapid in the Five Falls section, and the worst—a funnel of water into which the whole river cramped and shot over a seven-foot drop into a nasty hole, blizzarding through the stones and beating and fuming like some enormous force chained to the spot.

"Paddle hard," I yelled over the thunder as we bolted down the spillway and crashed into the hydraulic. We were buried in whitewater, tons of it, pouring like cement from all sides. Under the avalanche, I felt a constant trembling of awareness in a thousand places that added up to a kind of equilibrium. When we shoved our way out, John Yost was missing from his perch to the left.

"Where's John?" I howled.

Heads spun in a frantic search. My stomach fell like a stone. We were in the recovery pool below the rapid. It was quiet, just the muffled base note of the falls behind. And no sign of John. I threw my paddle in the raft and dove in. John was my best surviving friend. I had already lost one to the river. I had spent months in mental preparation to rejoin the river, to accept what had happened in Africa as a freak accident, to re-embrace the sport I had once loved so much. John was missing. It couldn't happen again. But it could . . . the river is totally implacable.

I dove in and probed with my arms. I was in a room of varying shades of green, beautifully graduated from light to dark, but there was no sign of life. When I resurfaced for a breath, John still hadn't showed. It had been half a minute. I thought the worst. Then, at the far end of the pool, downstream of our raft, just at the head of Shoulderbone Rapid, John surfaced, like a porpoise in a show. Water washed down his face, and he gasped for breath. We quickly paddled over and pulled him in. He had been stuck in the hydraulic, sucked down deep, and spit back up at the river's whim. After some wet coughing he was fine, not much ruffled by the close call.

"Let's get going." He grinned his famous cat-ate-the-canary grin. "This is what it's all about."

He was right.

We broke out into song: "Summertime," from *Porgy and Bess.* We tortured the tune, but the feelings were never better expressed.

There was a new tone in the river—an old one—something I recognized. We paddled through a few more small rapids before we lost our current in Lake Tugaloo. As we eased into the anesthetized water of the reservoir, hundreds of swallows flittered between us and the setting sun, making silver splashes as they dipped at the water. It was a pretty sight, but set against the ugliness of a constructed lake, where the quick life of moving water was choked to death behind a dam.

Ed Gentry, the protagonist in *Deliverance,* let such a lake bury three people, and with them the shame, the horror, the hatred he had encountered on the river. I would bury the same sentiments. For two miles we paddled across a landscape that evoked death: debris littered the shore like skeletons. Stripped trees were bent over as though crying. It was here I saw the difference. The river upstream was a celebration of life, full of sparkle and exhilaration, brimming with beauty, bursting with challenge and the promise of attainment, and an agent for renewal. This is what drew me to the river in the first place; this is what had called Lew.

He had made a sacrifice, the supreme sacrifice, but it was in search of life, not sitting in stagnant, polluted waters behind a dam or a desk. If only for a moment, he lived life to its fullest, rode along the keen edge between water and sky. And I knew then he would want me to do the same. As we pulled our raft up on the bank, I turned to John, cocked my hand over the blade of my paddle as though playing a banjo, and said, "Someday we have to run the Tekeze."

For half a year my spirit had been hijacked. Now, I was back.

It was August 25, 1975. As I emerged from the river reborn, on the other side of the world Mengistu Haile Mariam was smothering to death with an ether-soaked pillow his prisoner of almost a year, the 225th consecutive monarch in a royal line tracing to Solomon the First, the son of David: Emperor Haile Selassie. The remains would be secretly buried under a latrine.

CHAPTER 16

# WATER WORLD

"We shall not cease from exploration. And at the end of all our exploring will be
to arrive where we started and know the place for the first time."

—T. S. Eliot, "Little Gidding," 1942

That fall I returned to graduate school and became reengaged in
SOBEK, designing a new brochure, plotting new expeditions in
New Guinea and Turkey, running a few western rivers over the week-
ends. I wasn't sure, though, whether I would ever go back to Ethiopia.
The deaths still haunted me.

In November of that year, 1975, I got a call from a friend, a tour operator. A trek he'd organized to the Sahara had been canceled by the Al-
gerian government, and his clients wanted an alternative. Would I be
interested in taking them to Ethiopia for a trek? Two weeks later I arrived in Addis Ababa, where I met up with John Yost, Jim Slade, and a
trainee guide, Gary Bolton, fresh from a SOBEK raft tour of the Omo
River. They were surprised to see me there, where nobody expected I
would return.

By late December, after escorting a commercial trek through the Bale
Mountains of southern Ethiopia, John, Jim, and I were wondering what
to do next, and the subject of the unfinished Baro came up. The mystery
of Angus still gnawed at all of us. I confessed that over the months, some-

times in the middle of a mundane chore—taking out the trash, doing the laundry—I'd stop and see Angus's frozen features as I'd cut him loose. In weak moments I would wonder if there just might be a chance that he was still alive. And I'd be pressed with a feeling of guilt that I hadn't done enough, that I had waded in waist deep, then turned back. And I wondered how Angus had felt in those last few minutes—about himself, about me. Jim and John admitted to similar feelings, and we collectively decided to try the Baro once again. We needed a fourth, and Gary Bolton agreed to join as well.

This time we put in where I had taken out almost two years before, at the terminus of a long jungle path. Again, we had a single raft, with the minimum of gear to make portaging easier. The river pummeled us, as it had before, randomly tossing portages and major rapids in our path. But during the next few days, the trip gradually, almost imperceptibly became easier. On Christmas morning I decorated a bush with my socks and passed out presents of party favors and sweets. Under an ebony sapling I placed a package of confections for Angus. It was a curiously satisfying holiday, being surrounded by primeval beauty and accompanied by three other men with a common quest. No one expected to find Angus alive, but I thought that the journey—at least for me—might expunge all doubt, exorcise guilt. I wanted to think that I had done all that was humanly possible to explore a death I was partly responsible for. And somehow I wanted him to know this.

As we tumbled off the Abyssinian massif into the Great Rift Valley of Africa, taking on tributaries every few miles, the river and its rapids grew. At times we even allowed ourselves to enjoy the experience, to shriek with delight, to throw heads back in laughter as we bounced through Colorado-style whitewater and soaked in the scenery. Again, we found remnants of the first trip—a broken oar here, a smashed pan there. Never, though, a hint of Angus.

After one long day of portaging, I went to gather my wetbag, holding my clothes, sleeping bag, and toilet kit, and it was nowhere to be found. Apparently, it had been tossed out during one of the grueling portages. I trekked back upstream for a couple miles, but could find nothing, and it was getting dark, so I picked my way back to the raft and the plain pasta dinner John was cooking. At that moment, I had no worldly possessions, save the torn shorts I was wearing, my socks and tennis shoes, and the Buck knife that hung from my pants. I slept in a small cave that night, rolled up like a hedgehog, with no sleeping bag, no pad, but I slept well. With the morning, I awoke fresh and energized, ready for the day, and though I had practically nothing to call my own, I felt a richness for the moment. I was with friends, on a mission, and was touching something primal. In an odd way, this all seemed liberating—no accoutrements to weigh down the soul, just a clear, present reason for going forward, for being. And I allowed something that would be called joy to wash over me.

On New Year's Eve we camped at the confluence of the Baro and the Bir-Bir rivers, pulling in as dusk was thickening to darkness. A lorry track crossed the Baro opposite our camp. It was there that Conrad Hirsh, the professor from the second Baro attempt, had said he would try to meet us with supplies. We couldn't see him, but Jim thought there might be a message waiting for us across the river. "I think I'll go check it out," he said.

"Don't be a fool," John warned. "We're in croc country now. You don't want to swim across this river." We weren't far from where Bill Olsen, the Peace Corps volunteer, was chomped in half while swimming.

An hour later, just after dark, Jim had not returned. We shouted his name, first individually, then as a chorus. No answer. Jim had become a close friend in the two years since we shared a tent on the upper Baro; he had been a partner in ordeal and elation, in failure and success. Now John and I swept our weak flashlight beams along the dark river. We gave up. We were tired, and we sat around the low licks of our campfire, ready to accept another loss, mapping out the ramifications in our minds. Suddenly Jim walked in from the shadows and thrust a note at us.

"Conrad arrived three day ago, waited two, and left this morning," he said, his body still dripping from the swim.

"You fool! I knew you couldn't disappear now—you owe me $3.30 in backgammon debts." I clucked with all the disciplinary tone I could muster.

The following day we spun from the vortex of the last rapid into the wide, Mississippi-like reaches of the lower Baro. Where rocks and whirlpools were once the enemy, now there were crocodiles and hippos. We hurled rocks, made threatening gestures, and yelled banshee shrieks to keep them away. Late in the day on January 3, 1976, we glided into the outpost town of Gambella. The villagers there had neither seen nor heard of Angus Macleod.

I never told Angus's relatives of our last search; we didn't find what might have given them solace. What I found I kept to myself, hidden like buried treasure in my soul. It was the knowledge of the precious and innate value of endeavor.

I wanted to believe that when Angus boarded my tiny boat and committed himself, he was sparked with life and light, that his blood raced with the passion of existence—perhaps more than ever before. On that first Friday in October of 1973, ten of us thought we knew what we were doing: another expedition, another raft trip, another river. Only Angus was exploring beyond his being. Maybe his was a senseless death, moments after launching, in the very first rapid. I would never forget the look of horror in his eyes as he struggled there in the water. But there were other ways to think about it. He took the dare and contacted the outermost boundaries. He lost, but so do we all, eventually. The difference—and it is an enormous one—is that he reached for it, wholly.

〰〰〰

After the last Baro expedition I returned to graduate school and completed the master's in journalism, a program that provided me with a skill I found useful in promoting SOBEK by writing articles about our adventures. I then enrolled in a doctoral program in cinema, thinking the craft of filmmaking might also aid in advancing SOBEK. But the academics of cinematography bored me, and I hungered to get my hands dirty again with real expeditions. So a year into the program I quit and moved back to Angels Camp, where George Wendt offered me a bedroom, rent free, as I plotted new exploratories, and tried to turn SOBEK into a real concern.

During this time my father continued to be in and out of hospitals and sanitariums, and I would tramp home over the holidays to attempt a connection or understanding. But he seemed impenetrable, inscrutable. Once I asked about the film he made in Iran back in the fifties, and he perked up a bit. He said that the finished work was in a vault at CIA headquarters in Langley, and that someday he wanted to show it to me.

"What's in the film?"

"I can't tell you, but I can say we recruited a famous Hollywood director for the job. I was very proud of that."

In June 1978, John Yost, Jim Slade, and I were at the airport in Istanbul, having just completed the first descent of the upper Euphrates River in Turkey. We were about to board the Pan Am flight to Frankfurt that would connect us back to San Francisco, but we were on standby tickets, school was just out, and the flight was full. I studied the OAG and saw that we could catch a flight to Tehran that would require an overnight, but then the following day it connected via Bombay and Hong Kong across the Pacific back to San Francisco. It didn't take much convincing for Yost and Slade to join the plan, and a few hours later we were at the airport in Tehran. It was middle afternoon, and the continuing flight was scheduled for 6:00 A.M. the following morning, so Jim and John elected to stay in the airport and read, play backgammon, and sleep on the plastic chairs rather than venture to town. I had private reasons for going, though, so I grabbed the bus and made my way to the city center and the public library. Though the capital was renowned for being the closest thing to a Western city in the Middle East, it was choked with cars and smog and angry faces. As I walked down the streets, I stood out as a foreigner with my blond hair and backpack, and passersby stooped to pick up stones and toss them at me, or spat at me. Outside of our brief encounter with natives on the Blue Nile, it was the most hostile place I'd ever been. Little known to me, a cycle of protest and violence was under way, and I was walking through a time bomb. I passed an English newspaper, and its headlines quoted the shah: "Nobody can overthrow me. I have the support of 7,000,000 troops, all of the workers, and most of the people. I have the power."

In the library, I found the bound copies of the English-language newspaper going back to the early fifties. There I read about how Mohammad Reza Pahlavi, an imperial leader in much the same mode as Haile Selassie, was forced into a brief exile by domestic opponents in 1953. This I knew, from readings stateside, as well as the fact that the CIA had engineered and stage-managed the return of the shah to the Peacock throne in a covert coup operation headed by Kermit Roosevelt. Those were the salad days of the CIA, when clandestine operations were carried out against the North Koreans, in support of Japan's Liberal Democratic Party; the agency orchestrated a coup in Guatemala, and assisted the Tibetan uprising against China. The year I was looking for was 1956, when my father was in Tehran. I found nothing, except two unrelated items— a mention that an American documentary film crew was in the city for several weeks, and that a new secret police force had been formed by the shah, called SAVAK, to combat the pro-Moscow Tudeh (Communist) Party, which had been declared illegal.

The next morning we couldn't get on the Pan Am flight to Bombay, it too being overbooked. Instead, we caught a flight back to Istanbul, and there were upgraded to first class to take the last remaining seats on a flight to New York. It was a thrill to be in the front of the plane, but also an embarrassment when I took off the hiking boots I'd been wearing for weeks, and a smelly cloud billowed through the cabin. I sunk into my seat to avoid the stares and coughs.

Seven months later, on January 16, 1979, the shah was forced to flee the gathering storm of revolution in Iran, fueled by the corrupt way he used his country's oil wealth, and perhaps more because of the brutalities of SAVAK, his secret police, which was blamed for thousands of deaths and unspeakable acts of human savagery.

The shah moved from country to country in search of secure asylum: first to Egypt, then Morocco, the Bahamas, and Mexico. On October 22, 1979, just as John Yost, Jim Slade, and I were making the first descent of Pakistan's Indus River, the shah came to the U.S. for a gallbladder operation and treatment of cancer. Thirteen days later, militant Iranian Moslems invaded the U.S. embassy in Tehran and took Americans there hostage to demand the shah's extradition, and a confession of his "crimes" in Iran, especially those concerning SAVAK. Secret documents were discovered in the U.S. embassy after its seizure, including ones describing the CIA coming to Iran in 1956 with a clandestine operation to set up and train SAVAK, the secret police that terrorized the country during the shah's reign.

That same month my father, after twenty-five years of service, took an early retirement from the CIA, and moved as far away from Washington, D.C., as one can and still be in the continental U.S.: San Diego. After finishing his doctorate there he became a family counselor, specializing in sex therapy.

Seven years later by chance I saw an item from the Associated Press. Former President Jimmy Carter admitted that a small documentary film company, financed by the CIA, helped six Americans escape from Iran during the hostage crisis early in 1980. After Iranians stormed the U.S. embassy in 1979, six embassy employees hid at the Canadian embassy, and the film company was able to perform its cloak-and-dagger rescue under Ayatollah Khomeini's nose, as the leader wanted as much publicity as possible about his revolution, and gave the filmmakers wide berth.

I then called my father and asked once more if he could tell me about his documentary film in Iran in 1956, and he said he couldn't. His voice cracked a bit. He sounded angry and sad at once. He said if it hadn't been for Iran, his life would have been different, the world might have been different, his life with me would have been different, we would have spent more time . . . His voice trailed away as he handed the phone to my mother. He wouldn't, couldn't talk about it. I sensed that my father, like myself, had been involved in an adventure gone wrong, one that spilled blood and left families bereft—only there was a difference of scale, perhaps an enormous differential, and I understood at that moment that he had not, and would never really recover.

〜〜〜

The years from 1976 to 1990 I spent roaming the globe, exploring wild rivers and landscapes, many with some combination of the Baro River survivors. All under the SOBEK imprimatur I made the first descent of the Indus with Slade and Yost; the Waghi and Purari of New Guinea with Fuller; the Euphrates with Yost and Slade; the Tatshenshini in Alaska and Canada with Bart Henderson; the Yangtze with Yost and Slade; the Kilombero and Rufiji rivers in Tanzania with Slade and Bart; the Zambezi with Yost and Slade; the Alas in Sumatra with Bart, Fuller, and Slade; the Yuat and Watut of New Guinea with Slade and Yost. In 1982 Yost and I even made the first descent of the Congo . . . actually, it was a ride called Congo River Rapids in Florida's Busch Gardens, and some PR flack had recruited John, myself, and George Plimpton to make an Electric Cowboyish "first descent" in front of the evening news.

But never once, in all those years, did the surviving guides from the Baro gather together on a river, or even in the same room. The last trip I took with any combination of the original five was the Amazon with Slade, Bart, and Fuller in 1989. After that, we all drifted in different directions, and suffered individually for our early adventures in Africa.

John Yost left SOBEK, spent eighteen months driving around the country with his family, climbing the highest peak in thirty states, and spent six months in Mexico in an isolated village. Professionally, he became a consultant to groups interested in investing in or building ecolodges. On a float trip in Alaska he was stricken with malaria he had picked up in Ethiopia (it has a long incubation period) and was flown out to a hospital in the nick of time.

On the way back from a commercial Omo trip, Bart Henderson looked at his hands and saw they had turned yellow. In the airplane toilet he saw his stool was white. And he could barely stay awake. When the plane landed in San Francisco, he somehow made his way to a hospital, where he was diagnosed with hepatitis. He came within a hair of dying, and on his recovery moved to Alaska, about as far from the tropic heat of Africa as he could find, and there he founded his own rafting company.

Jim Slade was felled with a severe case of schistosomiasis, the snail-borne disease that slowly kills an untreated victim. He checked into the National Institute of Health in Bethesda, Maryland. I visited him there as he was undergoing a seventeen-day toxic-flush treatment that brought him to the brink of death. His physician, Dr. Nash, came into the room and announced to both of us that Jim should never, ever travel to

Ethiopia again. For ten years, as Jim guided around the world, he had no worldly possessions save his broken Ford van that was permanently parked behind the SOBEK offices. In 1995 Jim took the plunge and bought a house in Carson City with his girlfriend, Barbara Bean, but swore it wouldn't tie him down, that he would continue to guide until he dropped.

George Fuller also was infected with schistosomiasis and was haunted by his near-death encounter with armed bandits on the lower Tekeze. As the years wore on, George designed his life to allow him to pursue his primary passion: the creation of art. He took a job as an ER doc near Fresno and would work a stretch shift so that he could be home for several days on end to tinker in his studio. There he mastered various hallucinogenic art forms, including computer fractal art. Crowding the walls and shelves of George's externally ordinary house were scores of products of his singular, antic, often bizarre mind: psychedelic oil paintings, phantasmagoric clay sculptures, fun-house-mirror bronzes, and a chimerical assortment of masks, scrolls, wire works, etchings, and enlarged photographs. As the nineties rolled, George became obsessed with government conspiracy theories, and legal hallucinogenic drugs, and didn't get out on many rivers.

And I, knock on wood, never fell seriously ill from my forays in Ethiopia, but something else intruded, clinging like a barnacle to the underside of my memory, the anamnesis of a good friend lost. I hung an eight-by-ten color photo of Lew rowing the Omo with a shit-eating grin on his face on my wall. I would look into Lew's delighted eyes every day as I set about the business of SOBEK in our tiny offices in Angels Camp, concocting, marketing, and operating new adventures for our ever-expanding coterie of clients.

In 1983, after returning from New Guinea, I gave a slide show at the Fullers' home on our expedition. A photographer, Pamela Roberson, who had spent years roaming the globe capturing faraway cultures on film, approached me after the show and asked for my number. I was with a date, but sheepishly gave Pamela my number. The next day she called and asked if I would like to see a movie, *Raiders of the Lost Ark*. I agreed, and found myself swept away with the story, but disturbed and relieved they didn't place the Ark where it belonged, in Ethiopia. Something else came from viewing the film. How could I not fall in love with a woman who designed a first date this way? She became my wife.

Pamela lived in the San Francisco Bay area, and we decided to live there together, so I set up a branch office of SOBEK near Oakland's Lake

Merritt. Between the chores of the adventure-travel business, Pamela and I traveled the world and published several large-format travel books, illustrated with her images and my words. It was a rich time. But always a subterranean current coursed, a hidden stream that splashed with regrets of things not done.

As the years unfolded I occasionally ran more rivers, the Chatkal in south-central Asia, the Franklin in Tasmania, the San Juan in Utah. Mostly, though, I found myself rowing a desk, climbing the ever-higher mountain of paper that came with a growing business. There was a pause in 1991, when the Gulf War brought international leisure travel to its lowest levels since WWII. In the wake of the war, SOBEK, as did many tour operators, found itself floating in a precarious financial boat. Safe harbor came when SOBEK merged with its longtime competitor, Mountain Travel, and I was suddenly in a much larger company, with higher rent, more demands, and less time to run rivers.

But, in all this time, and after all these travails, none of us fell to the wasting illness of conformity.

# CHAPTER 17

# THE MAN WITH MISSING FINGERS

"We are all pilgrims on the same journey . . . but some pilgrims have better road maps."

—Nelson De Mille

In the early 1990s I put together a multiprojector slide show called "Endangered Rivers" and took it on the road, to universities, museums, aquariums, hiking clubs, libraries, any place or anyone who would take a look. It was born from a frustration that emerged with my twenty-year career running wild rivers and seeing them threatened, compromised, or destroyed. The Euphrates in Turkey, down which I had made the first descent, was now dammed. The Colorado, where I had begun my raft guiding, was so polluted from a nearby power plant that there were days one couldn't see across the world's most famous canyon, and at river level, the daily flushing from the Glen Canyon dam was eroding the beaches away. The Tatshenshini in Alaska/Canada was being prepped to shoulder North America's largest open-pit copper mine. Core samples were being taken on the walls of the Zambezi canyon to test for strength to hold a proposed dam that would flood the river to the base of Victoria Falls, one of the seven natural wonders of the world. Then there was the Chatkal in Kirghizistan and Uzbekistan, running into the Aral Sea. Because of diversion for cotton growing, there was virtually no water in its lower bed, and the Aral was drying up.

But the river that concerned me most was the Bío-Bío in Chile, cascading down the eastern slope of the Andes. I had pioneered it in 1977 and was spellbound with its beauty and strength. Beyond the rivers of Ethiopia, the Bío-Bío was my favorite waterway. And I had watched it grow in popularity over the years, so that it was now perhaps the most famous South American river after the Amazon. But a private dam was about to slit its throat, killing one of the finest whitewater runs in the world. And as such, the Bío-Bío was the centerpiece of my show, and my appeal.

In February of 1992 I was preparing to make a presentation of "Endangered Rivers" at the Denver Museum of Natural History, and I noticed a small item in the paper. It said a skeleton, almost certainly that of Haile Selassie, had been dug up beneath a latrine in the palace grounds on guidance from those who had buried him. The bones were placed in St. Mary's (Beta Maryam) Orthodox Church, the mausoleum for Haile Selassie's great-uncle, Emperor Menelik II—the warrior king who carved out the borders of modern Ethiopia and founded Addis Ababa in the late nineteenth century. The royal family in exile would not bury Haile Selassie's remains until he was given a state funeral in recognition of his nearly half-century reign, but Meles Zenawi, the new prime minister, refused.

My slide show was a success, even though my mind drifted as I flashed images of the Omo River on the big IMAX screen. After the show a tall, nut-brown, intense-looking man came up to me and extended a right hand missing a portion of three fingers. I tried not to notice the gap in his grip and stared into his eyes. He had a pioneer face, long, sinewy, and hollow, and a habit of flicking his eyes to the horizon, as though searching for a distant mountain. He introduced himself as Pasquale Scaturro. I recognized his name as a private mountain and river guide who the summer before organized and led an expedition down the Alsek River in Canada, during which a client drowned. The river rumor mill had put the blame on Pasquale as being too reckless, and having heard such, I was wary when he approached me. But he told me he was active in the fight to save the Bío-Bío, that he had donated thousands of dollars to the Bío-Bío Action Committee, and its successor organization, River Conservation International, headed by our mutual friend Steve Gates. In fact, Steve had asked me to join the board as a director, and I had accepted.

Pasquale mentioned that he was a founding director, so despite any reservations, I was connected to Pasquale.

We went out for pizza at some dive, and over a beer Pasquale told me about the Alsek accident. It was his first time on the infamous ice river, and his eldest son, eighteen-year-old Tim, was also rowing a boat, his first on a big river. Pasquale was rowing his girlfriend, Kim, and a couple, Mike and Harriet, who days before had become engaged at the Halsinglad Hotel in Haines, Alaska. The weather was cold and rainy. From the topo maps, Pasquale was pretty sure he was approaching Lava North Rapid, the worst on the river, so he pulled over to scout. But as he did, he saw Tim in the middle of the river being pulled into the maw. Pasquale quickly reversed, pumped his oars to get midstream to help his son, but instead was sucked into the main of the rapid. Tim made it through without mishap. But his dad's raft flipped in the glacial water, and Pasquale climbed on the upside-down floor and pulled Kim and Mike up with him, but Harriet was trying to swim to shore and he couldn't reach her. Several miles downriver Pasquale got his boat to shore, and a long time later another raft came down with Harriet's body wrapped in a tarp. She had apparently hit her head on the frame when the boat went over, and drowned in an eddy as she was trying to get to shore. Pasquale set up a distress sign with oars, and waited a day and a half until the helicopter shuttle they had prehired to portage them around Turn Back Canyon, an unrunnable section pinched by glacier, noticed them and landed. Pasquale said it was months before he could go near a big rapid after the incident. "What hurt most about the accident," he reflected, "was that my mission in life is to make sure I don't hurt anyone along the way, and that I help everyone I can . . . and I failed in a big way on the Alsek."

"Did you lose your fingers on the Alsek?" I wondered aloud.

"No, I was in Flagstaff after discharge from the air force and was building a house out of the forest since I couldn't afford one. I went to school during the day, and built at night, while trying to raise three small kids. One evening I was working late, and was very tired, and while cutting trim on a table saw, my hand slipped into the saw. I was in the hospital two days, and finished the house with one hand. And it was in Flagstaff I met Gary Mercado, who had been with you in Ethiopia, and he told me wild tales of your adventures there. After that, I always wanted to do a river expedition with you. . . ."

After a slug of beer and a moment to switch gears, I asked Pasquale what he did when not adventuring. He said by trade he was a geophysicist, and that he had gone to Ethiopia in 1991 as field manager of a geo-physical operation in the Ogaden Desert adjacent to Somalia for Maxus Energy, a division of Diamond Shamrock. He also said he was going back to Ethiopia in a few weeks. After his survey work, he was planning to or-ganize a private expedition down the Omo. This captured my attention. In the late 1980s, with the collapse of communism and the end of the Cold War, I often wondered how the brutal Marxist regime in Ethiopia could continue. Then I had read that in May 1991, $35 million was de-posited by the Israeli government in a bank account of the bankrupt Ethiopian government in New York City in exchange for Mengistu al-lowing fifteen thousand Ethiopian Jews to immigrate to Israel. A week later Addis Ababa was overwhelmed by the rebel forces, the Ethiopian Peoples' Revolutionary Democratic Front (EPRDF), led by Meles Zenawi. The socialist regime, one of the most oppressive in modern-day Africa, melted like a wax witch, and the so-called "Red Emperor," or "Black Lenin," Lieutenant Colonel Mengistu Haile Mariam, a man who required parents of his victims to pay police for the bullets used to kill their children, fled the country. Now in exile in Zimbabwe, he was liv-ing in a plush state-owned villa in a neighborhood called Millionaire's Mile. Besides the millions in cash, gold, and jewels with which he fled, he also took the late emperor's Rolls-Royce. This was the man who boasted, "We can control not only the reactionaries, but nature itself." He may not have been able to control nature, but he scarred the land with napalm and used famine as a weapon of war. The photographs of starving children that galvanized the world in 1984 were the direct re-sults of Mengistu's deliberate slowness to respond to the looming disas-ter in Tigre, where rebels were plotting his overthrow. Ultimately, Mengistu Haile Mariam, trained by the U.S. military, was credited with killing millions of people.

The new rulers, a patchwork alliance of several rebel groups led by Meles Zenawi, suggested Ethiopia would be returning to a democracy, and to me that implied the area so long sealed from the outside world might soon reopen, including the Tekeze valley. Knowing this, I found myself in hydraulic musings, imagining the long-lost wild river run down the Tekeze.

Now, with Pasquale telling me he was off to Ethiopia, I told him about the Tekeze, the last great unrun river in Africa, spilling through the con-tinent's deepest gorge. I told him that as far as I could tell, no explorer had ever done more than cross the grand canyons of the Tekeze, and there was no record of any attempt at navigation. I asked him if he might be able to drive up to the Tekeze and take a look. He scrutinized me with the mesmeric gaze of a cobra.

"I'm in. If I can scout that river, I will. And I want to be there when you run it."

〰〰〰

I didn't hear from Pasquale for a couple years. But then in late 1994 Conrad Hirsh, the professor who had joined me on the second attempt of the Baro, sent me a couple of videos. The first was an aerial scout he had made of a section of the upper White Nile above Murchison Falls. He had been hired by a development agency to make an evaluation of its potential as a commercial whitewater run. But, it was clear looking at the video, this was not a waterway soon to see boatloads of happy clients—the rapids were huge, sharp, dangerous, impossible. The other video was unmarked, but when I slipped it into the VCR I was transfixed. It showed a dry canyon, deep and steep, with a clear river winding its way past buttes and mesas, much like the landscape of the Colorado. Giant waterfalls leapt from canyon walls, and some rapids, with their white scars, interrupted the flow. Every now and then a voice that could sand wood made some remark, and I thought I recognized it: it sounded like Gary Lemmer, a longtime SOBEK guide who had spent several seasons on the Bío-Bío and the Zambezi rivers. Gary was a man blessed with intrinsic whitewater talent and a big heart. He was a founder of the Bío-Bío Action Committee and had spent weeks, months, of volunteer time organizing and overseeing efforts to stop the Pangue Dam. With his dark, piratical features and deep, penetrating eyes, Gary took on a menacing intensity after a few drinks, one that made him seem absolutely scary, as though on the brink of something terribly violent. Once on the Zambezi he so impressed a couple of vacationing Hollywood screenwriters (they had penned several Chuck Norris and Charles Bronson action vehicles) that they wrote a film loosely based on him, imagining a scenario in which the Gary character goes over the edge and becomes a psychopathic killer, taking out several of his passengers on a Zambezi tour. The resulting film, *Damned River,* had since become a cult video classic among river runners.

Gary no longer worked for SOBEK. He had a chronic back problem that made Class V rowing sometimes painful, and enough clients had complained about Gary and his drinking that his leaving the fold was mutually agreed upon. He lived in Colorado, working as an occasional bartender and sometimes as a guide on private river trips. I had heard he had been a guide on a private Omo tour, but didn't know details.

When Gary swung the camera around to the front seat of the small propeller plane, I recognized the face and voice of the man next to the pilot—Pasquale Scaturro. That meant that I must have been looking at the Tekeze. I sat up and played the video again and again. The date on the time code was October 22, 1994. Jim Slade was in town, so I invited him to my home for a viewing. We both leaned forward on the edge of the couch as I pressed the play button. It was clear we were looking at one of the great suture lines of the world, a river that defined the Great Rift Valley. This graphic subduction zone, formed by the colliding of tectonic plates, had spewed andesites, granites, and dolerites into the sky to make a wild confusion of raw geology. It didn't look real; it looked painted. The water was low, but still seemed powerful. The upper section was marked by Class VI rapids, killer waterfalls, and souse holes. But suddenly, as though by an invisible marker, the river turned friendly—long stretches of ribbon-flat water, inviting pools and meanders. This continued for miles. And when the camera panned up we could see the magnificent vistas of the Ras Dashan plateau. But, just as the river seemed to speed up, and the inner canyon walls darkened, suggesting more rapids ahead, the plane veered away from the canyon: reconnaissance interruptus. Someone mentioned refueling, and a few minutes later the video showed the plane filling up at Mekele, the capital of Tigre Province, which borders much of the Tekeze. Then the plane returned to Addis.

It was enough to inspire me to move into a higher gear. At the office I talked to Perry Robertson, the river operations director, and suggested we should try and organize a proper scout of the Tekeze, with the goal of determining its feasibility as an expedition, and returning at an opportune time to actually make the run. "Why not just go and do a commercial exploratory? Why the extra step? You've done exploratories for years without a scout," Perry said. I didn't have a ready answer, except that unscouted Ethiopian rivers had ripped lives close to me away, and I still bore scars. Less was known about the Tekeze than the Blue Nile or the Baro. More was known about the far side of the moon than what lay at the bottom of the Tekeze Gorge. Besides, these were the postillusional nineties. We didn't know when the water level might work; where we could start such an expedition; what the obstacles might be. I couldn't do it that way again.

That night I mulled over Perry's questions and wondered how I had changed. When I made my first foreign raft descent, down Ethiopia's Awash River, in 1973, I was fearless. Who needed a scout? I went rifling through the attic of my past and found the video George Fuller had produced of that first expedition, and I sat back to look at a younger, leaner, browner, more arrogant, more foolish, and perhaps freer version of myself and my friends. The video was old, a faded palimpsest, and the ghostly images were so tentative I could see right through my orange life jacket to the crude landscapes of the Awash, and it reminded me of long-lost love.

# CHAPTER 18

# THE LAST BOY SCOUTS

"At that time there were many blank spaces on the earth, and when I saw one that looked particularly inviting on a map I would put my finger on it and say, 'When I grow up I will go there.' "

—Joseph Conrad, *Heart of Darkness*

A short time later, on May 28, 1995, I gave a slide show of my favorite rivers and adventures to the Telluride MountainFilm festival. Afterward a small, peppery man came up and introduced himself: Thom Beers. I recognized the name. I'd seen it on end credits for Cousteau specials, *National Geographic Explorer* presentations, and Audubon shows. He was executive producer for Turner Original Productions, and he was at the festival to show a film he made on rafting the Grand Canyon with James Taylor. Thom suggested we retreat for a drink, and for an hour we traded stories and ideas. We hit it off, and by meeting's end we vowed we would get together in a less-crowded milieu and explore possibilities.

The get-together came that August when Thom joined me on a two-day raft run down the South Fork of the American River in northern California. Around the campfire Thom regaled me with stories of his adventures in documentary filmmaking: how he lost the bid to Fox to acquire the "alien autopsy" film; how he did battle with Ted Turner over the skin quotient in his biker women documentary (Ted wanted less and won); how he fought with Jacques Cousteau over just about everything. When talk turned to me the embers were on their final fuss, and most of the crew had slipped into sleeping bags. Thom asked about career highlights, and I deferred, saying I would rather dwell on the future. "Well, then, what's next?" Thom asked.

"I've been thinking a lot lately about the Tekeze. It runs through the deepest gorge in Africa, a half mile deeper than the Grand Canyon of the Colorado. Because of a civil war it's been sealed from the outside world for twenty years, but it's just opened. I would love to run it." Thom was transfixed and wanted to know everything. I told him I had pored over a set of Italian maps, and a take-out was clear. The mystery was where to begin, as the upper sections of river had no bridges, no roads, no paths, no native settlements marked. Just a jumbled witchery of steep gorges and canyons. I said that unlike the old days, when we would just show up with our gear, find a put-in, and head down into the unknown, I now wanted to conduct a proper scout first. And I went into some detail on how I thought a scout might work. We talked for hours. By morning we had a deal. I would head over that October to scout the river, and Thom would send a cameraperson to capture it on video, and throw in some seed monies. In fact, Lili Schad, a Bay area videographer with periwinkle blue eyes and blond hair, was on our American raft trip, and over breakfast Thom asked if she might do the job. Thom had somewhat of a Louis Leakey reputation for finding young, promising, talented blondes and dispatching them into the field. Lili looked to be the latest beneficiary of his largess. I didn't argue.

So, with Thom on board I set about putting together our scout team. Pasquale was the first call. He had made the partial aerial scout, had now spent almost three years in-country, loved Ethiopia, and wanted in. The next call was to Chris Haines. Chris had been on six SOBEK trips as a client, including the exploratory down Pakistan's Ghizar River with one of the new breed of uber-guides, Mike Speaks. Chris had been a contractor in Columbus, Ohio, until his mother passed away, leaving an inheritance large enough for Chris to quit his job and become, as he put it, "an experience artist." He had stopped by my office several weeks back and asked if he could join an upcoming exploratory. I mentioned I was thinking of a scout of the Tekeze, and he said he would love to join in. I wanted to keep the scout small, so we could be fast and nimble, and four or five was an ideal number. I did call my friend Bill Broyles, former editor of *Newsweek,* producer of *China Beach,* screenwriter for *Apollo 13,* and partner in an ABC Television project on adventure guides we had developed, but which tanked before production. He had the nerve to go off and get married again, his fourth time, and couldn't get away. So, that left the four of us, splitting expenses to make the scout.

On Thursday, October 5, 1995, we all convened at the Bole International Airport. Lili's luggage did not arrive. At my urging she checked her bags all the way through from San Francisco, and in Frankfurt, security pulled them, suspicious of the video batteries in her bags. After a frustrating hour of phone calls and telexes we determined her bags would arrive on the next Lufthansa flight, Saturday evening, which would put us a day behind schedule. But, that's Third World travel. For the rest of us, customs was rigorous, despite the unplumbed lethargy of the officials. The year previous, deposed dictator Mengistu Haile Mariam, from his asylum in Zimbabwe, called for a coup against President Meles Zenawi, claiming that human rights organizations that criticized his years of military rule failed to protest new rights abuses in Ethiopia, and charged that tens of thousands of his supporters were killed or imprisoned after his ouster. In the wake of the war, and Mengistu's long-distance threats, paranoia was still institutionalized. Still, the process was an otiose relic of a clogged, oppressive culture gone south. Every piece of baggage was opened and checked, and the serial numbers for both our video cameras were written on our visas, with a note we could not leave the country without taking out the gear.

Abadi Haile, a moon-faced forty-nine-year-old businessman with smallpox pits on his cheeks, met us outside the airport. Eritrean by birth, he lived most of his life in Addis Ababa, working first for the Ethiopian Distribution Company, and then for the sugar-agro industry. In October 1978, he was at work when soldiers walked in and asked him to come to the police station. Once there they tortured him. They took off his shoes, tied him in a fetal position, put a ball in his mouth, and poked his feet with an electric prod while beating him. They wanted him to confess to involvement with the EPLF, the Eritrean Peoples' Liberation Front. And though he had distributed some pamphlets questioning the Dergue, he had never been an active member of the EPLF, and as such refused to confess. So, he was thrown into a jail known as Alem Bakayne, "the End of the World," a dark, damp place that offered no food or medical supplies. For the first three years he was in a twelve-by-twelve dark room shared with forty other prisoners. It was so small they had to take shifts sleeping, as the floor could only accommodate about half at a time. There was no food or clothing provided. His wife had to bring him what he ate and wore. They were all let outside once a day for five minutes to go to the bathroom. Some prisoners had been castrated by their interrogators; others had their eyes gouged out, ears and fingers cut off. Every morning soldiers would open up the cell door and call out a few names. They would then take those called outside and shoot them, and replace the dead with new prisoners. Because not everyone had relatives to bring food and clothing, when someone was shot they would grab his clothes, wipe them in the mud to make them look used, and trade them in for clean ones with the dead's relatives each week, never letting on the fate of the true wearer. For three more years he sat in the darkness in his own cell, periodically tortured. Finally, he was set free. Now, he was making a living in support services for oil and gas companies, and he had outfitted Pasquale in his explorations. They had become close friends, and he was here to help us.

In his Toyota Land Cruiser, vested to him by Pasquale, Abadi drove us down the Bole Road, pointing out where the assassination attempt on Egypt's President Hosni Mubarak was made a few months back. And he swung into the Karamara Club (which used to be the Three Tukuls disco), where he treated us to *injera* and *wat,* the national dish of Ethiopia. Injera is a flaccid gray substance, looking a bit like a pizza made of foam rubber (it tastes much better than it sounds), and it comes in large round sheets, or folded like heavy napkins. Made from teff, or *Eragrostis abyssinica,* a kind of millet, it is laid before diners on a special circular, basketwork table. Then bowls of hot, spiced meats in a highly seasoned sauce are ladled out into the center of the bread. This is the wat. Using only the right hand, one plucks a napkin-sized piece of injera, seizes chunks of wat as though with a cootie catcher, then stuffs it all in the mouth Viking-style. It's a very tasty meal, though we took it in smaller doses than most Ethiopians who sup on injera and wat three or four times a day every day of their thirteen-month year. As we were swiping our fingers around the gooey wat, several very beautiful women in chitonlike dresses, quite similar in appearance to the model Iman, performed traditional dances to the national music. One of the dancers reminded me very much of Diamond. But it couldn't have been. She would be in her forties now, I thought, if even alive. This could be her daughter. This time I kept my distance.

〰〰

The next morning, with the faintly familiar sounds of wild street dogs yelping and yammering, I awoke, and unwound the stairs to the flagstone restaurant to meet my little band of conspirators. A waiter, whose red

jacket had so many patches the original fabric could barely be seen, rat-
tled plates like castanets, and served his guests on starched but stained
tablecloths. A lazy fan threw shadow plays against the wall, and conversa-
tions from neighboring tables spiraled up like smoke, disappearing into a
square of sky. Breakfast consisted of eggs fried in fish oil, sausage so well
cooked it looked like a cigar, warm brioche, a tomato garnish, white toast
with a big knob of butter on a metal dish, and thick coffee heavy with
tinned cream and floating grounds. Afterward we drove to the EAL
(Ethiopian Airlines) head offices at the airport. Though I had sent a
number of faxes beginning several weeks prior, asking for consideration
in regards to a charter flight for this scout, I had received no replies. Jerry
Maizel, the longtime North American sales representative for EAL, based
in Chicago, also sent faxes on our behalf. No replies. This was worri-
some, but not unlike normal business practices in Ethiopia as I remembered them: deals were not done long-distance, but in person, over *chai*
(tea). While I had some misgivings about traveling all the way to Ethiopia
without assurances we could charter a flight for an aerial recce (I pledged
to myself I would not tackle the Tekeze without a full fly-over), I also felt
fairly certain we would resolve the matter on the spot. So, we entered the
EAL offices not knowing if we would emerge with a flight.

The corridors of the Ethiopian Airlines building were dark and stark,
the minimalist look of socialist governments. However, in contrast to
most of the decrepit airlines in Africa, Ethiopian Airlines—founded by
TWA in 1945 under a contract from Emperor Haile Selassie, and for unknown reasons left alone by Mengistu—boasted a fleet of Boeing 767
aircraft and was considered a world-class carrier.

We met with a raft of officials before being told no Cessnas were
available (all four in-country were being used for training), but that they
could take a Dash-6 twin otter off a scheduled flight and offer us a 25
percent discount, as well as give us four free commercial tickets to return
from Gondar to Addis Ababa at the scout's conclusion. The price, with
the discount, was $2,672 in U.S. cash, more than I was carrying. Pasquale
had paid less than $1,000 for his nosewheel Cessna 172 the previous year,
but then the flight only made it a third of the way down the river, across
from Ras Dashan, before the plane had to refuel in Mekele and return to
Addis Ababa, so perhaps this asking price was not unreasonable.

Nonetheless, it was more than I had budgeted. So I called MAF (Mission Aviation Fellowship), and asked if the organization could help. The
director declined, saying his mission prohibited carriage that wasn't religious or relief. Pasquale suggested we meet with an old acquaintance, so

we drove to town and found General Tafessa, former head of EAL, now a private businessman. He controlled a private helicopter, and offered us a price of $500 an hour, and estimated ten hours for the aerial scout.

From my rough calculations back in the U.S., everyone had pitched in a share of the cash estimated to make this scout viable, and Turner Original Productions had sweetened the pot a bit. But chartering the EAL plane put us a grand short, so I asked if anyone in our group could help make up the difference. Lili Schad volunteered the shortfall from the Turner kitty, and we were good to go.

Later that evening we met Conrad Hirsh for drinks. He was preparing for an Omo expedition departing a few days hence. He told us he was recently approached by an Italian group, under contract from the Ethiopian government, that wanted to hire him to set up camps for a survey team that hoped to come in and look at three possible sites for hydropower dams on the Tekeze. He even had the coordinates. I couldn't believe it. Over the years so many of the rivers I had touched were now dammed, diverted, developed, or in the process of such. Now the Tekeze, to which I hadn't been within a couple hundred miles, was on the block. I bit my lip. I had to run this river, and soon.

Next day we went to the downtown EAL offices and picked up our tickets for the charter. Since we had many more seats on the plane than for the four of us, we invited Abadi and every Ethiopian Airlines official in the office. One accepted. We needed names on the tickets in order for them to be issued, so we made up a list, including David Livingstone, Henry Morton Stanley, Mungo Park, James Bruce, John Speke, Richard Burton, and Elizabeth Taylor. We figured if we met anyone between now and departure who might want to join the flight, he or she could assume one of the ticketed names and join us.

We needed some maps of the Simiens, so we made our way over to NTO, the National Tourist Organization, formerly the Ethiopian Tourism Organization, once headed by Hapte Selassie, who had been whisked away during my last visit. But now it was closed. Its windows showcased the same posters from photographer James P. Blair's 1968 *National Geographic* magazine feature that papered the tourist offices and airports in 1973. We next drove to the Victory Store, which used to be the American embassy commissary, and bought $170 worth of food, or what might pass for such. The barely populated shelves offered pasta, cans of tuna, canned hot dogs, peanuts, canned tomatoes, and peanut butter, both chunky and smooth.

We needed more food, so we trucked up the hill to the Ketema district of western Addis Ababa where sprawls the Mercato, billed as the largest open-air market in the world. Out of the seething mass emerged Abdu, an old friend of Pasquale's, and he volunteered to act as guide and bodyguard, as the Mercato was a busy, dangerous place, especially for fer- enjis. Even with the local muscle, I watched from behind as Lili was hit in the face by a rock, and a thief tried to wrest away a tripod from Chris.

Yet the place was magical and abstruse. We poured garlic, onions, and several unidentifiable spices for the pasta onto mechanical weighing scales, and then haggled over prices. Behind an abattoir draped with in- testines, brains, and guts, we found a room packed with a stoned-out group chewing chat and joined in. To wash down the bitter taste, we swilled fresh avocado and papaya juices. Our last stop was a curio shop. It sold faux ebony carvings (actually *wonza* wood, coated with Kiwi shoe polish), fake amber necklaces (plastic beads without the honey smell), and Maria Theresa talers, the eighteenth-century silver coins that for a time were used as currency in East Africa. But the great travesty was in a back room displaying endangered-species skins, including a rug made from twenty leopards and another from cheetah hides. Sitting on a hide- covered couch, we played the part of interested buyers while surrepti- tiously videotaping a lavish presentation by the shop owners, a tape we would turn over to the World Wildlife Fund.

That evening we supped at the Ghion Hotel, indulged in *tej*, a tasty and potent local brew, akin to mead, fermented with honey and the leaves and bitter roots of the *saddo* (*Rhamnus saddo*) or *gesho* (*Rhamnus pauciflorus*) trees. Of this puissant drink Baudelaire wrote, "*Le plus grand delice, c'est de boire l'hydromel dans le crâne d'un enfant.*" ("The greatest del- icacy is to drink the fluid in the skull of a child.") A couple glasses and I could feel it glow inside me. Sometime in the evening we met a similarly sweetened Sue Mathewson, just arrived to take the Omo River expedi- tion Conrad was leading. She said she had called the SOBEK office when she saw a talk show on which I talked about the Tekeze, and she had hoped to sign up. When the office told her the Tekeze was just a scout, and would be run earliest in 1996, she signed for the Omo instead. As the Omo didn't depart for several days, I invited Sue to join us on the aerial scout . . . so, she joined, as Elizabeth Taylor.

〰〰〰

Lili's bags arrived as scheduled on Saturday night, and so Sunday at 7:00 A.M. we made our way to the airport, where we each underwent a full- body search before being admitted to the waiting area. Once inside, we waited forty-five extra minutes as Prime Minister Meles Zenawi, who was famous for being a shut-in at the palace, ceremoniously boarded a plane to Uganda.

By nine we were off the ground, leaving the scrub-colored hills and looking up at the first harbinger of the great highlands of Ethiopia. An hour later we were over the Shafartak Bridge, the take-out on our 1974 Blue Nile expedition. The pilot agreed to fly up the length of the Blue Nile, and I pressed hard against the Plexiglas window, straining to drink in every detail. We passed the broken Second Portuguese Bridge, where Jim, John, and Conrad exited after the accident, and then, there, *there,* I was sure I saw it—after hearing the description of the rapid for so many years, I thought I saw it—the river split, it split again, with a wall on the right to which the water pressed. That must be the rapid where Lew drowned. Then it was gone, and in minutes we passed over the Blue Nile Falls, though the fantastic sight was lost on me. As we headed up the eastern edge of Lake Tana, I remained stuck at the window, staring still at something long ago gone.

We refueled at Gondar, the ancient imperial capital, then made the final hop to the Tekeze. With each mile the scenery grew more impressive, stunning, even, to a point where it had to be seen to be disbelieved. Herds of puffy cumulus scudded across the sky, torn by the sharp mountains, each one catching a dull red glint from the sun, as though bleeding. To the east, the great massif of Ras Dashan reared its head as the greatest cloud eater of all.

It all had a southwestern U.S. look, only with higher and more pronounced monument-style formations. Then we found the road that switchbacked downward, and we dipped into the Tekeze Canyon at the umbilical bridge connecting Gondar to the Queen of Sheba's city, Axum. This was the only fold in the mountains on either side of the river that would allow a major crossing. In fact, this was one of the few places Europeans had touched the Tekeze. When Queen Victoria asked Lieutenant General Sir Robert Napier to lead a punitive expedition against Emperor Theodore of Abyssinia in 1867, his army crossed here. I had read every reference I could find about the Tekeze, which amounted to less than a dozen, yet the river had been prefigured in my mind long before it met my eye. It was a shimmering band that coiled away into a private myth.

〰〰

As we banked and began flying up the canyon, the surrounding landscapes became more and more spectacular: a combination of the Grand

Canyon and Monument Valley overlaid by the silk renditions of the
Yangtze spires. The enfolding mountains had the appearance of a muddy
sea frozen in the midst of a storm. The river looked to be running fast,
perhaps 15,000 cubic feet per second in the lower reaches, but I spied no
unnavigable stretches. The rapids, which were interrupted by long sections of quiet water, all seemed of the convergence style, with interfer-
ence waves and uniform nodal lines—not unlike the famous rapid
Hermit on the Colorado when seen from the air, which is at river level
all big, buffy waves and no bite. We saw some debris-fan rapids, but they
all looked runnable. There appeared to be no technical or obstruction-
style rapids through the first one hundred miles, no Scyllas and Charyb-
dises, and wide, white beaches glinted invitations at regular intervals.

But I also knew from years of aerial scouts that what is seen from five
thousand feet above the ground is in no way related to what is on the
ground. The high view flattens reality, and something that looks like a
bathtub ripple from a mile up can turn out to be Niagara on the river.
Still, what I saw gave me hope.

Continuing up the aerial staircase we dipped between high buttes,
mesas, table mountains, cathedral spires, stone minarets, tortuous towers,
and palisades that seemed to break the sky. And always, on one side of the
river, the imposing, near-fifteen-thousand-foot-high brooding presence
of Ras Dashan. This was Arizona ten million years ago, before the erosion. There were dozens of places where waterfalls leapt over the rim,
some hundreds of feet high. We saw no villages or signs of habitation
along the river or in the main canyon, and this gave us pause. This was
desert country, and the Tekeze was water—why weren't people living on
the Tekeze? Ebola? Crocodiles? It was a mystery. About a third of the
way upriver we did see faint traces of animal trails, and then across from
an uplands village, called Agezba on my map, I saw a cable or vine crossing of the river, the only man-made ford for the entire length of the river
upstream of the Gondar-Axum Bridge. This appeared as the only path to
the middle section of river on our 1979 Topographic Center 1:250,000
scale maps, the most accurate we could find. This could be a resupply
point, except for the fact that Agezba looked to be about 150 miles from
the Lalibela airport, with no clear road, and it perhaps would take a
ground crew longer to reach this point by land than we might by river.

As we flew farther upstream there was more evidence of human cross-
ings, though no manifest point to which we could feasibly bring boats
and begin the expedition. We saw cattle, goats, and sheep sprinkled across
the fulvous plateau like drops of paint, and we saw farming settlements

back from the rim. But we never saw a single village or habitation along the Tekeze itself. We also never saw any signs of crocodiles or hippos, though at our altitude we likely could not have spotted them. At one point we passed a clear tributary that disembogued from the southwest into the turbid main river. The map called it Tota Bahar. Just upstream of this confluence the Tekeze ran through a steep gorge packed with what appeared to be unrunnable rapids. So, the starting point, I felt, must be at the confluence, or below, if we could reach it. The terrain became labyrinthine at this point, with a number of steep tributary gorges feeding the mother river, and it was difficult to orient ourselves. The put-in was a puzzle in a maze.

The confluence was just a few air minutes from Lalibela, so as the plane met its shadow on the dirt strip, we said good-bye to the Ethiopian Airlines crew, and Elizabeth Taylor, who had spent most of the flight exploring an air bag, but seemed genuinely pleased to have participated in our little scout. We caught a taxi to downtown Lalibela, about a forty-minute trundle up to a higher plateau. Here we were to rendezvous with Berhanu, Abadi's driver, who left the day previous to negotiate the Land Cruiser up from Addis Ababa. However, at 2:00 P.M. there was no sign of Berhanu at the 7 Olives Hotel, where we had agreed to meet. Perhaps he failed to defeat the mud on the way north. To pass time we hired a local guide to show us around, Haptewold Belay, a man who seemed dangerously brittle, as if hard work would snap him like a twig. We got as far as the River Jordan, a tributary of the Tekeze, when Berhanu trundled up. We loaded up on Ambo and began to drive south. As far as we could tell, the closest village to the intended starting point was Abtate on the south side of the river, or Inkway Beret on the north. Haptewold said he used to teach at Inkway Beret, but had never been in the canyon, nor seen the river. Whether we could reach either village by road was an unknown, but we rumbled out in search of a put-in.

We started driving south of Lalibela airport, and had to slow our already deliberate pace to negotiate around farmers sorting their barley harvest on the road. Women hauling stacks of wood and twigs, sometimes three feet high, weaved back and forth in front of our bumper, as did haystacks with donkeys' heads sticking out. About 5:30 P.M. we crossed the upper reaches of the Ketchn Abeba Wenz, a tributary that joined the Tekeze about ten miles below our targeted put-in. The Ketchn Abeba was almost dry; just a trickle. Another hour later we crossed the upper Tekeze, also a very small and unimpressive stream. Only thirty feet across, less than three feet deep, it was quietly meandering across the plateau before it plunged into its savage gorges. This was a disappointing sight, not the sort of current I would ordinarily fly twelve thousand miles to float. Between two fields of teff, under a stand of aca-cia trees, crooked, dry, and burnt, like the colors of pottery, we unrolled our sleeping bags and fell into fitful sleep, wondering if this had been a fool's pursuit.

# CHAPTER 19

# PUZZLE IN A MAZE

"Men go out into the void spaces of the world for various reasons. Some are ac-
tuated simply by a love of adventure, some have the keen thirst for scientific
knowledge, and others again are drawn away from the trodden path by the 'lure
of little voices,' the mysterious fascination of the unknown."

—Sir Ernest Shackleton

A searing red dawn. We crossed the Tekeze to its southern side and
continued to creep in four-wheel drive along the tableland.
Berhanu wrestled the wheel of the Land Cruiser like a captain in a ty-
phoon. The ungraded dirt track created a clumsy and confusing imposi-
tion on a terrain that did without for millions of years, and may do so
again. There was no logic to this road. It took sudden detours around
trees, split off in two or three erratic directions at once, which then convened again like participants in a square dance of the mad. Often only a
tremor of human instinct told Berhanu whether he was still following
the track or had veered off on an illusion, or worse, toward one of the
craterlike fissures caused by erosion that opens twisted mouths in the
earth and waits for a catch.

We met some locals en route, who told us to park and begin hiking if
we hoped to reach Abtate. We figured we would make a day hike out of
it, and return to the vehicle for more strategy, so we asked Berhanu to

meet us at this point at sundown. We brought packs with sleeping bags and some food, just in case.

The hike proved to be nothing short of breathtaking, the effects of our mile-and-a-half-high elevation notwithstanding. We could see the Tekeze Gorge ahead, and it looked like a Maxfield Parrish painting, or a Spielberg matte. The Afro-alpine desert was carpeted with cushions of helichrysum, Alchemilla, and the tall spike of the endemic Lobelia rynchopetalum. Big, bearded lammergeiers (the "bone-dropping birds") soared overhead, while shiny thick-billed ravens, white-collared pigeons, and wattled ibis occupied the lower air space. Along the way Chris found a white quartz flake (collecting points is his hobby), perhaps a projectile point, used with a bow or small spear. Chris believed it might be six thousand to eight thousand years old.

Around noon we picked up a boy guide, perhaps twelve years old, who was wearing a cowskin cape and two spent AK-47 shells around his neck, tiny reminders of the $11 billion worth of weapons the former Soviet Union poured into Mengistu's war machine. After following his airy footfalls for three hours we reached Abtate, a perfectly unspoiled African village. As we entered the circular thorned fence, children broke out in tears at the sight of us and ran away. The chief greeted us with hands so dry they felt like crushed leaves, and with a wave of his thin wrist invited us into his *tukul,* a conical grass hut. He told us no white-skinned people had ever visited here, and the children thought we were ghosts. Inside a woman sporting a brass bracelet beaten from old cartridge cases prepared a formal coffee ceremony, roasting green beans to black (coffee originated in Ethiopia, in Kaffa Province to the south), while burning frankincense filled the room. Her son brought in a wooden bowl and water in a gourd, which he poured over each of our hands in turn. We were then offered roasted corn on the cob and a nasty-looking yogurt wat sprinkled with dead flies. I reciprocated with our own peanut butter wat, and our hosts chomped it gently, like tortoises at dinnertime.

As we were leaving the village, a woman motioned us to a dark tukul, and we followed and peered inside. There was an old woman, puss pouring from a leathery eye, with legs so thin if she fell they would go snap. And there was a baby with a bloated stomach, scabies, and worms. They asked for our help, and Pasquale was only too willing to oblige. He left some antibiotic ophthalmic drops for the woman, and some oral amoxicillin for the child, explaining through Haptewold the correct dosages. The village chief bowed low three times and thanked Pasquale as we departed.

From Abtate it was a ninety-minute descent into the gorge, more of a slow fall than a hike. Several times we went tobogganing on our asses down scree. From the map we determined the tributary that conflued at our drop-in point was called the K'oga Shet. It was not the clear tributary we were seeking. Nonetheless, I ran the final fifty feet to the tributary, and splashed it on my face, my first taste of the Tekeze watershed. We were in a steep gorge with walls perhaps two thousand feet sheer, and we reminded ourselves this was the section on the aerial scout that had looked least impressive. It reminded me of Marble Canyon in the Grand Canyon of Arizona.

The river at the loamy confluence was running about five hundred cubic feet per second, actually enough to float rafts upon, except the drop was clearly too severe. As far downstream as we could see there were rapids, mostly Class VI, unrunnable. We were in the gorge that we had seen from the air was not in any way navigable. So, our goal, we believed, would be the next major southern tributary downstream. That was where we thought the manageable water began. But how to get there? We could either hike back out and around and attempt to punch in downstream, or try to canyoneer down the gorge. Our guides and porters told us nobody had ever traversed this gorge; that it was too dangerous, not possible, filled with hippogriffs and evil spirits, and they feared for our lives if we attempted to continue. We tried to entice them with more money, but they were adamant. With the Abyssinian standoff in play, I decided to take a conspicuous hike downstream to show how it could be done, and I charged down boulders and across the river until out of sight. When I returned, Pasquale had performed his magic, and negotiated, with the offer of a month's salary each (about $12), for five porters to accompany us into the gorge the following day. Haptewold refused under any circumstances, but agreed to hike back to the Land Cruiser and arrange for the extra supplies we needed to be carried back in by 9:00 A.M. The porters wanted to hike back to their villages for the night, and as they started up the cliff a snake shot out from under a boulder. The porters sliced it several times with their machetes, and Haptewold declared it was a boomslang, a deadly poisonous snake, and said runically its presence was a bad sign. We wondered if any of the porters would really return.

The great white disc of the full moon seemed so close that night I almost touched the craters on its face. Its light on the canyon walls glowed like phosphorous, and it spread a golden, mobile sheen across the water. When a plane passed over, I guessed that for an instant its passengers were my nearest neighbors. It took some time to fall asleep, but when I did I had nightmares about dead-of-night attacks by wild animals and shifta-wielding machetes. I awoke once and looked at my watch. It was midnight. The moon, like a silver clasp, was uniting tomorrow with yesterday. I turned, buried my face in my balled T-shirt I used as a pillow, and drifted away. In the morning the heart-shaped hoof tracks of an antelope and the tracks of a big cat littered the beach, crossing just a few feet from our bags.

Around 7:00 A.M. three guides from Abtate showed: Adam Merequol, Worku Mohammed, and Asntca Mohammed. It turned out Abtate was a Jabarti Muslim village in the heart of the ancient Christian empire. None of the guides spoke English, so we couldn't communicate well, but smiles and gestures and pictures in the sand seemed to work. At nine o'clock three more porters showed, carrying a cache of food and supplies (including a case of Ambo and another of Amstel beer) from the Land Cruiser.

By nine-thirty we were hiking downstream. We saw spotted-leopard prints along several small beaches, and antelope spore. In a pool we spied a four-foot-long Nile perch. Sodden cormorants hung themselves out to dry on overhanging branches, throats wildly shivering as if with a dreadful ague. Beneath them waded big, solitary Goliath herons, nearly five feet tall, impeccably neat and dry, with pink necks, black legs, and round, yellow eyes. In the air we saw rainbows of birds, including malachite kingfishers, coots, moorhens, hornbills, and all manner of unfamiliar avifauna. A few hours into the gorge we came across several troops of shaggy-coiffed gelada (bleeding heart) baboons, also known as lionmonkeys, digging rhizomes and picking up seeds with a precision grip that rivals humans'. There were hundreds of them, and they collectively seemed to have a third sense of Lili's camera. When she faced away, they would bare their teeth, jiggle like Saint Vitus, and make impertinent remarks. Then, when she turned her lens on them, they would duck and hide. She never got a single shot. In honor of our elusive hosts we named the canyon Baboon Gorge, but doubted it would ever see a map, or even another human visitor. At one point a small animal darted across a cobble beach in front of me and splashed into the water (a crocodile? monitor lizard?). Our lead guide seemed to be saying it was something like a big rat with jaws. That made me wonder if it might be the legendary Osgood's swamp rat, a mythic creature something like Ethiopia's version of Sasquatch, the monster of Loch Ness, or the Yeti. There are no recorded sightings of the infamous rat; we may have been the first.

The canyon was a continual cascade of boulders and waterfalls, and the traverse was a zigzag back and forth across the river, up and down the granite and basalt slabs and debris. Everyone fell in at one point or another. If the river had been just a foot higher, the traverse would have been impossible. Whenever a side canyon found the river, a waterfall splashed over the edge into the gorge.

At about 5:00 P.M. we broke through to the other side of Baboon Gorge, and found the clear tributary, Tota Bahar. It was warm, so much so we thought it might be fed by a hot springs. It was across from a tributary canyon and waterfall, and a shepherd was at its mouth. He told us there was a path up the side canyon to Inkway Beret, just three hours' walk. This was our put-in! The puzzle solved!

We celebrated with a pasta dinner, generously mixed with the unknown spices from the Mercato; spices that made salsa seem like vanilla ice cream. The porters awkwardly tried to learn how to use our utensils, spilling good portions on the beach. One ripped open a Lipton tea bag and poured it into a samovar to make tea. Others were transfixed by the bubbles in the Ambo. Another played plaintive tunes on a bamboo flute, while a shepherd offered us a huge white squash, the size of a Gott cooler. Two women with three children appeared from the Abtate side, and when they saw us, they precipitated away in fear.

As far as I could tell from the map, we were about five thousand feet above the level of the sea; from the contour lines it appeared the gradient averaged about fourteen feet per mile. The Colorado through the Grand Canyon drops about eleven feet. So, this seemed entirely doable.

As the sun painted the red-rock walls with honey light, I looked downstream to a river enticing, seductive. There was an imponderable nature to the Tekeze: nothing but the attempt itself would really prove if we could stand up to it. Suddenly I had a plan: "Pasquale . . . Conrad has got rafts. What do you say we hike out, fetch a raft, come back and run this thing, guerrilla style. The four of us. We could bag it now." Pasquale, a man capable of swift, certain decisions uncorroded by self-consciousness or second thoughts, was all for it. Lew would have liked the wild idea, too. Pasquale started devising the menu, the fishing line we would get, the logistics of the take-out (we'd just wait for a truck or local bus to pass). Lili and Chris didn't quite know what to make of this, but sat through the discussion with equal parts fear and excitement that we were serious.

Then I had second thoughts and put on the brakes. "You know, I'd like nothing better than to do this alpine style, quick, simple, light, the way we used to, but we can't. We have no defenses against shifta, no safety support for big rapids, no backup if a croc chomps our raft. Besides, we have an obligation to Turner." Sanity prevailed, not, though, without regrets. I dreamt a cycloramic dream that night, of floating, drifting on a river of honey light, companioned by time.

The following morning we hiked out of the canyon. In the cool shadows of cliffs we passed sacred datura plants, whose seeds contain a powerful hallucinogenic sometimes used by the Hopi and other southwest Indians for vision quests. We couldn't help but wonder if the plant was used in any similar fashion here. Near the top of the canyon the path took a deep breath, and we passed a walled Coptic church ringed with trees sprouting thumb-size bananas, and populated with sprightly vervet monkeys. Our only Christian porter stopped to kiss the wall. The sun, translucent as fine china, stood well-nigh vertical at noon as we entered the flyblown thorp of Mitk, which didn't exist on any maps, but which had as its showpiece an impressive triple-walled church called Hawa Mikael, which we were not allowed to enter. Come back on Sunday, a guardian priest seemed to be saying, and I made a note to try and schedule arrival next year to coincide with services there.

Another hour hiking through vast sorghum fields and we entered Inkway Beret. We resupplied with water and graciously refused offers of sour goat's milk. Two hours later we arrived at the Lalibela airport with the great geographical riddle solved and a plan at hand. We would return a year hence with all our crew and gear, fly to Lalibela, trek to the Tekeze confluence with the Tota Bahar, launch our rafts, and hopefully emerge 250 miles downstream at the egress of the Tekeze Gorge.

# CHAPTER 20

# VIRTUAL
# ADVENTURES

"Life can only be understood backwards, but it must be lived forwards."
—Søren Kierkegaard

I returned to the United States confident we could run the Tekeze and called Thom Beers to let him know. Thom was euphoric. "We'll make this the *Deliverance* of the nineties," he said.

After going over volume statistics that Conrad had dug up, I decided to schedule the expedition for early September 1996, a month earlier than the scout. The river was notoriously fickle when it came to volume. In some years in August it appeared to be running five times the volume of the Colorado; in others it was bone dry by October. September seemed the safest month. So, that left me eleven months to get everything together.

And what an eleven months it was. My world took directions I never imagined.

It started in December, in Antarctica. During the previous few years I had been playing with New Media, dynamic digital representations of traditional static print media. It had always been a point of frustration over the years when I set out to convince the uninitiated that adventure travel was a good thing, with alchemic transformational qualities and positive consequences. The universe of adults, though, who would leave the comfort zone and step off the beaten path into the wildness of adventure was small, very small. Over and over I met with glazed eyes as I tried to describe the delight and aperçus that came from my latest foray into the field. I felt it was a question of accessibility; to most, rafting the Zambezi or trekking in Nepal seemed like something mythopoeic. So, I wanted to communicate the message that adventure was for everyone . . . unless you craved concrete and enjoyed seeing the air you breathe.

For years John Yost and I did this by producing an annual SOBEK catalog of adventures dripping with gorgeous photos of everyday people in exotic locales, challenging themselves, having fun, interacting with people from distant cultures, and with wildlife rare and beautiful. And, to a degree, it worked. SOBEK grew and, while it didn't exactly prosper, it allowed us to pursue the mission of adventure, our passion. The catalog concept never really realized its potential. We would spend the better part of a year creating the catalog; we would print and distribute 200,000 copies, and would garner 3,000 clients. Part of the problem, I subliminally assumed, was the basic shortcomings of a print publication. Because of space and cost considerations we could use only one or two thumbnail photographs to illustrate all the diverse sights and sensations of a three-week trek in the Himalaya, or a two-week rafting run down the Bío-Bío. Somehow that seemed a travesty. And one of the most compelling facets of an adventure trip—the sounds, the ethnic music, the wildlife calls—could never be properly portrayed. Try as I might, I could never describe the rainbow qualities of the gamelan music of Indonesia; one had to hear it to grasp it, to appreciate it. The same with the hunting cries of the Masai, or the haunting wail of a gibbon.

So, when I read about the coming age of New Media I became enthused and jumped in. In 1993 with Kodak as a partner, I produced the first Photo CD of adventure travel, featuring the original photographs (restored in PhotoShop) of Ed Hillary and Sherpa Tenzing Norgay's successful first ascent of Mount Everest in 1953, replete with narration from Ed. It also featured dozens of high-quality photos of our key trips, and full-bodied, digital stereo sound. You could hear the lions and the Kechek dance, waterfalls thundering and glaciers calving. In my mind, it was a huge leap forward in grabbing an audience, and conveying the wonders of adventure travel; in motivating the next step. We bundled the CD in the back of 100,000 copies of our annual catalog, with hopes that our well-heeled and qualified clientele were so passionate about the subject of adventure they would go out and buy the necessary proprietary $200 Kodak Photo CD players that attached to TV sets like VCRs. The theory seemed sound: our clients were proven explorers, early adapters, photography lovers. It didn't work. Once again, I was out exploring the sharp outer edge of the curve, but this time I was working in what would become a Betamax format. Photo CD players never caught on. As far as we could tell, only about fifty people actually saw the Adventure Disc in their own homes.

But a side effect was brewing. In 1994, because of my early efforts at exploring New Media applications for marketing and selling adventure, I had been asked to emcee a travel and technology conference in New York. But it was in early December, and Pamela was pregnant with our son, Walker Taylor, who was due about that time. So, I bowed out of the emcee slot, but volunteered that if Walker came early, I would be happy to fly out and make a presentation.

As it turned out Pam went into labor November 17, 1994, while I was in the middle of a speech in Washington, D.C. When informed by an aide, I made a hasty excuse to the audience, ran off the stage, caught the last flight back, and arrived in time for the birth, in the early morning of the eighteenth. I was hooked up to the Internet, so I broadcast my son's arrival to the wired world.

With Walker's early arrival I was able to make the conference, and showed the Adventure Disc to great fanfare. Afterward a young man approached me in the back of the room and slipped me his card: Richard Barton, Travel Product Services, Microsoft. "We should talk," he suggested.

And we did, periodically, over the months and weeks that followed, exploring different ways Microsoft might work with my company. By this time I had produced several CD ROM's and realized their own shortcomings: long development time, static content once created, and ultimately limited space (although with 600 megabytes, CD ROM's held room for the equivalent of several hundred catalogs). I had read about a new interface/application on the Internet, the World Wide Web, which would allow multimedia presentations and cross-linkage to pages anywhere on the Internet, anywhere in the world. This seemed the ultimate application for travel, with near infinite space, and the ability to update information at any time. So again I jumped in and produced the first travel site on the World Wide Web, an interactive, multimedia version of the SOBEK catalog that even featured electronic postcards. It was pioneering of a new sort for me, a whole different exploratory, but in some ways not unlike running unrun rivers. There was no road map, no marker for what lay around the next bend.

The website was a hit, receiving notices in national magazines and newspapers, and Rich Barton increased his phone calls to me. He even flew down to my offices and we spent a couple hours talking of ways our companies might work together. Still, nothing concrete emerged.

〜〜〜

Then a new idea dawned in early 1995. Why not take the power of the World Wide Web into the field and allow virtual travelers to join an expedition, follow it and participate from the portals of their computer screens, be they at offices, schools, or homes? I was scheduled to travel to Antarctica in December to escort a Mountain Travel★SOBEK commercial expedition. Why not make that a trial run for a virtual expedition? I enlisted the help of four key players: Jonathan Chester, author, filmmaker, photographer, Antarctic explorer, mountaineer, and recently a fanatical webizen: he would be the field producer; Christian Kallen, who had collaborated with me on several books, films, and recently the CD projects: he would be the project director and editor at Mission Control at our offices in El Cerrito; Gary Schumacher, a VP at World Travel Partners, a top-ten corporate travel agency looking to explore downstream possibilities with the Internet, and willing to invest in crazy ideas such as this one; and Kevin Twidle, a research fellow in computer science at Imperial College outside London, and co-owner of 7-E Communications. He had set up satellite links in the Sudan, Siberia, Afghanistan, and other countries he was not free to divulge. He spoke six languages, including Perl, C++, and English. Kevin was our communications wizard who could make all the satellite equipment buzz and sing. Christian and Jonathan brought in a fifth key player, brilliant web designer Brad Johnson, who took the site and made it transcendental. We called our enterprise TerraQuest.

Just before I flew to Antarctica, Gary Schumacher and I visited the Microsoft campus for an attempt at a deal. We described in detail what we hoped to do with TerraQuest, and invited Microsoft to license the concept, offering several virtual expeditions a year. We presented a budget, and Rich Barton and his confrere, travel product unit manager Greg Slyngstad, seemed to think it reasonable. We left the meeting with a handshake and a promise that Microsoft would send a letter of intent before I departed for Antarctica.

The letter never came. But I was almost too busy to notice, putting together the ambitious Antarctica project. Miraculously all the gear arrived in Ushuaia, Argentina, intact, and we set sail to the White Continent wired to the world. Every day we would send back dispatches, digital photos, answer e-mail, and engage in Live Chats, wherein any webizen could converse with us via text. It was a successful exploratory, and mentions of the project made *Newsweek, The Wall Street Journal, The New York Times,* and many other publications. One man in Israel who had religiously followed the trip sent a post-expedition e-mail: "Thank you, thank you, thank you. I am a paraplegic, and this was the closest I will ever come to visiting Antarctica, and it was wonderful." And the project didn't go unnoticed in Redmond, on the sylvan campus of Microsoft.

With our Christmas return from Antarctica I was set to start organizing the Tekeze, which at this point would be a commercial exploratory with a Turner crew on board to document the descent. Turner didn't have the resources to pay all the expenses for a private exploratory, so we agreed to sell seats to proven SOBEK clients to help underwrite the project. The response was overwhelming, and before we turned around a dozen clients had signed.

At the same time I wondered why we never heard from Microsoft and called Rich Barton. He said he was sorry, but there had been a "major reorg" at the company, and he would have to get back to me in due time.

In February I got a call from Rich, suggesting I come up for a meeting with Nathan Myhrvold, whose name I recognized as the chief technology officer of Microsoft. Nathan was also a former colleague of Stephen Hawking and the coauthor of *The Road Ahead,* the best-selling book mapping out Bill Gates's vision of the digital future. Rich also said Melinda French would join the meeting. Who is Melinda French? I asked. "She's Melinda French Gates, Bill's wife," Rich informed me. This sounded like a serious meeting.

At the meeting it was explained that on December 7, Pearl Harbor Day, Bill Gates had announced a major reorganization of the company, revamping his corporate starship to "embrace and extend" the web. Microsoft, theretofore a software company, was going to commit its vast resources to developing "content" for the Internet. One of the first deals the company made was signing Michael Kinsley to come to Redmond to create an on-line political policy magazine, which became *Slate.* Now Rich Barton and company were asking if I would come up and create an on-line adventure travel and exploration magazine. "But this is a full-time job," Rich reminded me. "You'll have to leave SOBEK behind."

"What about TerraQuest?" I asked. "We'd rather have you, and own the magazine."

It was the offer of a lifetime. I struggled a bit, having spent twenty-three years in the adventure business in my own company, and being excited about the birth of TerraQuest, which was owned equally by Mountain Travel★SOBEK and World Travel Partners and was brimming with promise. But this was too much of an opportunity, a chance to give birth to a twenty-first-century magazine with deep pockets behind me. Now I could create my own vision of a geographical and discovery magazine, a publication using tools that would make the stories come alive in a multimedia and interactive way. And I would not only contribute words and photos, sounds and video, but would edit as well.

I would retain an ownership in Mountain Travel★SOBEK, sit on the board, but would leave the day-to-day of commercial adventure travel behind. TerraQuest would be purchased by World Travel Partners, to run a couple more virtual adventures before being parked as an archive site, a marker stone for the beginnings of virtual expeditions. I didn't dwell on history, though. I was training my field glasses on a new species.

I did wonder how accepting the job would affect the Tekeze, a trip I knew I could never miss. I showed Rich Barton and Greg Slyngstad Lili Schad's exploratory video, and suggested if I joined up that I devote the first issue to the Tekeze, partnering with Turner and making it a live, interactive expedition from the bottom of the deepest gorge in Africa. I had no idea if the satellite equipment would work from such a depth, surrounded by mile-high walls, but I threw out the concept. They loved it. I signed up and moved into my Redmond office April Fool's Day, 1996. The first thing I placed in the windowsill was a skull I had found in a cave on Easter Island some years back, with a small hole in one temple and a large chunk of its occiput missing. The tiny hole was where a bullet had entered, the big one where it exited. But I knew nothing more of the fate of this man. I kept the skull as a reminder of the impermanence of all things living, and of how we all ultimately become anonymous. It also was a great conversation piece in a world of e-mails, software, code, and killer apps.

This twist put the Tekeze into a whole new light. I had been hoping the expedition might be a chance to reunite surviving friends of the 1973 Baro and Omo expeditions, as we had all vowed back then to run the Tekeze. But a commercial exploratory concept wouldn't allow such a reunion—it would be too expensive. Now, however, with Microsoft and Turner on board, we could organize a dedicated expedition with no commercial clients, just the reuniting five, plus four professional rafting guides, the Turner film crew, and a production crew from my new web-zine, *Mungo Park,* named after the eighteenth-century Scottish explorer who disappeared while pioneering the Niger River in West Africa. For *Mungo Park* there would be Jonathan Chester and Kevin Twidle, who had made the Antarctica expedition such a success, and *Mungo Park* in-house producer Steve Lee, as well as my friend David Roberts, a co-field cor-respondent who would file regular dispatches from the expedition to the *Mungo Park* website. I had known David for years, had traveled through Yemen with him in 1980, and made the first descent of the Waghi-Purari River in New Guinea with him in 1983. The latter always im-pressed me, as David cannot swim, and I cottoned to his keening spirit of adventure. David was a great writer, with many books to his credit, and he had been doing some virtual correspondence for Discovery On-line. So, I figured David would be our guy. Pasquale Scaturro would also join us, though he had reservations. Two months after we returned from the scout, his seventeen-year-old son, Adam, broke his neck while wrestling at high school, and became paralyzed from the waist down. Pasquale wondered if he should join an extended expedition under the circum-stances, but I urged him on. "I've been there. It's good to go." And he said yes. We also had a translator, Daniel Mehari, and a Turner Produc-tion manager, Jackie Frank. That put our total to twenty-three people, huge by exploratory standards. And just two days behind us would be the commercial exploratory, led by Conrad Hirsh, also with twenty-three people. My offering of the Tekeze to veteran clients as a first descent some months earlier had yielded an overwhelming response, and some-how we needed to accommodate the commercial explorers. So, we de-vised a tricky plan that would allow the Turner/Microsoft expedition to launch first, but only by a couple days, so that everyone could claim to being on the river during its first descent. It was all outlandish, bordering on being unmanageable, and was very risky. But I committed to go for-ward, knowing that the Tekeze would go from a million years of solitude to being a media phenomenon in one fell swoop. I wondered, some-times, if a year ago, when I had the chance, if I should have taken Con-rad's raft and just headed downstream with our little crew of four.

〜〜〜

The weeks before the expedition diaspora were crazy, organizing all the expedition equipment, the film gear, the satellite gear, securing the per-mits, working with sponsors, and building a website. But the biggest argument we had during the prep stage of the expedition was over the spelling. I had always heard the river pronounced Takeze (TAK-ee-zee), and promoted that official spelling. Jim Slade, however, with his penchant for thorough research, dug up a raft of published spellings for the river: Takazee; Tekezee; Takeze; Tekaze; Tekkaze; Takazze; Tekkazee, Tekezo, Takkazye, and Alan Moorehead's summons, Takkaze. All of them meant "terrible" in the local language. He tallied their appearances as well, and Tekeze won by a half-dozen citations. So Tekeze it would be. Abadi Haile, Pasquale's friend who had helped us on the exploratory, now did prodigies on our behalf during the planning of the actual expedition, and without him we would not have had a trip. His role was all the more vital because, although we had the blessings of the prime minister, certain conditions prevailed in Ethiopia that made expedition planning tedious and frustrating: demands for paper authorization, insistence on signatures and rubber stamps, the difficulties of actually tracking down Ethiopian officials. Whatever the obstacle thrown in our path, Abadi cleared it, made it correct in every punctilio of diplomatic procedure. If we needed the moon, Abadi would have arranged for it. We were off and running.

Things started to heat up as departure day grew nearer. In July, the Al-Itibad, a guerrilla faction fighting for the independence of Ethiopia's barren Ogadan region bordering Somalia, made an assassination attempt on the transport minister, one of the men who had advised Jim Slade and Pasquale during a diplomatic call they made prior to the expedition's launch. The gunfire killed his driver, and shot off part of his hand, but he was still behind our effort. On August 9, three weeks before D-day, a bomb exploded in the Wabi Shebele Hotel in Addis Ababa, where we had thought of staying, killing one person and wounding at least ten others. The next day Ethiopian troops invaded Somalia, in a region long in tribal dispute and reportedly harboring oil reserves. Hundreds of civilians were killed. Was the country about to once again become a warzone? On August 28 there was a small headline in the paper, "Egypt braces for largest floods on record," and it went on to say that in the Sudan, where the Blue Nile and Tekeze rivers spill their waters, floods had already destroyed hundreds of houses and driven thousands from their homes.

Ten days before my flight I went to see my doctor. She looked me over and pronounced I had spent too much of my life in the sun. "You're at risk. You really can't expose yourself to any more intense sun if you hope to avoid skin cancer." It was all I needed to hear. Unlike my early river days in which I was sometimes called "the Banana Tan Man," I would stay pale and unexposed this round, beneath hat, glacier glasses, and long-sleeved shirt and pants.

〰〰〰

The night before departure uncertainty spread outward like unblotted ink. I was anxious, anxious as I had been on the eve of departure twenty-three years before. Back then I thought the chances I might die were quite high; now I felt the same, but the stakes seemed higher. I had a young son I wanted to know. My father was unwell and I wanted to see him again. The news of flooding in Ethiopia meant we could be getting into something over our heads. And I was no longer young and spry. I felt friable and trackless. Worse, with my new job at Microsoft I hadn't found the time to get into shape. Where once I ran every day, I was down to a day a week. My thews and sinews were not exactly to par. My emotions ran red hot and ice cold—one day I was as excited as a kid on Christmas Eve, the next wondering why I had set this juggernaut in motion, and how could I stop it. And, I was all too aware that I was at the same age as my father when he had his nervous breakdown, a condition his doctor warned might be genetic. But I was committed. I would run the Tekeze, or at least attempt it.

I repacked my old wetpack, taking out the original SOBEK T-shirts and shorts, knowing I was going to make a keen effort to avoid direct sun exposure. I threw in the knife I used on the Baro, a couple old blue SOBEK hats, and the SOBEK flag that flew exploratories on six continents. And, I packed my journal. Once again, I would keep a daily log of our adventure, of our discoveries, of my thoughts and feelings. Then I settled back to watch some TV and take my mind off the expedition. I pushed the remote and on came TBS, the primary sponsor of our expedition. Behind a disco beat the announcer intoned that the evening's programming was a seventies tribute. And then the music jumped to a familiar theme song, playing over a scene I recognized. The movie was *Shaft in Africa,* and there was Richard Roundtree hurdling through Addis Ababa. And yes, behind him in the crowd were fleeting faces I recognized, faces from the American embassy, faces I had long lost touch with, faces with names no longer remembered, faces white and cracked like a crocodile's belly.

As I slumped deeper into the couch the phone rang—it was my mother. She was worried. I could hear her brow crinkle. My dad, who suffered a stroke in February 1994, leaving him partially paralyzed and speech impaired, took a fall to the head. They would have to operate. My mother feared he might not survive. She didn't say it, but I knew she wanted me to come to Albuquerque, where she and my father had recently retired, and be there. For an instant I considered the option . . . it would be a graceful way of getting out of this million-dollar scheme I had put in motion, a project I now worried might turn to disaster. Who could fault me, bowing out to be at my father's side? But I told my mother that I prayed for the best, and that I was on a plane in the morning to Africa. Once there, I lied, I would be out of touch. When we hung up, I called and left a voice-mail for my assistant. Even though we would be connected by e-mail, please, I said, don't send me any messages of a personal nature—none at all. I knew if the worst happened to my father while I was on expedition, I couldn't help. Once in, there was no exit from the Tekeze Gorge until its end. There would be nothing I could do, except cry and vex. It would be better not to know until we were safely out the other side.

CHAPTER 21

# PRIME TIME

"Only desire makes the story errant, flickering like a compass needle."
—Michael Ondaatje, *The English Patient*

*September 4*

At last I am back, about to embark on a river exploratory in Ethiopia, twenty-three years after our ill-fated Baro expedition. I check into the Ghion Hotel, named for the river in the Garden of Eden. It was once the grandest hotel on the horn of Africa. Now an 80-mm Howitzer shell acting as an umbrella case meets visitors in the lobby, and beyond is a musty, threadbare grotto partially barricaded, prohibiting guests from a section destroyed by a bomb eight months earlier. The floor of my room is stripped of its carpet, and the parquet is buckled and warped. Patches of damp discolor the paint on the walls, and here and there plaster has cracked and flaked away. The curtains are tattered, and an unglazed windowpane is broken. There are no flowers, no mints on the pillow, and no outsized baskets of fruit. I set a plastic bag of duty-free whisky I had brought for bribes, and my computer pack, into the camphorwood cabinet in the tiny room, as this is all I have. Lufthansa lost my dry bag containing my sleeping bag, clothes, toilet kit, medications, spare glasses, and air mattress.

I feel a bit naked without my accessories, or a change of clothes, but I also feel an odd sense of liberation. It reminds me of the Baro when I lost my only bag and was reduced to what I had on my waist and feet. It was as free as I had ever felt.

After a quick shower I step downstairs into the bar where I find most of the lost crew, people I haven't seen in years. Bart Henderson, George Fuller, Jim Slade, and others are there slugging tej, flirting with the bar girls, who dance about tossing bundles of plaited hair, and fluttering shoulders as though there are two birds under their robes. The only missing are John Yost, who because of a schedule conflict won't arrive for several days, and Lew Greenwald.

*September 5*

Jet lag, too much tej, and thoughts of Lew keep me in bed until late morning. A wave of sorrow for a time long ago, when Lew and I giddily scrambled about Addis Ababa putting our trips together, washes over me. For a moment, the reservoir of grief seems so deep, I think if I open the floodgates I will drown . . . so, I park these memories, and stumble out of bed.

After lunch I ride down Yohanis Street, past the unfinished Sheraton with its stained cement and paralyzed cranes, over to a bridge that crosses the headwaters of the Awash, and look down into its muddy maw. This is supposed to be the end of the big rains, but there is no evidence here that the country is moving to a drier season. The Awash is in spate, stewing with sewage, and it looks ugly, chocolate-brown waves biting the air. Trash tossed from the street above litters its banks. It is so putrid even the stray dogs avoid it. It is hard to believe this was the flow that gave so much satisfaction and transcendence; that this was the first flow I shared with Lew as my partner. A barefooted woman drives a train of donkeys laden with brushwood by me, and she stops and looks over the cement railing to see what I am staring at. She considers the sight for a second, then makes a loud spit that arcs in the river, and proceeds on her way.

I walk up the hill to where a young friend used to live, a metalsmith named Abba Wedaje. I knock on the metal door, and a pygmy-sized woman answers. I ask if she knows where I might find Ato ("Mr.") Abba. She turns away and lets loose a muffled sob. Then she invites me in for tea. As we sip from handleless Chinese cups, she tells me in broken English that after surviving ten years of brutality under Mengistu, in the summer of 1984 Abba had made his way to the Sudanese border to be airlifted by Operation Moses. But within sight of the border, he was grabbed by other Ethiopian refugees and accused of being a *buda,* a possessor of the evil eye. He was drawn and quartered in front of hundreds of witnesses. I turn the Coptic cross–engraved bracelet on my left wrist Abba had given me in 1974, and which I've worn ever since. I thank the old woman and drift back to the hotel.

I decide to take a shower, to wash away the grime of memory, yet the spigot emits an impressive metallic sound, but no water. So, I spray myself and my clothes with the water mist that came with my airline kit, and head to the lobby for a trip to the palace. There I am to conduct the first Internet Live Chat with a prime minister, His Excellency Meles Zenawi. The high-tech satellite gear we need to make the expedition interactive and accessible through the Internet is basically a couple of spy sat-phones linked to laptops. Knowing that the Ethiopian government, just emerging from a twenty-year civil war that saw no shortage of foreign machination and spying, would not likely be keen to grant us permits to take our gear into the region that was a critical battleground and still harbored residual conflicts, I concocted a wild plan that might ease the way. Pasquale, who had faced similar challenges trying to bring in communications gear for his oil research, was an advocate of doing the whole expedition "under the radar." He had smuggled in high-tech gear several times by disguising it, and by using his many friends in high places. I considered that a serious option. But with so much at stake, including a half-million-dollar film budget, the launch of my on-line magazine, and our safety, I decided to attempt the "high road" approach. This meant going to the top and asking for highest-level permissions. This had huge risks as well, and if we received a no from the top, it would effectively squelch our efforts; it would be near impossible for us to sneak the effort if the government was on the lookout. I had successfully employed the top-down method before, most conspicuously in 1981 when I put together the first descent of the Zambezi from the base of Victoria Falls. I had convinced Zambian president Kenneth Kaunda to bless the expedition, and join us at the launch with a speech and ceremony. It didn't hurt that we had crews from ABC television and *National Geographic* magazine along, and the media-savvy president seized the moment for a piece of international limelight.

So, several months prior to scheduled departure I crafted a letter to the prime minister, and sent it via the U.S. embassy. In it I invited the prime minister to participate in an historic event, the first Internet Live Chat with a prime minister, which would be available for an audience around the world to join. I pointed out that Microsoft had just done the first Live Chat with a national president, Bill Clinton, through its MSNBC website, and it had been a big success. Here was the chance to follow in such company. The only requirement would be issuance of a permit to bring in the necessary gear. And, by the way, we would love to have a helicopter for safety while we conducted our expedition. I even sent Jim Slade and Pasquale over in early May for meetings with the U.S. ambassador and various Ethiopian ministers to pave the way.

To my great delight, the prime minister answered in the affirmative, with an official letter replete with rubber stamps of purple ink. I photocopied the letter and gave it to Jim Slade and Pasquale to use whenever they came upon bureaucratic blockades. In the letter the prime minister sanctioned our project and added he was personally thrilled we were attempting the Tekeze. He was from the Tekeze region, knew the river, and even fought there during the civil war. His regret was he couldn't join us.

Abadi picks me up a bit late for the appointment with the prime minister. He brings a cheap tie for me to wear, and I sling it around my neck as he negotiates traffic, occasionally touching a string of worry beads swaying from his rearview mirror. At the palace Abadi is denied entrance. He fumes and argues while I am waved inside. There an aide ushers me up the stairs, down a grand hallway, and into a room where the prime minister is waiting to begin.

The forty-one-year-old Meles Zenawi is a balding, short man with distinctive arched eyebrows, a black goatee, and impeccable English. He was born second child to thirteen in the Tigrean town of Adwa, where Emperor Menelik defeated the invading Italians in 1896, and Ethiopian independence was preserved. A brilliant student, he went to the Wingate School in Addis Ababa, then the nation's elite scholastic school. His given first name is Legesse, but he joined the rebels during his third year in medical school and adopted the *nom de guerre* Meles. After the forces he commanded seized power in May 1991, he did not, in the tradition of most revolutionary leaders, assume dictatorial powers. Instead, in early July that year he convened and presided over a national conference, out of which emerged a new government. Representatives from many of the country's eighty or so ethnic groups, which have never been represented in the central government, were allotted seats in a new legislature. In May of 1991 representatives of Amnesty International were allowed to visit Ethiopia, the first delegation of the human-rights organization to do so since 1974. In July of that year Meles declared that public demonstrations could be held, a right that doesn't exist in many African countries, and never existed in Ethiopia.

Though we had made much of the fact that we needed permits and customs clearance to bring in our satellite systems for the Live Chat, the truth is the easiest way to conduct it is with what we call "Sneaker Net," meaning we would conduct the interview via phone. As people on the Internet typed questions, we would read them to the prime minister, and as he responded over the phone a team back in Redmond would transcribe his answers. Still, we set up the satellite system and computer so it all looks very techy, and then dial the white plastic phone. The prime minister settles back on the overstuffed couch and for an hour answers questions from around the world. He talks of his involvement in the war, and how between 1975 and 1991 he spent time in the Tekeze Gorge as a guerrilla fighter, where he was wounded in the head trying to overthrow the military regime. After defeating the military in a bloody, long battle he became president of the transitional government, and finally in 1995 he was elected, for a five-year term, to be prime minister. He explains there are nine states in Ethiopia, and that Addis Ababa, the capital, which used to be a state, is now a special designated area, something like Washington, D.C. He proudly describes the recent medal wins at the Olympics, and even answers questions about the weather. He talks about how the government is once again trying to promote tourism, protect its parks and unique wildlife, and that a road is being built into the Simien Park adjacent to the Tekeze, and there is encouragement for the building of private hotels and lodges. He describes some of the musical instruments, the national food, and fields a question from a netizen inquiring whether there is a McDonald's yet in-country: "Not yet."

The touchiest moment comes when someone starts a line of questioning concerning the royal family, some of whom, in exile, have been raising monies to finance a return to power. In fact, I am carrying a letter from Princess Rahel Fikre-Selassie, the San Francisco–based great-granddaughter of Emperor Haile Selassie, requesting blessings for her to return and make a documentary about her mother, and I wonder if a hidden agenda is written between the lines.

NETIZEN: Would members of the royal family be allowed to return and live in Ethiopia in peace?

MZ (shifting on the couch): They're very welcome to visit. It's their country. I'm not aware if they've visited since the war. But there's no reason they shouldn't visit.

NETIZEN: Very generous attitude, sir. But would the government allow members of the royal family to live in Ethiopia and guarantee their safety and freedom?

MZ: There again, there's no problem. It's not up to me to tell them where to live. If they want to live here, they're welcome. I think there are close relatives of the royal family living here. I am a bit surprised by these questions. There should not be any problem.

NETIZEN: If some of the royal family did live there, could the government guarantee their safety?

MZ: There would not be a problem. Shortly after 1991 we recovered the remains of the last emperor. The royal family wanted to have a state burial; we said they could have a family burial. That's the only conflict that I know of. In any case, I would be very glad to welcome all members of the royal family to come here, live here, work here. Their safety and security is guaranteed.

Then the questioning drifts to another subject altogether, one about which I am eager to hear how the prime minister will answer.

NETIZEN: Do armed guards protect the St. Mary's Church in Axum, where the Ark of the Covenant is said to be?

MZ: It's not armed guards who protect the relic. It's an old priest—sort of a selected person. He's given the responsibility of protecting the Ark for life. It's very dangerous to see it, according to legend.

NETIZEN: Some sources say that a Dr. J. O. Kinnaman, who organized the National Museum for Haile Selassie over twenty-five years ago, was allowed to see the Ark of the Covenant. Have you ever heard of this person?

MZ: I've not heard of that, but I find it difficult to believe. He'd have to kill the priest to do that—he's the keeper of the relic and would not allow anyone to see it.

NETIZEN: Was *Raiders of the Lost Ark* a popular movie in Addis Ababa?

MZ: Not to my knowledge.

NETIZEN: Does the present government have any plans to make a public display of the Ark at any time in the near future?

MZ: The legend says that if anyone is exposed to the Ark, he or she immediately dies. The other point is that the Ark is considered a precious relic. The government has no control of the relic; it's under the control of the Ethiopian Orthodox Church. As far as I know they have no plans to display it.

NETIZEN: Then why hasn't the guardian of the Ark died?

MZ: The legend of the Ark is that the guardian is selected by his virtuous being. Secondly, even that person does not come into contact with the Ark. It's covered and stored in the basement of the church. Consequently, he has not touched the Ark.

The prime minister patiently answers several silly questions, and repeats answers to ones asked previously. He concludes with a question from an elementary school district in Phoenix that asks if their students could interact with students in Ethiopia. Not yet, he confesses, but he is hoping to bring the Internet to Ethiopian schools soon and implement a distance-learning program, and then he hopes they will tune in and interact. Then he makes a closing remark: "I think Ethiopia is one of the least-explored and least-known places and perhaps one of the most fascinating places to see. I'd like to welcome all to come see us when they travel. We're very welcoming people. I'd like as many people to come as can. I hope your Tekeze project will be a success. I'll follow the expedition on the Internet."

With that, he hangs up, and we exchange pleasantries and a few memories of old Ethiopia. I then give him a copy of *Rivergods,* a book I had cowritten with Christian Kallen many years ago that features a chapter on the Omo River. And I give him a copy of Bill Gates's book, *The Road Ahead.* At this gift he smiles, as this is the third copy he has been given, he tells me. In fact, Bill Clinton had given him one at the anniversary celebration for the UN some months earlier. Then he shakes my hand and walks out of the room.

# CHAPTER 22

# INTO THICK AIR

"We rose up, and in a few minutes were ready, and yet we hesitated a little, as human nature is prone to hesitate on the threshold of an irrevocable step."
—H. Rider Haggard, *King Solomon's Mines* (1885)

*September 6*

We awake early and bus to the airport to catch our chartered flight north to Lalibela, where we will trek to the start of the river expedition. But when we arrive at the domestic terminal we find Stan Boor and Kate Rineer gloomily sitting in the molded plastic waiting chairs. They are here as the lead team for the commercial trip down the river, which will leave two days after ours. Both are longtime SOBEK guides who have rafted rivers around the world. Stan will forever in my mind be remembered for the river he didn't do. He signed up with me to make the first descent of the Bío-Bío in Chile back in 1977, but at the airport he decided to turn back—he had a bad feeling, was spooked with some aspect of the exploratory, and so we went on without him. And discovered one of the classics of whitewater.

Now Stan has turned back again, but not at his beck. He and Kate had actually taken off a couple hours earlier, and were well on the way to Lalibela when the pilot announced they were going back to Addis; the weather was just too bad.

Our flight is delayed as well. As do millions of Ethiopians, we sit and watch the rain outside. In the flat light the drops look like silver threads, like static on an old film. The air seems almost thick enough to drink. My feelings are mixed when during this wait someone shows up with my missing bag. I sort of enjoyed the notion of rafting the Tekeze with just my blazer and airline wear. At last, we file onto the Dash 5 "Buffalo" and take off. In the 1920s Haile Selassie brought the first airplane to Ethiopia, and this looks to be that. Actually, the plane was used by the Americans in the Korean War, and it is worse for the wear. The pilots don't even have working seat belts. After takeoff we look down to sheep grazing in the tussocky grass of the Entoto Hills and see tall clusters of blue gum trees swaying with the wind. They seem to be moving, migrating, like the Danakil and their camels. Looking up I see the underbelly of great gray frigate clouds, and higher still a sky nearly black, pulling into nothingness. We turn north as the last edifices of Addis dissolve into the distance. Moving out over the plateau, the land spreads in shelves, in ripples, in straggling eaves. The road looks like an infected scratch across the weathered skin of the plateau, curvilinear in some places, sharply angled in others. In the wake of the big rains, the landscape sparkles, more Ireland than Africa, interrupted with checkerboard squares of bright yellow barley and circles of gray thornbush compounds. Villages stand in red moons of cleared land. The tukuls look like moles or freckles on the face of an oversubscribed plain. The farther north we travel, the less forest we see. A century ago about 40 percent of Ethiopia was covered with trees; today it is 4 percent.

After an hour we cross the transit of the Blue Nile, the river where Lew drowned. I stare transfixed through the portal as we wind up the river and wonder for an instant what piece of sky Lew saw as his last. The plane wheezes suddenly, does a sloppy seesaw, as if in response to my thought. The quadruple rows of dials in the cockpit, which I can see through the open cabin door, appear to go wild. The pilot's hands fly for a moment, then the hiccup subsides as quickly as it erupted. I look outside and see we are crossing Lake Tana, shining like a huge silver coin set in the escarpment. Finally, we are above a lacerated, folding landscape, creased with chasms, at the bottom of which streaks of water flash . . . the watershed of the Tekeze.

At the Lalibela airport we meet Mike Speaks, who has been here a week preparing for the expedition. Mike claims to be descended from the great African explorer John Spekes, rival to Richard Burton, and perhaps the true discoverer of the source of the Nile. I had never run a river with Mike, though our fates were entwined. Several years ago I had gone to central Borneo and scouted a river called the Boh. I was convinced it would make a great exploratory and packaged it as such. I didn't return for the expedition; Mike Speaks went in my stead, and it turned into a nightmare of sweat flies, heat, capsizes, portages, and delays. There were two bright spots. One was that Mike enjoyed one of the greatest river romances of all time with a famous fashion model who then followed him to his cabin in Alaska, before realizing living long-term without electricity or running water was more romantic scrim than reality, and fleeing back to New York. For this I was jealous I didn't make the run. The other bright effect was that I sent Tracy Johnston on the trip, a writer and editor friend, and asked her to author an article on the adventure. She endured several unexpected challenges on the trip, not the least of which was the onset of menopause, and her article of the experience was expanded to become a best-selling book, *Shooting the Boh*.

Mike tells us it has been raining every day since his arrival and the tributaries are in flood. With spirits a bit soggy with this news, we pile to the back of a rusted Mercedes panel truck and grind up to town. We check into the bungalow-style Roha Hotel, a big, cool ship above the sea of village-life commotion. As far as we can tell the hotel has only one other party, a young German couple driving across East Africa. The manager seems a bit overwhelmed with our entourage and mountains of gear, and he suggests we're the biggest thing to hit Lalibela since the Muslims invaded in the twelfth century.

After lunch I meet up with Haptewold Belay, our lead guide last October who abandoned us in the unexplored upper gorge. Now he says he wants to join the expedition; he is no longer afraid. He is not someone I would trust for anything more than a city tour, and so that's our compromise—I agree to hire him to take David Roberts and myself up for a tour of the troglodyte churches of Lalibela.

As Haptewold tells the story, around 1200 A.D., Lalibela was born to a royal family, and a swarm of bees hung over his cradle, a prophecy of future greatness and wealth. Sometime later in life his brother, Harby, became jealous with this augury, and attempted fratricide by poisoning. But a deacon in Lalibela's service first sipped the tainted liquid and died immediately. Overcome with grief, Lalibela seized the goblet and swallowed the rest of the brew. But instead of dying, he drifted into a deep three-day sleep filled with celestial visions. When he awoke he found he was cured of a chronic worm disease that had been troubling him. In addition, he remembered that in his slumber angels had showed him magnificent churches that God commanded to be built. The next twenty-four years were spent creating the churches, the heavy lifting done by Lalibela's subjects, the carving done by angels.

Though lore claims angels carved the sunken edifices, history writes a Christian emperor of the Zagwe dynasty built them. They were not built at all in the conventional sense, but instead were excavated and hewn directly out of the solid red volcanic tuff on which they stand. In consequence, they seem superhuman—not only in scale, but also in artistry and in innovation. They remain places of living worship eight hundred years after they received their first prayers.

Close examination is required before the full extent of the achievement can be appreciated. This is because considerable efforts have been made to cloak their real natures: some lie almost completely concealed within deep trenches, while others hide in the open mouths of huge, quarried caves. Connecting them all is a bewildering labyrinth of tunnels and passageways with offset crypts, grottoes, baptismal fonts, and galleries—a cool, lichen-enshrouded subterranean world, shaded and damp, silent but for the faint echoes of the voices of priests and deacons as they go about their timeless business.

The most striking of the churches is Beta Gioghis (Church of Saint George). Standing more than forty feet high in the center of a deep, almost well-like pit, it has been hewn to resemble a cross. It is here, in this pit of Christianity, that I say a quick, silent prayer for our safety on the Tekeze.

With darkness, we assume Jim Slade never made it out of Addis Ababa, and that we will rendezvous with him the following morning. Yet at around 9:00 P.M. Slade arrives with the rest of our eight thousand pounds of gear. A master at cortex-based problem solving, Slade had been hung up at the airport over some of our gear. It had been another Keystone Guides comedy. The driver first took him to the wrong terminal, then every piece had to be weighed, then a customs inspector insisted on looking at every piece, even though this was a domestic flight. He flagged the kayaks, recognizing them as boats, and forbade Jim to take them to Tekeze, saying he was afraid they could be used to paddle into the Sudan "and escape from Ethiopia." But Jim produced the "atomic bomb," the prime minister's letter of support, and the customs agent waved the kayaks through. But this wasn't the last hurdle. Now everything had to be rolled through a giant X-ray machine that had a conveyer belt on the front end that was outside, exposed to the weather, with the other end under a roof. Because it was pouring rain, the X-ray inspector took pity on Jim, and the supplies that were in cardboard boxes. The inspector allowed Jim to place all the gear under the roof at the exit side of the conveyor, and he then rolled it into the machine backward, and then out again, a process that kept things dry but took twice as long. As Jim feared, the X-ray man stopped the belt and asked about the giant propane canister that would be used for cooking, and the plastic containers of kerosene and gasoline, all of which are illegal to carry on an unpressurized flight.

"Are these safe?" the inspector asked Jim.

"Yes, they're fine," Jim lied.

"Okay, I trust you," and he waved it through.

After a dinner of curried rice, chicken, and crème caramel, Jim Slade tents his hands and with an admonitory gaze makes a speech about fining down our personal kits to the absolute minimum. Collectively we just have too much weight. I retreat to my room and dispose of several books, as well as my collection of PowerBars, which I hate anyway (so much for any sponsorship there). Steve Lee and Kevin Twidle set up the satellite systems on the balcony of the hotel, and we make our first contact with mission control in Redmond. We answer questions from people who have joined in the expedition, and send back some digital photos, video and audio reports. It works. We're twelve thousand miles away, but not yet at the bottom of a mile-and-a-half-deep gorge.

〜〜〜

*September 7*

The war of attrition is at our door this morning. David Linstrom, a Turner assistant cameraman, vomited all night. Bill Anderson, the director, has a G.I. problem. Eric Magneson and John Armstrong, kayaking cameramen, hiked up the western slope of Abuna Josef (13,747 feet) to a ridge last night to get some sunset shots and never returned.

Saturday is market day, so before beginning the trek Bart and I wander over to the open-air bazaar, enclosed with a euphorbia and thorn fence and filled with dozens of haphazard lean-tos made from burlap and branches, under which people are trading for bloody slabs of goat or tiny bags of salt or chat. This was not long ago a war zone, and pairs of soldiers still walk the muddy aisles with loose-jointed strides, holding hands by one finger, like paper dolls. And the merchants still have the darting, lateral eyes of a hunted species. With an elderly entrepreneur, brittle as snakeskin, I haggle over a hand-woven cotton *shamma* (shawl) to sleep in, and a box of Blue Omo laundry soap, in tribute to the namesake.

After lunch we divide the group into two, an advance party that will trek the twenty miles to the river today, and a follow-up party that will make final arrangements in Lalibela and catch up tomorrow. I am anxious to get to the river, but also keen to witness the Sunday church service that will take place at Hawa Mikael, the church about halfway through the trek that we had visited on the scout. And so I take off with the first group, consisting of Bart, Pasquale, George, some of the Turner crew, and myself. We drive the thirteen miles to the airport runway, unload the truck, and Pasquale goes about hiring forty porters. Then, just as did Mungo Park, and the great African explorers of the eighteenth and nineteenth centuries, we head out single file, the porters with our two tons of gear balanced on their heads, singing as we march southwest toward the Tekeze. The day is clear, the first in weeks, and the mud paths have begun to congeal a little. In a matter of minutes we reach the Ketchn Abeba, the Tekeze tributary we must cross. It is broad and fast, like a glacial stream, and we set up a rope system to help everyone cross in the waist-deep water. A gentle descent begins into a massive canyon bowl and we head out across fields of yellow maskal daisies and brilliant green teff. In a region where everything would seem to conspire to make life a misery, the tail of the wet season has made every tree and shrub burst into hectic leaf, and it is staggeringly beautiful. It feels like we're in an oversized diorama, or in the middle of an IMAX film—everything is exaggerated, the colors more brilliant than enhanced photos, or HDTV.

After a couple hours George is moving stiffly, like a tin man, and beginning to limp. In April he was in a car accident that fractured three tarsels in his foot, and now he is using a special brace to allow plantar-dorsal inflection, but he is clearly in pain, especially when descending.

Late in the afternoon we walk up a rise to the village of Mitk, and at the crest the Tekeze unveils its otherworldly panorama—it is breathtaking. I call for camp here so we can soak in the beauty of the Tekeze with the setting sun, and visit the nearby church in the morning. The only problem is that this pass is the Chisholm Trail. As we go about setting up our "no-hitch pitch" Lunar Ship North Face tents, hundreds of lowing cattle are herded through, and not a few fat-tailed sheep. The dense odor is of milk and manure. A line of slender, grubby boys stands in permanent enfilade at our perimeter, and flies like paparazzi descend upon us. We retreat to the reliquaries of our tents until dark, when the flies retreat to wherever flies go. In the cool, night air we emerge to share a dinner of steak and egg sandwiches, packed by the Roha Hotel. Then Steve Lee unpacks the M-system satellite, and positions it to hit the geostationary satellite 22,000 miles above the Indian Ocean. We make a connection, our first in the field, and try to call Peter Beardow, our communications expert in England. We get a wrong number, someone's answering machine in London. The expensive connection has already been made, so we go ahead and leave a message. "Hi. You don't know us, but we're calling on a sat-phone from a remote village in Ethiopia. Have a nice day." Then we proceed to call our loved ones. Pasquale calls his recently paralyzed son, George Fuller calls his kids, and I call Pam. All receive the calls with a measure of disbelief—"Are you really calling from a village in Africa?"

After we've used our communications allotment for the night, we are invited to join a village couple in their circular mud and dung hut with a high beehive-shaped roof. We are ushered into the semidarkness, where the small cooking fire highlights motes of dust hanging in the air. From the newly brushed earth floor a loamy fragrance rises, complicated by a faint note of sandalwood. Here the wife performs a coffee ceremony, authoring a brew that would bankrupt Starbucks. I can't help but notice the beautiful, silver pectoral cross, worn on a leather thong around her neck, as she pours the coffee from its earthen pot. We all sip her offer to the last drop. Then, she turns to the back of the kitchen, and returns with another container and some new vessels. She now serves us toothglasses full of thick, cloudy *tella* (a crude and unfiltered barley beer), which George knocks back while simultaneously telling us that when he was in jail in Hamar some years ago for having the wrong protocol stamp he watched them brew tella . . . from the laundry water. I pass on the brew, but sip another cup of joe, then head for bed. On the way I step over our porters, who are sprawled out on portable cowhides, the original Therm-a-Rests. Once tucked into my bag I find I can't cross the frontier between consciousness and unconsciousness, not because of the caffeine fix, but because we hired *zabanas,* locals armed with ancient Italian rifles, to look over us. Two of them perch on my tent portico and chat, chant, and sing all night to keep themselves awake; I suffer their success.

CHAPTER 23

# THE TEKEZE FOUND

"We named this place 'The Abyss,' and it will always make me think of Dante's Inferno."

—Major H. C. Maydon upon seeing the Tekeze Gorge, 1925

*September 8*

We emerge on Sunday to the sound of a liturgical drum coming from the nearby church. Only our zabanas are late to the day, rolled like moths in cocoons in their coarse shammas. After breaking camp we step over to the outer wall of Hawa Mikael church, which is girdled with thorn trees. The outside ambulatory of the three concentric parts of the Abyssinian church is called *k'ene mahlet,* the place where hymns are sung, and it corresponds to the *ulam,* of Solomon's Temple in Israel, where the Ark of Covenant sat from the tenth century B.C. until spirited away by Menelik I. The next chamber is the *k'eddest,* where Communion is administered to the people; and the innermost part is the *mak'das,* where the *tabot* (the replica of the Ark of the Covenant) rests, and to which only archpriests have access. This division into three chambers applies to all twenty thousand Orthodox Ethiopian churches.

Inside the first circle about a hundred women and men are praying and turning beads and genuflecting about the circular chapel. A fragrant cloud of incense billows from the open door, and a priest wearing a *Matab* (a neck cord that signifies membership in the Ethiopian Orthodox

Church) offers to escort us inside the dark second chamber. Walking in stockinged feet—since it is considered sacrilege to wear shoes inside any Ethiopian church—we follow the priest inside. There I see a man, seated cross-legged on the dirt floor, creating the slow, deep throb of a *kebero,* the large oblong drum, made of cowskin stretched over a wooden bowl, that features in much of the music of the Ethiopian Orthodox Church. To this sound is added a nasal chorus of voices chanting a hymn. This is a mysterious scene: nothing about it belongs in the neoteric world, and as I watch I feel transported into the past, traveling the weird waveforms of the music, which seem to belong to some other place and to some ar- chaic faith. Dressed in traditional white robes and black shoulder capes, the deacons lean on tall staffs with curved silver handles. They sway and chant, sway and chant, absorbed in the primal cadence of the dance. Each holds in his hand a silver sistrum, which, in the silent interstices between the drumbeats, he raises and then lets fall, producing a clear and melodi- ous tintinnabulation.

Inside we make a circuit of the ambulatory, where we see Coptic crosses, faded friezes of biblical scenes, and hundreds of thousands of flies and fleas. I strain my eyes to look through the fumes of darkness and can just make out, at the very center of the k'eddest, the curtained entrance hiding the replica of the "Holy of the Holies," or perhaps the real thing. Some in Ethiopia believe the authentic Ark is moved around, for its own protection, among the twenty thousand churches in a giant shell game, and if so it could be here. But we will never know.

As we break camp to make the final descent to the river, a village chief shows up brandishing a Steyr M.95 rifle, dating back to about the time of the battle of Adwa (1896), during which 4,000 Italians died, the great- est defeat ever suffered by a European colonial army. He is corseted with two rows of bullets in a bandoleer. He demands we cease and desist un- less we produce a permit. We pull out the letter from the prime minis- ter. He inspects it closely, then waves us on.

A giant ground ibis stands at the rim of the canyon, pointing the way. We follow its beak, and begin the drop into *aqua incognita.*

〰〰〰

A gash in the skin of the continent, the gorge of the Tekeze bleeds brown. The first sighting of the river comes at noon on our second day of trekking, as we're descending a tributary gorge. It washes away my deepest fears.

For days I've been unable to sleep, thinking this may have been an awful mistake, one of a scale never imagined when I first thought of running the Tekeze back in 1973. The reports of record floods throughout the region had many of us spooked as the beast of this expedition lurched forward. Ever since our arrival in Ethiopia it has rained, and almost everyone with whom we shared our plans sneered at the prospects of success in this deluge.

As Bart Henderson, George Fuller, and I drop down, step by step, into the gorge, the world seems smaller, more closed in: civilization ceases and the heat covers us like a balm. The gradient is more suited to centipede than human. When the Irish explorer Dervla Murphy crossed the Tekeze Gorge in 1966, she wrote, "This was the toughest descent I have ever experienced. I tend to accuse the highlanders of exaggerating the difficulties of my trek, but they certainly have not exaggerated the difficulties of crossing the Tekeze Gorge here; if it were even a degree more difficult it would be impassable to humans."

Finally we round a hairpin and there is the full-bodied Tekeze below us, translucent brown, like yellow garnet or topaz, fast moving, but not so terrible: it has gravel bars and wet-sand beaches, indicating the river level has been dropping rapidly. The current is fast but not overwhelming. The volume looks like that of a California river in spring runoff; friendly, inviting, doable.

George is suffering with his injured right foot and is using as a crutch the stem of a broken paddle, a paddle that broke on the Omo expedition twenty-three years ago. Despite his handicap, even George steps up his pace upon seeing the river. Minutes later we're at the gravel bar, and I throw off my pack and jump like a flame into the river for a baptism. For a score and three years, I have been hoping to reach this river; at last it wraps around me and pulls me downstream. It's cold, and fast, and wonderful.

It is even more of a delight to find we can actually uplink to the satellite from the bottom of this very deep canyon. We use the Thrane M 3030 satellite system to call Kevin Twidle, who is still in Lalibela, by reaching a satellite over the Indian Ocean, bouncing the signal to an earth station in Norway, then back up to a satellite over the Atlantic, and finally down to Lalibela, which is just thirty miles away. Kevin sounds like he's underwater, but the damn thing works! Pasquale pulls out the Global Positioning System (GPS) and calculates our whereabouts to within thirty feet. The only kink is a near accident when David Linstrom, like a monkey, climbs a wall behind camp, rappels dizzily over a crusty crag, then slips, knocking down a large rock that just misses the group and the gear. He finds himself clinging at the edge, and David Roberts, a veteran mountaineer, works his way up the cliff to belay the other David down. Roberts thinks it a close call, that we might have come close to a serious accident even before launching on the river.

A short time later an uneven whir echoes up the canyon through the still, thin air, and with a whoosh an MI-8 single-rotor Russian helicopter appears around the bend, hovers above us like a giant insect, and settles on the bar one hundred feet from our packs. A door drops down and out jump John Yost and Jim Slade. John had just made the marathon flight from the States and barely made the connecting flight to Lalibela. There he caught up with Jim, who was loading the chopper with some of the eight thousand pounds of expedition gear he was ferrying to the river.

Now the knot of surviving original SOBEK members is reunited, twenty-three years, nine kids, several strained backs, dislocated shoulders, broken bones and hearts, fifty first descents, capsizes on six continents, countless insect bites, dozens of diseases, and a quarter million river miles later.

We all look the same, and different. We all put out our hands in the SOBEK crocodile handshake; smiles spread and crow's-feet crinkle. George's wild red beard is now flecked with gray, and he seems thinner and smaller than before. Bart, who in 1973 sported shoulder-length severely sun-bleached white hair, now has a short GQ cut, and, with his strong cleft jaw, looks like a Hollywood version of a hero river guide. Jim is still vertically challenged; I'm still tall. We're both a bit wider. And gray streaks our temples. John Yost's face seems hardly written on, and he is wearing one of our original SOBEK T-shirts. It doesn't quite seem real that we are in the country where we began as a rafting team in 1973; now on the banks of the Tekeze, likely our last river exploratory. Back then we were beginning life's journey and anything was possible. George now is an emergency room doctor in Los Banos, California, a horticulturist, and a pleiad of artists on the side. John gave up the adventure business four years ago and is now executive director of the Conservation Lodge Foundation, a project of the Pew Charitable Trusts, which is planning on opening a series of ecolodges in North America. Bart is owner and operator of Chilkat Guides, an Alaskan river and hiking outfitter that specializes in taking cruise ship passengers floating through a bald eagle reserve. Jim is the only remaining active river guide and probably holds the world record for miles rowed and exploratories run. And I'm now a nerd at Microsoft.

After the greetings and exchanges Jim Slade rolls out the map, and simultaneously all five of us pull out our reading glasses.

〰〰〰

*September 9*

I awake to the gentle susurration of the swift river, and the eructation from someone suffering the effects of last night's freeze-dried curry. Today is the day.

The morning is spent in final organization of the mountain of gear, the "attack of the Pelican cases," as Bart calls it. We may, in fact, be the heaviest river expedition in history. If importance is synonymous with baggage bulk, we are kings.

The six self-bailing Wing Inflatable rafts are topped with air. Collectively they look like a shock of sunlight against the strong brown god, the river Tekeze. At the crack of noon we push each into the water, peel off downstream like fighter planes, and with hoots and hollers echoing across the canyon, we swirl into unknown Africa. The movement has a timeless quality, a ritual we have all shared with one another, and with many other friends.

It is a bony river. A minute into the trip a crack rings out, and I look back to see Pasquale holding a broken oar; a few minutes later another crack reverberates, and this time it is Bart's oar snapped, just as happened in 1973 when Bart first pulled the sticks on the Omo. We began with a total of eighteen oars, so if this keeps up it could be a very short trip. About ten miles downstream we stop at the Ketchn Abebe tributary for lunch and spread out our international smorgasbord: Spanish sardines, Kenyan cheese, Danish lunch meats, Israeli jam, Ethiopian honey, Japanese tuna, Norwegian kippers, peanut butter from the People's Republic of China, French mustard, and American Crystal Light. While noshing, we gaze up the tributary watershed to a cupped valley that could be Yosemite, except for the shrieking baboons sauntering along the banks, and the leopard tracks crisscrossing the beach.

Back on the river, the journey unfolds pleasantly—the neighboring mountains are majestic, the weather is fine, the air quiet and balmy, the river fast and cool. Just when I am beginning to think the water is going to be safe we see the radial-tire skin of a croc. Then another. On the right a massive tail plated with heavy, pointed scales lashes from side to side, exploding into the water. We've traveled about fifteen miles down the

Tekeze, as far as we know the first time anyone has traveled by boat down this river. And while we expected, dreaded any number of dangers, we never seriously considered crocodiles to be an obstacle. While some in Addis Ababa and Lalibela warned of Nile crocodiles, we all pooh-poohed it, and worried about high water and shifta, even schistosomiasis, which George Fuller is certain exists here. It just doesn't make sense. The Tekeze virtually dries up in the eight-month dry season leaving little room for water reptiles, or their primary food source, fish. I had seen no evidence of crocs on the aerial scout, and I knew the nearby Blue Nile was practically void of the creatures, they having long ago been poached. So, when Daniel Mehari, our Ethiopian interpreter, yells *"Azzo!"* and we turn to see a ten-footer slide into the enveloping murk of the river, and watch him watch us with his periscopic eyes, it is a chilling moment. Then another crocodile shoots into the river, as though jet propelled, not far from the kayakers Eric Magneson and John Armstrong. This doesn't bode well for downstream, as from past experience the size of crocodiles increases proportionately with river volume. The river here is small, perhaps two thousand cubic feet per second, and we expect it to increase ten- to twenty-fold by take-out. There is no shortage of croc tales in the SOBEK archives. The two we just saw remind me of the Zambezi. In 1981, on the first descent of the Zambezi, we were showing actor Levar Burton (who was hosting an ABC documentary being made of our effort) how to kayak, when we heard a loud *pop* and saw a tube on John Yost's raft burst apart; a ten-foot croc had done the deed. Minutes later Levar called in the helicopter and flew away, never to be seen on the Zambezi again. There are rafts of stories of the mingled destinies of crocodiles and men, most ending with torn flesh or lost parts, or worse.

The six rafts are divided in a way unfamiliar to our earlier expeditions, in which gear and crew were distributed pell-mell, with little thought to how it all might appear on camera. Now we have two "talent" boats, carrying the surviving SOBEK guides, and we are instructed never to ride on other boats for fear of messing up a shot. Then there is the official Turner boat, carrying all the camera and sound gear, and the crew. Pasquale is rowing the *Mungo Park* boat, the heaviest with all the high-tech tackle to do our daily multimedia uplinks as well as producers Steve Lee, Jonathan Chester, and Kevin Twidle. Finally, there are the two expedition boats, rowed by current SOBEK guides Brian Stevenson and Greg Findley, carrying all the food and normal equipage that would go into an expedition without massive media coverage.

All this makes for a less than nimble fleet. On exploratories, such as the lower Baro, if we came to an obstacle, we could simply lift up our conveyance and kits and carry them around in a matter of minutes; it would take hours, days, perhaps, to portage this argosy. And, in the past, in our light and limber boats, we'd been able to outrun the hesitant hippos and crocodiles. Not now, not here—we were burdened with the weight of media, and ambition.

# CHAPTER 24

# JUNGLE FEVER

"Those who will not reason perish in the act. Those who will not act perish for that reason."

—W. H. Auden

*September 10*

Reveille brings a merry mood for everyone, save George, who spent the night in Bart's tent puking. Bart moved out. George doesn't feel well. He says he was scorified by last night's sauce beriberi, a very potent Ethiopian pepper generously mixed into the meal. I wonder if it might be the tella he drank in Mitk.

George climbs on the boat I am sharing with Bart, sprawls across the thwart, and begins to snore. From its abundance of tributaries the river is gathering more water, and going is better. We pass several local peoples on both banks. Some stand with raised arms and bow to the ground a number of times, in case we are of importance, or are an invading army. Others run along the margins of their teff fields encouraging us to stop, but our rafts in the swiftly moving river soon outstrip them. Spry gray monkeys scatter along one bank, while troops of noisy gelada baboons scamper down the other, both moving faster across the uneven terrain than humans ever could, and for a moment I contemplate the disadvantages of having evolved.

Around noon we pull over to the western shore at a tributary, and all but George make a short hike up to a sparkling waterfall. As Bart moves under the cascade the force of the water has a concertina effect on his skin, and he becomes for a moment a sea monster.

Back at the boats I look over and see George, his thin shoulders slumped, his face ashen, staggering to a nearby tree, where he stoops and drops his trousers in front of the group and begins to squirt from both ends. He begins shaking uncontrollably. I step over to feel his head. He's burning up. His voice, attempting simple reassurance, catches the edge of something more: "I'm okay," George insists, but I have to help him walk back to the raft and lift him on board. He does not look okay; this seems more than mere dyspepsia. We rig an umbrella over George, wrap his head in a wet bandanna, and head downstream. A cloudburst brings down a hail of cold rain, and George begins to shake like a dying dog. We cover him with a sleeping bag and several towels.

Then, sometime in late afternoon I hear several shouts. John Yost and Jim Slade are screaming. Yost and Slade don't scream unless it's serious. I look downriver and see Yost frantically slapping the water with a paddle. I'd seen this scene before. It is a crocodile attack. I can see the business end of the croc, its long, dark snout, and it is repeatedly charging the raft that Slade is rowing. And it is resisting John's water pounding and the commotion. It just keeps charging, again and again. This is a serious attack. Slade spins the raft around and heads for shore. The crocodile follows, and John continues to yell and slap. Slade is swept into a small rapid, and the crocodile shoots the first half, then eddies out. Slade continues the run, then quickly pulls to shore.

My heart pounds as I follow Jim's course. Unlike our past African river expeditions, we have no metal protection, no guns, on this expedition. The only way to stop a charging croc is with noise, paddles, and what we can hurl. As I pull up next to Slade's raft I ask, "How big?" "Ten-footer," John replies, eyes wide. This is scary news. Finding large crocs this far upriver is one thing; finding aggressive crocs is another thing altogether.

The other boats soon beach, and virtually everyone jumps out with still, video, and 16mm cameras and races upstream to get a shot of the crocodile. The only ones left behind are George, who has collapsed in the bilge, vomiting, and me. George rolls over and looks up at me. His face is formless, like a pricked balloon. He suddenly looks old, as if mortality had seeped to the surface of his skin. I pull him out of the boat and carry him like a sack of potatoes up on the beach. George has always been a small man, but now he feels like a skeleton—there is no flesh on the man. He is in a severe delirium, mumbling incoherently, and his skin is burning. He's soiled his clothes, so I pull them off and wrap him in wet towels. We have no trip doctor on the expedition, the closest being George, who refused the honor. The next closest we have are Mike Speaks and Eric Magneson, both trained in river rescue and advanced first aid. Together we set up a tent to get George out of the heat and try to get him to drink water. Mike takes his temperature: 106 degrees, the edge of death. Eric gives George Imodium and Tylenol, and asks a series of questions about his condition, but George just chunters.

"Look, George, we can call a helicopter," I bellow into his glazed face. "It can be here in a few hours. You're the doctor. You've got to let me know how serious this is."

"It's only viral. It will pass," George mumbles as he spits up the water Eric gives him. He can't keep anything down. He looks like a crustacean with its shell off.

I can't believe the rude and welling ironies here. George was the one with the bad premonitions, and yet I persuaded him to join. An avid collector of tropical insects, he may now be the victim of one. We didn't bring a trip doc because, despite George's insistence that he not be the appointed one, we all knew he would come through in a pinch. Now he is caught in the vortex of scenes he has decried. Now I am afraid Dr. George Fuller, my good friend for twenty-three years, is going to die on the Tekeze, another casualty of my African misadventures.

Night pitches its black tent over our camp as George slips into a deep sleep. I tuck him into his bag and shine a light on his face. His freckled skin looks thin as rice paper. His face shudders like the hide of a horse disturbed by flies. But there is nothing we can do except wait. Jim Slade sets up the single-band radio, hitches the skywave dipole aerial to a planted oar, and calls Stan Boor, who is with the commercial expedition upstream. There's an emergency room doctor on that trip, Lee Meyers, with whom I climbed Kilimanjaro a couple years back. But Stan says it would take more than a day to catch up with us. By that time, George could be gone.

After dinner, George is sleeping soundly, and there is no more we can do for him until morning. So, four of us set out upstream to where the crocodile charged Slade's raft. We're anxious to find whether the reptile is alone, so we can grasp the potential risk this unexpected danger brings to the equation. We carry a Q-Beam spot floodlight, which emits 200,000-candle power, and sweep it along the banks. As the beam travels it catches the bright red eyes of half a dozen crocs hovering a few feet from shore, waiting for some potential prey to visit the river for a final drink. At one sweep we catch a huge Verreaux's eagle owl, perhaps a yardstick high, perched on a river rock, also waiting for some dinner to pass, perhaps a mouse or other rodent. It's a spooky scene, and even more so when we trek back to camp and find a large crocodile hanging in an eddy just ten feet from the moored rafts.

As we sit in a witches' circle around the campfire, I watch the milky light dance on the faces of Bart Henderson, Jim Slade, and John Yost. It seems to come from some other evening. We muse over the afternoon's crocodile charge and swap stories of croc and hippo bites our rafts have suffered over the years.

SOBEK has a long history with croc attacks. John remembers he has been in three rafts deflated by croc bites: one on the Omo in 1975, another on the first descent of the Zambezi in 1981, and a third on the exploration of the Kuhnene River on the Angola/Namibia border in 1992. Bart decides to change the subject to happier memories, and tells how he was once invited to join a New Year's Day trip down the Awash River by some ex-pats he'd met at the patisserie. But he partied too hard the night before, and a hangover kept him from making the trip. The Land Rover carrying his new friends was attacked en route and two of the Awash-bound were shot dead.

Other tales of ripped fabric and close calls that seemed exotic and even a bit of a thrill back then now seem serious, and a pall hangs over the barbs and brittle laughs. John's leg is shaking like a sewing machine, a nervous habit he's had since high school.

As on the other nights on this trip, I roll out my sleeping bag under the marquee tarp covering the *Mungo Park* gear, including laptops (five Toshiba Tecras 700 Cts, a Compaq Contura 420CX, and an Apple PowerBook), satellite systems, DAT recorders, inverters, batteries, generators, a spaghetti plate of cables, and Kodak digital cameras, like a high-tech Bedouin establishment in the desert. Whereas everyone else has retreated to the tents, I feel a special responsibility to the hundreds of thousands of dollars of equipment, though I know the locals would rather steal a rope than anything with software. Yet I find I can't sleep: I'm haunted with images of the nearby crocodile stealing up to my bag and making the Gary Larson cartoon come true: "That was great! No hair, no claws, just soft and chewy on the inside." I had once eaten crocodile in New Guinea. Was now the time for poetic supper-justice?

Just before turning in, Bart saw the reflected blue eyes of a leopard just beyond the camp perimeter, and a dozen members had gone in search.

Now, as I turn in my sleeping bag, I wonder about nocturnal leopard behavior. Would one be bold enough to attack a sleeping camper?

During this thought a mosquito whines past my ear, and I switch to remembrances of malaria incidents. Back in 1973 John Yost and his college roommate, David Bohn, traveled the Zaire River, buying local art and shipping it back to their African goods import shop in Southampton, Long Island. Shortly after returning from one buying trip to Africa, John discovered his business partner unconscious in bed in their shared apartment. He rushed David to the hospital, but it was too late. David died hours later from falciparum malaria (black water fever), a virulent and fast-acting form of the disease.

Sometime in the mid-1980s Skip Horner, one of the most experienced SOBEK river and mountain guides, contracted the same malarial strain while rafting in Madagascar. An oil exploration company had the only helicopter in the country and sent it to save Skip, who, doctors said, was within hours of dying.

Then there was today's conversation as we were floating into crocodiled waters, with George wrapped in wet cloth to keep his fever down. I was wondering out loud why so few people live near the Tekeze although the valley appears fertile and water is abundant much of the year. George, in half delirium, stirred with my conjecture, and mumbled his professional opinion: "malaria." Then he rolled over and went to sleep.

Crocs, leopards, and malaria swamp my thoughts, forbidding sleep. I keep dreading the same things over and over again, as if the thoughts are a kind of cud, and I'm a cow chewing on it. But some cerebral voice tells me the fears are unfounded. So I rise, surround my sleeping bag with Pelican cases, pull the cover over my head, swallow a .25-milligram tablet of the anti-insomnia sedative Triazolam, and disappear into sleep.

# CHAPTER 25

# RIDERS OF THE STORM

"I was not a little exercised in my mind as to whether this mishap at the outset was or was not a bad omen for our journey."

—Ludwig Ritter von Hohnel, northern Kenya, 1888

*September 11*

The sharp morning air brings celebrations. First, that George is alive, though still quite ill. The plastic bucket we left in his tent is coated with a film of stinky vomit; most of his regurgitation missed and is spilled in puddles along the floor of the tent; some flecks his beard. In a slow, rheumy voice he answers my good morning with an indecipherable mumble, but it is music to my ears. Second, this is Happy New Year. Ethiopia follows a Julian calendar of thirteen months (one of them, Pagume, has just five intercalary days). Today is the first full day of Julian year 1989, and the official end of the rainy season. Against hopes, George still has a fever, so Slade announces we won't head downstream until after lunch.

For the first time, our interactive abilities help us: we contact Mission Aviation Fellowship (MAF) in Addis Ababa on our Inmarsat M in case George later needs to be evacuated by helicopter. This contact would have been impossible just a short time ago. Many people died in the field who could have been rescued had the communications technology been available.

After a breakfast of thin, lumpy, uncompromising porridge, an armed contingent from the village of Abia, seven hours away, marches into camp. The men have trekked all night to catch us after hearing about us through the African grapevine. Some are blue-turbaned, all are wrapped in dark shammas, and most are slinging Kalashnikov assault rifles. For a moment, as they approach, I feel a chill—despite our numbers and high-tech gear, we are really defenseless should this group decide to attack. We argued about bringing firearms, but decided not to. One reason was that firearms are so precious here they alone would be reason to kill. Yet, as they step to me, they bow in friendly greeting. I bow back, stick out my hand, and shake and smile. My lips are so badly cracked a trickle of blood runs down my chin.

Through Daniel, our Ethiopian dragoman, I ask if they know much about the river downstream.

"Crocodiles?"

"Yes, many and large."

"Hippos?"

"Yes."

"Rapids?"

"There are big waterfalls downriver."

We then ask about the shifta, the roaming groups of bandits. "We thought you were shifta. That's why we brought our rifles. We came to fight you but then found you came in peace."

Reassured, the men explore our gear, delighting in our rafts and kayaks, but our computers are treated as coldly as brass by a magnet. One man grabs a double-bladed paddle, jumps in the fast-moving river, and tries to maneuver himself like a boat, to the amusement of all on shore.

With the festive mood established, several villagers break into an ar-rhythmic song and dance. Daniel interprets the words:

*"Our village is Abia;*
*Our river is the Tekeze.*
*We can shout and jump,*
*And nothing will happen to us."*

By early afternoon more and more villagers are streaming into our camp, and the crowds are making Slade, Bart, and others uncomfortable. Many times on the Omo and other rivers, locals would steal from the rafts and tents if not watched, and it was becoming impossible to watch this many people. And with a swelling crowd of people for whom violence is still functional and honorable, there is always the possibility of aggression, and their numbers now quadrupled ours. George's temperature is down to ninety-nine, though now his rawboned frame seems to stretch his body to a painful thinness. It's also getting hot, and we know George will feel better with a river breeze washing across his face. So, Slade calls for us to decamp, and we begin to load the rafts. But the Abians seem disappointed with our actions, and like friends, they implore us to come stay in their village, saying it is a safe place; safer than the river, which floods quickly and has many dangers. We're thankful for the invitation but have appointments to keep downstream, and an hour later we're once again floating the Tekeze.

Tonight David Roberts and cameraman Bob Poole spend time sweeping the water with their lights, catching the bright red beads of crocodile eyes offshore. David wonders aloud why the crocs have such blood-red eyeballs, why the leopard Bart saw the night before had a blue reflection, and why a flashlight doesn't have that same color effect on a human. Nobody knows the answer, but I have an idea. I get on the Internet and ask the question. This is, after all, supposed to be an interactive expedition, and indeed we have been dutifully answering e-mail questions every evening. Now I'll see what comes back.

*September 12*

A sudden jerk of the line, then a greasy black catfish with a leathery mouth lies at the feet of Mike Speaks. A living fossil, it is wide-eyed, sides puffing and trembling with the shock of defeat, the terrible absence of water. Breakfast has arrived. Sir Richard Burton said catfish "tasted like animated mire," but today, expertly cooked, spiced and buttered, it tastes like ambrosia.

We're camped on the eastern bank, in a cove so idyllic it looks to be a groomed campground in a national park. Dense trees block the sun, filtering the slanting morning light as though in a cathedral. George emerges from his tent with a collected tsetse fly between thumb and forefinger, so we know he is on his way back. As we're preparing to disembark, a group of locals shows; they hiked down from their village three hours away. The leader of the group is carrying an old carbine, has large, slightly spatulate bare feet with virtually no toenails, and his long shorts have been patched copiously, and hang together by one vital safety pin. But above the waist he proudly sports a tattered old army jacket with a prominent patch that declares his authority: "Sheriff of Travis County." He acts the part and demands to see our papers. Ferenji are a potential liability to headmen such as the sheriff. They might be robbed or shot by shifta, and they are the responsibility of the local chief while in his territory. We understand the rationale, but take responsibility for our own safety and are anxious to proceed. Again, we pull out the prime minister's talismanic letter and present it to the sheriff. He stares at it intently, upside down. It's clear the sheriff can't read. Daniel explains its contents, and the sheriff agrees to let us move on.

The water dropped, drew its sleeve away last night, so the rafts are high and dry. That means we all have to get out and push. "*And, hulet, soust* [one, two, three]," Slade cries, and we wrestle the rafts back into the water. I hadn't heard that countdown since our last portage on the Baro.

Just before pushing off, a watery-eyed, toothless old man wades across the river to our boats, oblivious to the crocs we know are there. "Why don't they kill the crocs and eat them?" I ask Daniel as the old man approaches. "They are Christians, so they can't eat crocodiles," Daniel answers with an authority that tells me his statement makes complete sense to him. It means nothing to me. The old man stops in knee-deep water, his turkey neck rattling in the wind, and points imploringly to his eyes, and then back across the river to two children in waiting. He seems to be indicating eye infections, but as the rest of us are trying to interpret his hand gestures, Pasquale is rifling through his ammo box. Before there is even a consensus among the group, Pasquale is in the water next to the old man giving him a tube of infection medicine.

After a few hours floating, we pass into a dark columnar basalt gorge, with strangler fig vines crawling down the face like props in a Tarzan flick. The air has become hotter as we've dropped deeper into desert terrain, and where we saw evergreens on the upper slopes just a day before we now see cacti. The bird life is extraordinary, and though my ability to identify the avifauna is rusty, Mike Speaks's is honed. He points out wood storks, Abyssinian rollers, sacred ibis, hornbills, turacos, rails, Egyptian plovers (the crocodile birds mentioned by Herodotus), tits, and more.

We stop at a waterslide on the eastern bank, and just like old times, John and Jim scramble up to find a groove. We all used to love finding these slides on the Omo and other rivers, and spent hours in playful respite. George was the most fanatical, and in fact the greatest slide in Ethiopia, a thirty-yard twisting, lugelike run, is officially named (at least on my map) Fuller's Flume. But George is still too feeble to climb up the rocks; he fills his phials with snails he's plucked from the creekbed instead. I consider, but the run doesn't look feasible. I yell to Slade, "Aren't you too old for this?" "Gotta keep up with Yost," he retorts as they scramble higher. But the run isn't there. The stream is too shallow, the turns too reckless. Maybe twenty years ago . . .

## September 13

Dusty crepuscular rays splash light on a landscape that looks older than history, a river that seems to have gulped time. I half expect to see Lucy, or some other vintage hominid, stoop down to the current for a drink. Above the canyon walls I see table buttes and mesas reminiscent of the landscapes around Moab, and behind our camp a clear creek spills over a gray wall.

In the Ethiopian language, Amharic, a river is called *wenz,* and our maps show three different Tekeze wenzes, all converging in the next hundred miles. On our charts a creek is called a *shet,* and in our devolving states of mind, addled from too much heat and from our deeper descent into the map, we've had puerile fun with that appellation. One unnamed tributary, where a large crocodile hovered in the eddy, we named Croc-o'-Shet; a memorable dry creekbed was appointed "No shet, there it was."

Pardon our immaturity, but I guess even the most refined minds would descend to our level after four days of floating down a river that requires constant vigilance for reptiles indisposed to retreat. At this point we've seen over one hundred crocodiles and hurled as many croc rocks.

In the early 1970s, our fifteen-foot rafts had twenty-one-inch tubes, just wide enough for large Nile crocodiles to wrap their jaws around, as they did on ten separate occasions. Now the rafts are eighteen feet long and the inflatable tubes measure twenty-four inches, and the raft manufacturer, Wing, claims its Coolthane fabric is "croc resistant" (not croc-proof, however). We'll see.

The kayaks are a different story. I had guessed John Armstrong and Eric Magneson would abandon their boats a couple days ago, but they have hung in there and until today seemed fairly sanguine about sharing the river with armored lizards. This evening Eric seems close to reconsidering. He had two serious pursuits today, both by animals bigger than his boat. He shot a rock at the first charging croc, but it didn't pause. "I saw its dentures, and I felt like hamburger meat, like prey. It put me on my knees." When he pitched another rock the animal dived, just thirty feet from his Tupperware-thin plastic bow. (The color of Eric's kayak looks like marbled steak, and that may not help matters.)

At twilight Bart tosses a line into water that seems to glow with fluorescence. Using a piece of pepperoni sausage as bait, he gets a bite within a couple minutes. But it doesn't move like a fish. My first thought is he has snagged a crocodile. I grab my digital camera and position myself. This might be our chance to photograph a crocodile; a surprisingly difficult task, even in croc-filled waters. But Bart's catch of the day turns out to be a creature not quite terrapin, not quite turtle, rather something called a trionyx, the Tyrse of the Egyptians, with a bite as vicious.

It reminds me of our first Omo expedition, when I tossed out a similar line and pulled in my catch to find a three-foot croc flailing at my feet. I cut the line and ran for my camera, but missed the shot as the croc scurried back to the river.

Mike Speaks follows Bart's turtle catch with a catfish, one with feelers rather than eyes to guide it through the ooze of the Tekeze. We had been reminiscing about the electric catfish I had caught on the Awash twenty-three years back, and wondered, since we were so dependent upon batteries this trip, if we ran low whether we could string together enough catfish to power the cameras and computers. Mike flashes a pixie smile at the suggestion, then touches the fish gingerly to check its charge. It's a normal catfish after all.

Tonight we're camped in what looks to be a flash-flood path, and it feels like rain. Usually such intermittent streambeds are safe, but all it takes is a strong storm up-canyon for things to change dramatically. In 1974 on the Omo River, SOBEK clients Barbara and Tony Batelle camped in a similar creekbed. Just after dark, a flash flood came roaring through, washing the tent and all its contents, including sleeping bags and clothing, into the river. Jim Slade waded out and retrieved all but one item: an ammo can, a small metal waterproof case used to carry personal effects. Inside was a Nikonos, an underwater camera, loaded with its mostly exposed roll of film.

The following year Jim was leading another Omo trip, and fifty miles downriver from the site of the flash flood, he saw a shiny object on a beach. He pulled over and found it was the lost ammo box. A bullet hole had pierced the can, probably from a local villager armed with an old Italian carbine. When Jim opened the box he found the camera intact.

At the end of the trip he mailed the camera back to the Batelles, and they developed the film. When it came back from the lab, all the photos were intact, including an amazing photograph of a Nile crocodile.

We make an early camp, and after setting up our satellite system we spend time answering some of the e-mail arrived from several countries, several schools, even a hospital. A Joseph P. Flanagan, DVM, from the Houston Zoo Animal Hospital, answered the question about the bright red eyeshine of the lidless crocodiles. I had decided the explanation was simple: the devil lurks within. But, I was eager to read the elucidation of a scientist. He explained that the reptilian eye has a reflective layer, *tapetum lucidum* ("bright carpet"), that lies behind the retina. The cells of the tapetum contain guanin crystals, which form a mirrorlike layer reflecting most of the incoming light back through the light receptor cells. In man and other animals without a reflective tapetum, the back of the eye is pigmented to absorb light once it passes the rods and cones. Humans, as day-vision animals, need to see sharp images, and a reflection from the back of the eye would blur the primary image. Sometimes, however, when a photo is taken of a person the "red-eye" effect shows. This is a reflection from the back of the eye and is red because of the blood vessels in the area. Some dogs and cats, like leopards, who have blue irises (subalbinotic), lack a tapetum lucidum, and the flashlight merely reflects the color of their eyes.

I don't quite understand his explanation, but am thrilled to see that through interaction via the Internet, knowledge is being transferred from a professional at a medical facility to our curious adventurers in a remote camp in the bottom of a gorge in Ethiopia.

David Roberts, a natural skeptic with a keen mind, comes back from a solo predinner hike, looks at all our high-tech gear whirring away, and pronounces, "This is not a wilderness." I counter that indeed, this is a wilderness, but this isn't a true wilderness experience.

Just as I'm uttering these words a sharp, black wind seems to come down the canyon like an avalanche. It whips through camp, spinning dust and sending unanchored items flying. "Grab the computers!" I yell, but the wind tears my words away and swallows them. Jonathan Chester had constructed the shelter for *Mungo Park* like a gardener's cloche, and so we are not prepared for a storm coming at us virtually horizontally. Great drops fall, some being blown through the tent and out the other side. The roof fills like a sail. Like storm-wracked mariners, we hang on to spars and rigging to prevent the whole thing from taking off. The bright blue UNHCR (UN High Commission for Refugees) tarp, which Pasquale bought in the Mercato for $40, flaps angrily, and the wind's nightstick begins to clobber our little camp. We rush to pack up as fast we can, trying to cover all the sensitive electronic gear, and as we tie the last baton, the full force of the storm hits like a firehose. The illusion that we are connected to Technolopolis, or are a part of civilization, is shattered. Our existence here is fragile, at the whim of Nature. This is wilderness.


*September 14*


This morning all our food crunches with sand, and when I put on my shirt it feels like emery cloth. We lost a few floppy discs to the abrasive wind, but all the other stuff works. After breakfast I continue my discussion with David on whether bringing the Internet to the wilderness is a knell for its death, or its salvation. We agree to disagree, and I continue to muse about the matter as the day unfolds.

When Ed Hillary spoke out against commercial climbs up Everest, his words rang with remorse for a season lost to time: "How thankful I was that I was active in a pioneering era when we established the route, carried the loads, all worked together for the ultimate objective. The way things are now, I don't think I would have bothered." Even before this expedition, the same was being said about the appearance of the Internet on remote expeditions: that it somehow diminishes the experience, and those who climbed a mountain or ran an unrun river before the advent of GPS's and connections to the web were the real pioneers, with a much more authentic adventure. Many have complained that Yosemite, the Grand Canyon, Kilimanjaro, and Victoria Falls have lost some transcendence because of their manufactured and commercial accessibility, and that the backcountry is no longer so if one can call for help on a cell phone. Some argue, however, it is elitist to deny others what you have experienced, to preserve in private sanctuary the epiphany that came with a special effort, time, and place. In my years as a river guide I escorted blind children, senior citizens, and paraplegics down the Colorado River, and I can testify that the transformational aspects of the experience were as vital for them as for the young, hearty, do-it-yourself expeditioneers. It may be less of a feat now to climb Everest than in 1953, what with better gear, communications technology, and routes well described, but is the adventure really less, for the guides, for the clients, who feel the same elation and sense of personal achievement on top?

Twenty-nine years ago Dr. Rod Nash published *Wilderness and the American Mind,* a seminal work that explored the evolution of thought and behavior toward wilderness in the New World, from the European settlers, who viewed nature as something to be subdued, to today's urban romantics, who revere places that have escaped the human tap. In November 1995 I invited Rod to a demonstration of TerraQuest and its "virtual expedition" to Antarctica, in which a team I put together explored the edges of the White Continent and uplinked daily to a website, sending digital images, sounds, and dispatches to the wired world, as well as answering e-mail and engaging in Live Chats. "This is the death of wilderness," Rod proclaimed after the demo. And in the summer of 1995, when I brought a couple of digital cameras and a satellite communications system on a float trip down the San Juan River in the Four Corners region, several members of the party told me they considered canceling when they heard of the high-tech element, because they felt it would compromise the wilderness they loved and remembered from past trips. One called my project "a spiritual invasion of time set aside to explore one's soul," and compared the Internet in the wilderness to "a brass band running through a cemetery." And now David Roberts is wondering aloud about all our digital equipage, and whether with our link to the outside we can honestly call ourselves a wilderness expedition. In all of these outcries there is a cast of elitism: that what was a special place, a powerful experience for a singular soul at a singular time was the right experience; and all else is somehow something less.

Besides, the articulation of the concept is wrong. Wilderness, which is nature unchanged by the hand of man, is not generally adversely affected by small groups of softly stepping people passing quickly through, whether they carry tents, paddles, Gore-Tex, or computers and phones. As long as they leave only footprints and kill only time, the wilderness pretty much remains as such. What does change is the notion of the "wilderness experience." In my mind, the only absolute wilderness experience is one in which you cut the tether and surrender yourself to the elements. There is no nexus to the world of humans and machines; you're as raw as a feral dog. As such, if I went naked into just beyond my backyard, into a grove of old growth, my wilderness experience would be more genuine than anyone standing on the roof of Everest, wrapped in layers of manufactured apparel. If you accept this notion, then the wilderness experience becomes one of degree. Is it more or less so if you use the gear and clothing available in 1953? Is it less so if you carry a radio for emergencies, or a cell phone? What if you have Internet access, but you don't read your e-mail?

In fact, the Internet is not the death of wilderness. It may be its savior.

With its power to break the tyranny of geography, to allow people anywhere in the world to virtually join expeditions to wild places through the portals of their computer screens, and its capacity for information exchange and communications, the Internet can be a more effective tool than anything yet devised to preserve the wilderness. The ledger is long of wilderness areas gone down because there wasn't a constituency to do battle. Arizona and Utah's Glen Canyon, entombed beneath one of the largest artificial lakes in the world, is the poster child. A basic problem is that wilderness areas are hard to get to, and the numbers who see them, experience them, fall in love with them, are too often too small to make a difference. That's where the Net could be the instrument of awareness, appreciation, and activism that no oversized nature book ever could. For the first time we can showcase the beauty and magic of a wild place to a global audience, and millions can participate in a journey through it, without ever breaking a branch or stepping on cryptobiotic soil. To a degree *National Geographic* has done this for over a century in the pages of its august journal; and Discovery and others have done this on television and video. But those were passive, receiver experiences, where a publisher, editor, or producer added his or her own vision to the primary experience, passing it along to a quiescent audience. Now, for the first time, a worldwide audience can receive the data unfiltered from the primary reporter, in all its raw and brutal honesty. And members of that same audience can become players, become active on some levels, participating in the experience by asking questions, suggesting ideas, and sharing information.

It is the most powerful intercommunications tool yet, one that tears down the media power towers, erases the information filters of middlemen, and allows anyone to jump into the thick of things and asseverate a voice and opinion. Those who have joined, through the web, our expedition down the Tekeze so far have "experienced" canyons grander than the Grand, seen and heard baboons, monkeys, and riverside flutes, and rode along as we ran rapids and were chased by crocodiles. And, they've learned that a scheme exists to dam this extraordinary wilderness. I'm convinced that when the time comes for a call to action to stop the drowning of the Tekeze, the patronage for preservation will be that much greater because of the web. A couple of years ago we lost a fight to save Chile's crown jewel of a wild river, the Bío-Bío, from the concrete slug of a private big dam; but then only a few thousand had ever seen the river. Now more people than visit Yosemite in August, regardless of wallet size, physical abilities, age, or weight, can be introduced to a faraway wilderness in a more immediate way, and that means that many more who can fall in love with a wild place, grasp its issues, and perhaps lend a hand when it needs many.

〰〰〰

The river gorge tightens as we churn along this morning, turning first to Cretaceous limestone, then sandstone. Slade calls lunch at a spot in the river I recognize from the aerial scout. A ship-sized rock stands foursquare in the river. In very high water it splits the river, but now the current swings around the left side, and we find a lovely, shaded place to spread our peanut butter, sardines, and butter cookies. The beach is full of belly marks from crocs, the dark, round beads of antelope spoor, and animal tracks. Mike thinks he can identify bushbuck, duiker, hyena, jackal, mongoose, and porcupine. As we're setting up the lunch table, David Roberts, whose most recent book, *In Search of the Old Ones,* is an examination of Anasazi cliff dwellings in the American southwest, spies what he believes is a man-made cave high up a cliff about a quarter mile downstream. In front of the cave is a bleached log that looks strategically placed. So, with great enthusiasm David starts trekking toward the cave, with me in tow. We scramble up a talus slope to what looks like a trail at the seam of the vertical canyon wall, and we traverse to the entrance of the shallow cave. In fact, it is natural, and the log looks like a large branch that fell from above. So, a bit dispirited, David picks his way back to the boats.

But David's disappointment doesn't last long. An hour downstream Mike Speaks, who has the clear eyes of an eagle, spots what appear to be cliff dwellings up on the eastern cliff face. Passing binoculars around, we each scrutinize the site. It looks to be about two hundred feet above the high-water level, an eight-foot wall closing off a niche in the cliff visible through an open doorway in the wall, which has wooden doorposts and lintel. What is this? A frontier redoubt? Religious site? Granary? Shifta hideout? The dwelling of an ancient anchorite? We pull in, and David kicks up the scree slope to a cobbled path, which leads to the travertine alcove, and this time, the find is genuine. It is certainly not ancient—in fact, it is a cluster of four currently used abodes, though we can find nobody around. It is like a *Twilight Zone* episode, when the protagonist walks into a town, and it looks as though the population disappeared moments before, coffee still boiling, radios still on. The little neighborhood appears to have a religious purpose. In one wall a charcoal angel is drawn, while on another there are words in Ge'ez, the ancient ecclesiastical language used only by priests and monks. Outside one abode a Coptic cross hangs on a necklace of amber. A hermitage? A hidden church? Some scholars believe there may be hundreds of hidden rock churches in northern Ethiopia yet seen by outsiders. It was a young Syrian named Frumentius—captured by pirates, then marooned on the Red Sea coast—who brought Christianity to Ethiopia in the fourth century. In his old age he retreated to Abba Salama ("father of peace"), a monastic church hewn from a cliff face in Tigre that was never seen by foreigners until the 1960s. Could this be such a place?

Inside the hovel there are personal effects, a goatskin bed, a shamma with a broad red edge, earthen crocks and vessels, and some pale, dried injera. In a small cave there is a skull that appears to be looking down on all who might venture here. David thinks he sees a number of sealed human-sized vaults that could be tombs. This feels like a sacred place, and we're not sure if we belong here. Jim Slade climbs to the uppermost hovel, pulls back the cotton curtain, and stoops inside. There he finds an earthen jar covered with a stone. When he lifts the lid, out swarm a cloud of wasps, and one stings him sharply on the hand, dispatching Slade out the cave and down the hill.

We seem to be making discoveries about which we know nothing.

This evening we set up the Inmarsat B satellite system, and all gather around to call John Kramer. High school friend to John Yost and myself, and a member of the first Awash expedition in 1973 along with George Fuller and Lew Greenwald, he has also shared many adventures with me in Africa, Alaska, New Guinea, Pakistan, and other places over the years. But now he has a family and a new job as a hydrogeologist and couldn't break away for this expedition. It tore him up. We make the call on the speakerphone so he can hear all of us, and we get Renee, his wife, who says John is out with the kids. We tell her from where we're calling, and she refuses to believe us, thinking it's another high school prank, for which we were all a little notorious. But we insist, and finally she shares with us that one hope John had expressed was that we would name something after him.

I miss John Kramer—his infectious energy and boundless enthusiasm have been untempered by time—and I wonder for a moment how the dynamics of this expedition would be different were he here. And I vow to meet his request, and name something special for his clear spirit.

# CHAPTER 26

# THIRST FOR TRUTH

"Someone who doesn't see the Tekeze is very unlucky"

—From a song from a village along the Tekeze River

*September 15*

The *dabo,* our Ethiopian bread, has turned green. That's about the most exciting thing that happened today. That, and it threatened to rain, which would have been welcome respite from the pounding heat. In a way, this is refreshing, if not earth-shattering news. One of the controversies that has been salted to the Internet pot is the notion that website reportage of expeditions might provoke field members to push themselves to do things they ordinarily wouldn't, both because of the potential size of the global audience, and because of the need to keep a site fresh and entertaining each day, like a live television show, or the audience will go away. The first point harks to the 1996 Everest disaster, wherein some post mortem ratiocinations suggested leader Scott Fischer acted, with fatal consequences, less than professionally to take advantage of the promotional opportunity of his company being covered via the World Wide Web. I can say with authority that is not the case here, and today is a day to prove it. Since landing in Africa events have been unfurling at a bracing pace, but with a lag now, there is no compulsion to create drama. No one yet has volunteered to swim with the crocodiles.

On the second point, that expedition correspondence might feel obligated to cater to an audience that expects high entertainment with each transmission, I can only comment that I believe there is an honesty with this medium never before available, and I find that exciting, and believe savvy web visitors will as well. The truth of expeditions is that they don't suffer from an overabundance of excitement—there are typically many boring minutes, hours, days. A documentary film will, after months of postproduction, present to the world the sensationally crafted highlights of an interminable time in the field. A magazine article distills and accents in the same way. But here, for those keen to follow and participate, the raw reality of what happens, or doesn't, on an expedition is accessible.

The lack of action affects perhaps the film crew most. Pressure is on to come back with the goods, wild water action that outdoes *The River Wild* or *Deliverance*. But it just isn't here, at least not yet, so the Turner crew spends time setting up long-lens shots at low angles by some of the riffles we run, trying to stretch and magnify them so they appear thunderous. But, the reality is, not much is happening on or off the river.

That said, I must confess that the day is not unengaging. We meet a Christian villager who has walked an hour down from the rim to see us, and he reports that the collection of dwellings we visited yesterday is a monastery. Part of the thrill of this exploration is that we have no guidebook, no monographs, no reports to reference—we're starting from scratch. Through an interpreter we hear an explanation from the Christian villager. It's up to us to assemble as much information as we can and then guess. The villager tells us the monk in the monastery is invisible, that the cave is sacred, and that visitors, unless in need of healing, are not allowed. Bart, who claims not to be superstitious, wonders if the invisible monk might have been the wasp that stung Slade, and several members nod with the possibility. All guides claim they aren't superstitious, but each has his own talisman. Greg Findley, one of the boatmen on this expedition, wears a spiral-carved wooden performance of Nyaminnyami, the river god of the Zambezi, around his neck. It has given him good luck in his six years of running the Zambezi, and he's watched rafts flip all around him as he's sailed upright through maelstroms, as though steered by an unseen rudder. He says he's scared to ever raft without his phylactery. Jonathan Chester wears a gold piton, given to him by a jeweler friend before climbing Annapurna III, and during the climb he survived two avalanches (including one in which five died), and he's worn it ever since.

I, of course, am not in any way superstitious, though as I write this a bracelet patterned with Coptic crosses dangles from my left wrist, as it has for twenty-three years. While on our first visit to Ethiopia we rented a doss-house in Addis Ababa where the guides would crash between trips. While there I became friends with our houseboy, Abba Wedaje, and we shared laughs and sometimes spiritual and political discussions, and even personal problems. He told me by trade he was a metalsmith. In Ethiopia, smiths are associated with demonic spirits. Although his skills were desired because of his ability to repair farm implements and weapons, he was thought to have descended from those who fashioned the nails used to crucify Jesus Christ. He was accused of having super-natural powers and was called a *buda,* a warlock with an evil eye. So, he took this job of houseboy to keep a low profile. After several months, on the eve of my departure back to the U.S., I was awakened in the middle of the night as I felt someone grabbing my wrist. My first instinct was to slug the intruder, as the week before a thief had climbed in through an open window, and was rebuffed when he stepped on Lew Greenwald. But, as I balled my fist I heard Abba's voice—"It is a gift." I turned on the light and saw he had clasped a handmade bracelet around my wrist. I started to pull it off when Abba sternly said, "*Yellum! Yellum!* [No! No!] It is a gift of good luck. I made it for you. If you wear it always, you will have good fortune. If you take it off . . ." His voice trailed as he disappeared from the room.

Whatever might be said, or not, about the lack of happenings, there's no denying we're in cowboy country, except for the sight of trees with elephant skin—the baobabs—and trees that resemble delicatessens festooned with salami, the so-called sausage trees. At camp George Fuller and I venture up one of the countless dry, sedimentary rock–walled side canyons, only to discover a few hundred yards up it is spilling clear water, which then sinks into the sand before achieving a confluence, as happens with several major rivers in Ethiopia, such as the Awash and the Wabe Shebele. A hundred yards farther, the canyon narrows and begins a sinuous dance, like a slot canyon in Utah. Travertine springs leak down the walls, feeding maidenhair ferns, and overhead a flock of fantailed ravens wheel with updrafts. As I stoop to splash my face in a small waterfall, I remind myself again that our eyes are likely the first to admire this place, a rare trice in an overcharted world. But then, perhaps there is a reason this vault has been denied. A few steps farther up the canyon a baboon hurls a rock at me, then another, as though a warning. We scramble another hundred feet and a spur-winged plover circles over my head, then with a high-pitched screech dives at my head, just brushing my hat. The tiny bird repositions then attacks again, then again, and again. Neither George nor I are superstitious, but we decide to turn back to camp, as it is getting close to dinner.

There we find a freshly baked loaf of bread, prepared by John Yost, to replace the dabo that has gone bad. And as I write the wind is beginning to sough through the trees, auguring something to write about.

## September 16

I awake to the ashen voice of Van Morrison, and it disorients me, brings me back to another time. This is one of the casualties of sleeping close to the kitchen. Pasquale is up and cruising, making coffee, hydrating the freeze-dried eggs, and rocking out with the Sports Walkman attached to tiny speakers.

Early in the day we pass a wispy, dreamy waterfall spilling down the western canyon wall. It looks like Vasey's Paradise, named for a botanist who was supposed to make John Wesley Powell's exploration of the Colorado in 1869, but he missed the trip. I decide to name this falls Kramer's Paradise, in honor of our friend who missed the trip.

In the afternoon we encounter two members of the Agaw tribe. An ethnic group considered to represent the oldest stratum of population in the Horn of Africa, the Agaw are part of a tribal confederation to which the Falashas, the once indigenous black Jews of Ethiopia, also belonged. One local legend says the Falashas are the lost tribe of Israel, and they, not Menelik I, fled the Holy Land with the Ark of the Covenant, and found safe haven by traveling up the Tekeze and settling in the highlands. Virtually all the Falashas now live in Israel, and I was almost a part of their movement. In late 1982 I received a call from Marvin Josephson, then head of the giant talent agency ICM, and also a friend whom I had taken down the Zambezi River on the first descent a year previous. He was active in the Jewish Defense League, and was helping to put together a secret airlift, called "Operation Moses," that planned to move twelve thousand Falasha refugees from Khartoum to safety in Tel Aviv. The Ethiopian Jews believe Moses married the daughter of an Ethiopian king, and then ruled in Ethiopia, and as such they chose the namesake for the return-to-Israel operation. The hard part was getting the Ethiopian Jews across the Ethiopian/Sudanese border, and one covert route was down the goat trails along the Tekeze, which Marvin had heard me talk about. Marvin called and asked my help, assuming I would be keen to assist in a noble project that would bring me to the waters of my dreams. I briefly considered the offer, and had much empathy for the Falashas, and all Ethiopians under the "Red Terror" pogroms of Mengistu, but I felt a refugee myself of Ethiopia and didn't think I could yet return. I had read that Mengistu's Soviet advisors and his East German–controlled Department of State Security were summarily executing 100 to 150 "anarchists, feudalists, exploiters of the people and counter-revolutionaries" each day in the capital's streets. It was reported the state-run radio regularly broadcast long lists of the people the government had shot. I didn't think I could handle that music. In 1983 when we had a ten-year celebration for SOBEK, Slade and I and his sixty-nine-year-old mother and a few clients and friends went to Egypt and sailed the Nile to Kom Ombo, the island of the SOBEK temple. For a second part of the anniversary celebration, there was an Awash trip that John Yost would lead. I had heard the abundant wildlife we had seen while first floating the Awash in 1973 was all gone, shot by some of the eighteen thousand Cuban troops the Russians had dispatched to Ethiopia to support Mengistu. The group flew from Cairo to Addis, but I couldn't get on the plane. It just didn't feel right. Not then. I wasn't ready to return to the land that had taken away my friend.

*September 17*

The people at the put-in of a river trip come from all calls and runs, but as river-time takes over, individual histories, professional titles, net worth, and wardrobes all fade from meaning. A separate culture emerges: a floating tribe, with its own mores, orders, and consciousness. Here the knowledge of the whereabouts of an aloe vera plant, used to treat Jim's wasp sting and my chapped lips, is more important than any mastery of money market funds. Here the ability to read a map or river currents is infinitely more valuable than the cunning to interpret real estate law.

Yet with the emergence of new personalities and pecking orders, a natural deterioration occurs as well. Jim Slade, a good friend since 1973, has a testy side not often displayed in places with windows and walls. A few days ago his toilet kit, with razor, contact lens solution, comb, and so on, went missing. When it turned up in Jackie's bag yesterday, Jim blew up and publicly chastised the only woman on the expedition, forbidding her to ever board his boat again.

Lewis Wheeler, the still photographer on the Turner team, tripped over a bucket at breakfast and splashed boiling water over his right leg.

The second-degree burns condemned him to our milkweed-rimmed camp for the day. Three others have been squirted with the acid from blister beetles; several are smarting from an array of insect bites and their backs look like the raised map of a mountainous country; sunburn and diarrhea are pandemic. And this morning Bart groused loudly that he wasn't getting his e-mail. But then, everyone's a bit choleric with the heat, and a caustic word here is forgotten there.

And John Yost has been in a peculiar mood the last couple days, immersing himself in a book on quantum physics and deriding the trip for lack of rapids and too much media. Though I have known John my whole adult life, and we've shared so many rites of passage and significant experiences, he's a shy man, and I will never know his interior monologues; they remain under lock and key in his neocortex. To a few people—David Roberts, Bill Anderson, the film camera, but not me—John expresses his belief that media influences the experience, making it less pristine, and he cites the Heisenberg uncertainty principle. John, who has never carried a camera or kept a diary, who abjures television and rarely sees a movie, talks on camera about his take on this experience to the Turner film team: "With media, you can't get into river time." He asserts that the way we ran the final Baro trip, with just four people, four paddles, and four pillow-sized bags, was the purest, and therefore best way to run a river. In fact, he has brought the same amount and type of gear on this trip as he had on the Baro: a couple T-shirts, a pair of shorts patched and bleached to the last thread, and a toothbrush. The only difference, he asserts, is that back then, as did all guides, he wore tennis shoes, and now, like all river guides, he wears Teva sandals.

Though I found the simplicity of the lower Baro expedition extremely satisfying, when I hear of John's musings about the "purity" of experience I disagree. Since Galileo, scientists have adopted the view that they were objective observers of the natural world. That was implicit in every aspect of their behavior, even the way they wrote scientific papers, saying things like "It was observed . . ." For three hundred years that impersonal quality was the hallmark of science, and became the accepted rule of media. Scientists, writers, and reporters claimed to be objective, with the observer having little or no influence on the results.

But in the twentieth century a different perspective evolved. Physicists now believe one cannot even measure a single subatomic particle without affecting it totally. If one inserts an instrument to measure a particle's position, its velocity will change. If the velocity is measured, its position will change. This basic truth became the Heisenberg uncertainty principle: that whatever you study (or report) you also change.

The Internet, with its power to communicate and allow global interaction in real-time, is the latest medium to be criticized as intrusive, as something whose presence influences and reshapes events, perhaps in a negative way. Jon Krakauer, author of the best-seller *Into Thin Air*, is a proponent of this theory. Yet his presence on Everest, as a celebrity author writing for *Outside* magazine, may have had as much to do with leaders doing foolishly fatal things to impress the media as the Internet.

If one accepts Heisenberg's uncertainty principle as it was intended, then the universe of cause and effect is too complex to distill. It could be argued that if the Everest team had true connectivity to the Internet (they didn't; rather, they phoned in reports at base camp via a satellite phone, and had no direct access to the Net), then they could have seen the bad weather headed their way, and they would have postponed the summit attempt and saved lives. Would the Tekeze expedition have been a "purer" experience without laptops and digital cameras? In my mind, no . . . it just would have been simpler.

All the while, the mysteries of this place continue to accumulate. At every alcove in the cliffs we spy, we wonder what might be within. The discovery of the monastery two days ago and David Roberts's enthusiasm with the possibility of archaeological or prehistoric finds have infected us.

To the north of camp, over a sharp rise, a crystal-shaped pinnacle points to a satellite. Eric and I decide to see if we can reach the diamond-shaped spire, and we set off up a tributary canyon. After an hour's walk, we slew up a side canyon, where we find two rock-and-stick shelters, seemingly too small for a human. We scramble up to the plateau level and begin the overland trek toward the monument. The sun here is like thunder made visible, and there is not a square inch of shade in any direction. After an hour, with the goal seeming no closer, Eric, an expert in wilderness rescue, suggests the wise course is to turn back and drop down into a creekbed canyon for the return to camp. The risk of heat exhaustion or dehydration is just too high.

So we begin the shadeless march back, and by the time we reach a canyon to drop into, we are low on water. The water bottle, or rather the water within it, assumes the importance of a syringe of insulin to a diabetic in a place like this. We are desperate to replenish it. My mouth becomes too dry for conversation, and so we abridge ourselves to point.

There was water in the tributary creek we climbed out of, and ahead there is a crack in the landscape, so I point there, assuming it will lead us back. After thirty minutes walking my ears are buzzing, eyes are stinging from brow salt, and my head whirls dizzily. I can feel the hot earth suck my body's moisture from underneath, while the sun does the same from above. The canyon we reach, however, is different from the one out of which we climbed. Since all canyons drain to the Tekeze, though, we aren't too worried; that is, until the canyon narrows to shoulder width and makes serpentine bends to a darker domain, closing out the sky above us. Fruit bats start to flutter and screech, and it suddenly seems as if we've entered an underworld.

A spilling wall at our feet, thirty feet sheer, smooth as monument stone, checks us. Eric has a rope, and we consider the option, but if we lower into the next chamber, we don't know if we can retreat should another drop present itself. If we become locked in here, the chances of anyone ever finding us in the enormous wasteland of the Tekeze valley seem slim to none. We seem to have wandered into a circle of Hell Dante didn't know about.

We retrace our steps back to the sun-cooked plateau, nursing our remaining drops of water, and seek another route home. We both admit we're feeling the effects of the enervating heat and need to suck some water soon. In twenty minutes Eric finds a traverse into another canyon, and we drop down between its lips to find a grottolike path filled with travertine deposits flowing over stones, stalactites, and other formations characteristic of limestone caves. Thankfully, there is also dripping water, to which we cup our hands and greedily drink. We replenish our water bottles and continue the journey back.

Back at camp, I step behind a bush for relief and see my urine running dark red, a sign of advanced dehydration. It's a reminder how delicate our systems are in this wilderness: another hour lost in the heat could have spun the adventure to an unpleasant end.

Around the campfire, talk turns to our schedule. We're progressing faster than expected and have the opportunity to exit the river earlier than planned. Some like this idea, eager to return to family and outside obligations, but David Roberts urges that we take this time to explore the side canyons and landscapes presented to us. He points out that we may even find something prehistoric, which does not seem outrageous, as paleoanthropoligist Donald Johanson discovered the radiometrically dated 3.6-million-year-old partial skeleton of an upright-walking, small-brained ape-woman he named Lucy (*Australopithecus afarensis*) in the next watershed over, on the Awash River. Scores of fossils have been un-earthed along the Awash since. Because of the rapid burial of artifacts by rising lakes and falling volcanic ash over the millennia, the fossils have been well preserved and offer windows into the world's prehistory. Pale-ontologists call it "the cradle of humankind," and "the most significant hunting ground for prehuman fossils ever discovered." It's not a stretch to believe the two-legged creatures wandering the Awash millions of years ago made the trek over the hill to the Tekeze. But for now, we de-cide to stick to the river and its own time and see what the future brings.

# CHAPTER 27

# THE TEMPLE OF
# THE ARK

"Like a river that twists, evades, hesitates through slow miles, and then leaps violently down over a succession of cataracts, man can be called a crisis animal. Crisis is the most powerful element in his definition."

—Loren Eiseley, *The Night Country, 1971*

*September 18*

This morning, crocs again become the motif. It seems funny, now, that in advance of this expedition we were afraid of the wrong things, mostly rapids. It's the crocs that scare us now. As we launch, three men with Old Testament faces tell us that just down from our camp there is a popular river ford where ten men were eaten in the past three years. One of them was the brother of one of our visitors, traveling to fetch his wife, who hailed from a village on the other side. The wife watched in horror as the half-ton croc crunched her mate like a biscuit.

A few minutes later, as we float past this crossing, two enormous crocodiles charge our rafts. John Yost hurls a rock at the first and makes a direct hit on its nose at fifty feet. John breaks out into his own version of the Macarena, a hand flip here, a hip swivel there, and laughs his signature nervous laugh, the one that sounds like a baby croc in trouble. This nose hit is a first in SOBEK history. But John's celebration is short-lived: the second croc charge is more serious. With its mouth open, teeth bared like a rabid dog's, it motors toward the bow. We launch a total of four croc rocks, and he ignores them all, submerging just a few feet from the raft. There is a long silence, like an iridescent glass blown so fine that a ripple would shatter it.

Then a *BANG* as the croc surfaces right under my feet, just below the inflated floor of the raft. The surprise impact almost knocks me out of the boat. The reptile emerges again a moment later an arm's reach away, between the oar blade and the gunwale. Slade fires two more rocks at its head, and the croc at last retreats.

With this latest attack the kayakers pull out of the river and ride on the back of one of the rafts. Everyone is a bit spooked. The river slows. There is a monumental stillness in the hot air, the world seems strung taut. Even the birds seem stifled, the white egrets feeding slowly, the goliath herons and yellow-billed storks standing still in the shallows like decorations on a Japanese screen. Even the murderous thrust of the heron's beak, the upward jerk of the head and the swallowing of the fish, seems labored, strained. As the day progresses, it gets hotter and hotter, up to 120 degrees Fahrenheit. Shut in between the black rocks, choked by the wadding of dust that lines every ledge and crack, we feel as if we are being cremated. The only wind comes from the noisy weaver birds flitting about their condominiums hanging over the river.

At last we come to a rapid worthy of the name, though as a Class III it is nothing that would break a sweat with this crowd. But as the film is important, and Thom Beers envisions this being the "nineties version of *Deliverance*," we need whitewater, so we spend the afternoon setting up cameras with low angles and preparing to run this sucker through its worst holes to give the show some wild water. Since Ted Turner and Bill Gates are the two financiers behind this expedition, we begin calling our enterprise "Bill and Ted's Excellent Adventure." And we name this first rapid Turner Falls.

As we progress downstream we find a few more rapids, more gambol than threat, however. At every one Slade sternly lectures the team about wearing life jackets at all times on the river, and some are beginning to resent his close cosseting, which they feel to be overfussy and unnecessary. When Slade is out of sight, several rip off their jackets in acts of defiance.

Slade calls an early camp at the most spectacular campsite yet, with a high butte just above camp around which is a Grand Canyonesque panorama, with a backdrop of the Ras Dashan massif to the northeast.

Almost everyone climbs up the butte to photograph and admire, and Jonathan Chester shoots a Surround Video here that becomes the hit of the *Mungo Park* site. But while everyone is soaking in the high view, David Roberts is poking around a smaller mesa a few hundred yards away upstream. What he finds is more remarkable than any rapid run.

In a flat area David discovers a ring of fist-sized rocks surrounding a flat stone etched with rock art and writings. There is what looks like a Maltese cross, or a sun symbol, and something resembling a divertissement, tic-tac-toe of the gods, or perhaps *gabadea,* a popular game throughout Africa using pebbles in a kind of checkers. I reach over and touch the drawings, drinking in through the pores of my fingers the antiquity of the abstract engravings. George Fuller notices the commotion on the mesa and climbs up, even though his foot is hurting once again. As an anthropologist he, too, is quite interested in the petroglyphs, and examines the patterns closely. He announces they may be random patterns made as local peoples sharpened their flint. He sees no patina on the rock etchings, and to him it means they are likely not old. An Agaw boy wearing a goatskin wrap shows up and tells Daniel, our interpreter, that one rectangular sketch is merely the blueprint for a sandal, while the sunlike symbol is the local icon for bread.

But as we step around the little plateau we find more drawings, more kiva-type formations, pieces of flint, dolerite arrowheads, smaller implements of translucent chalcedony, and cobbles roughly the size of eggs that seemed to be pounded and split so the edges were sharp enough to slice and cut. River settlements along the Blue Nile have been dated back a quarter million years, and the Tekeze, the first major tributary encountered when traveling up the Nile from Egypt (the Blue Nile is second), would seem a natural ancient migration path to the fertile highlands. When Jim Slade and I found similar arrowheads and pottery shards, even an intact vessel, on the Blue Nile in 1974, I took it back to the Institute of Ethiopian Studies in Addis Ababa. A year later the curator wrote to say it was akin to early Neolithic material of about 3000 B.C. in the Khartoum area, though he had no way of accurately dating what we brought in. Chris Haines, on the commercial Tekeze expedition just behind us, found a stone chopper tool he believes might have been used by *Homo erectus* or other early peoples, hundreds of thousands of years ago. And a few months after this expedition a group of scientists in the nearby Gona region of Ethiopia found what they claimed to be the oldest known objects made by human ancestors, tools crafted more than 2.5 million years ago.

So, there is a fundamental problem with our discovery. I want to believe we have found a mystical exhibition in the tumbled gallery of fractured boulders and flat rocks. David wants to believe we have unearthed evidence of an African Anasazi, perhaps Paleolithic testimony of the earliest settlements in Ethiopia—it would be a significant find; yet for all we know this could be a contemporary Saturday marketplace with a view. Just before we leave a teenager tells Daniel the art was created by his friends as doodles just a few days before.

At lunch a few miles downstream we take a long respite from the heat, lingering over the *kolo* (grilled barley and peanuts), sardines, salami, cheese, and the thick chocolate spread called Nutella, the most popular lunch item, something John Yost calls "orgasm in a jar." We sit beneath the scant shade of an acacia and sip Tekeze punch, made with river water that is 80 degrees, buzzing with silt, and no doubt heavily laced with crocodile scat and pee, and stinking of the iodine we mix in to "purify" it. But for us, it tastes like fine wine.

Bob Poole, who lives in Sun Valley, Idaho, introduces a game he calls the Selway Rock Toss, in which contestants crouch with hands behind their butts holding a softball-sized rock, then hurl it for distance through the knees. This becomes quite the contest, and I hold the record early on for all of five minutes but am quickly outclassed. It boils down to a battle between Bart and Pasquale, and Pasquale takes the prize.

An easygoing discussion takes place about remoteness, and whether there is such a thing in this day and age. A couple years ago I shared a writers' workshop panel with author Jeff Greenwald. During the discussion he asserted there was no place left on the planet one couldn't get to within twenty-four hours, and as such there is no true remoteness left on the planet. I challenged him, and said remoteness often has to do with birthright and choices available therein, and conjectured that if he attempted to travel round the world without using plane transportation he would discover this a truth. He took my dare, and spent the next year circumnavigating the globe by foot, horse, mule, ship, bus, and other old-fashioned means, and the resulting book, *The Size of the World,* is a tribute to remoteness in the twentieth century. To bring home the point, I ask, through Daniel, a young Agaw man who wandered into our lunch spot, if he knows the world beyond the Tekeze valley. He says he has spent his whole life between the tributary upstream and the one downstream, and fears that as we venture downstream we are going to the edge of the earth. To him the world is flat, and finite. I ask him if he has ever heard of Mohammed Ali, Michael Jackson, or Michael Jordan. He has not, and I rest my case. We are in a remote place.

All this is belied just eight miles downstream. We pass beneath the cable I had seen on the aerial scout, a nexus to the outside world. As the canyon walls on both sides dip here, we're told this has been a traditional crossing for hundreds of years, and was the ford for the infamous Ethiopian Exodus of 1862. A false prophet, a monk from Dambya named Abba Mahari, persuaded thousands of his people to leave Ethiopia en masse for the Promised Land. He vowed that the miracles of the Exodus would recur for them. They crossed the Tekeze, and trekked to Axum, where they circled the Christian holy city that they maintained held the Ark of the Covenant. They believed they would be given the Ark to return it to Israel, but instead were stoned and beaten. They were stalemated, and those who didn't die from violence, hunger, or malaria returned to their villages in shame. Now, a rusty set of cables marks the crossing. We're told they were attached during the civil war as a way to get rebel troops and guns across the Tekeze. The men working the pulley are sporting Afros the likes of which I haven't seen since the Shaft movies, and several ask us for quinine, a traditional cure for malaria. They tell us many died from crocodiles during the war, many from guns and land mines, but ultimately more from malaria, which is extremely bad at the bottom of this gorge. It reminds us to take our 250-mg tab of Lariam, the malaria prophylactic of choice, and we ask one another if we've remembered. Only John Yost doesn't answer. He decided he was going the "pure" route this trip, and chooses not to take any antimalarials. And for a moment I imagine John in a bedroom with his roommate Dave Bohn, dying of malaria, and wonder how that changed my friend.

*September 19*

Like an ancient tool cutting through the bone of the earth, we're slicing through the ages. When we began the journey the river walls were basalt: the volcanic layer from the Tertiary and Quaternary periods, perhaps sixty million years old, that covers much of the highland regions of East Africa and forms the upper crust of the Great Rift Valley, the spectacular graben running right down the middle of the country like a grave. For days we wound down through 1,500 vertical feet of Vulcan's rock until we reached a band of fluted limestone, looking like broken Butterfingers, left from some long-ago sea. Then we spilled through a vertical half mile of Mesozoic-era sandstone, a strata that seemed to emanate soft light and was formed perhaps two hundred million years ago.

Today the walls at river level turn dark and hard, exposing another page in this living textbook. We ride into metamorphic shales, Precambrian stone six hundred million years old. This was a violent place back then, and evidence is everywhere. The landscape is bent, fractured, and torn; it has folds and faults, monoclines and synclines, dikes, sills, schist, all hundreds of millions of years old.

Now, at camp, we're even deeper in time. The gorge is steep and narrow, the rock is granitic, the core of the earth; and we can't cut much deeper without coming out the other side. Pasquale Scaturro, the sole geologist on the trip, sums it up: "I'm really turned on by this place."

After only an hour's float this morning, I spot a cobbled wall set a short way up the eastern bank. Downstream one hundred yards is what looks, to my unpracticed eye, like an Anasazi shelter. Searching farther we can see more masonry deep in an entering gully. Slade pulls over and hikes to the wall. He finds only a support system for a path, which he follows. He reports the path ends at a travertine spring just around the corner.

Curiosity piqued, several of us scale up to the shelter and crouch through an oven-sized door. A scant tangle of dead branches form the skeleton of a roof, and a yard-high pile of slate forms what appears to be an altar. But there is nothing else; no personal effects, no evidence of recent use. It looks like a sacrificial stone out of a legend.

While David Roberts climbs higher to explore the upper structures, the rest of us wait for two boys to navigate across the river on their state-of-the-art Tekeze raft, a native *jendie,* two stunted logs loosely strapped together. They kick their way over with powerful leg strokes, all the while ululating and slapping the water to scare away the crocodiles. With a current of three miles an hour or more, they pass down the river for several hundred yards in the course of getting across. The boys, black and dripping, shaking their hands like mop ends, climb to where we are exploring, and seem eager to explain the architectural mystery. Daniel Mehari is game to translate.

The structure is apparently a chancel for Timkat, the annual ceremony of Epiphany and the most important festival in the Ethiopian Orthodox Church. As part of the ritual, replicas of the Ark of the Covenant are wrapped in rich brocades and carried in procession to a holy altar. The boys tell us all the villages in the region congregate here on the eve of the January festival, and throughout the rest of the year those who are sick use the mineral springs for healing.

The altar, they tell us, is where the Ark of the Covenant is placed during the ceremony, carried from the nearby church of Beta Maryam. I ask the boys if the ark brought here each January is the real one, and they reply, "Of course."

It seems to me as likely that the true Ark is isolated here in the Tekeze Gorge as anywhere. As I take a closer look at the altar, I see it is made of a steep pile of slabs of gray slate, perhaps five hundred pieces in all. I snatch a small shinglelike piece, which I will take home and give to Michael Kinsley in honor of his new magazine, *Slate*. But, to make sure I don't offend the gods, I leave behind 100 birr and a package of dried fruit.

As we are examining the modest altar, David Roberts is exploring the higher ground, and he returns to our group with eyes wide and note-book filled:

From river level we could see stone structures 200 feet up, browing our horizon. I scrambled up a nasty, loose gully to emerge on a small grass shelf that might once have been a field. A continuous wall, four feet high and 50 feet long, made of slate flagstones cunningly fitted together without mortar, terraced the lower edge of the fallow shelf. But in the middle of the "field" stood a puzzling structure: a semicircular dwelling of the same neatly dry-laid stones, for all the world like an Anasazi kiva (though here in Ethiopia, its function must be utterly different from the ceremonial chambers of the Southwest).

Looking up, I saw yet another set of walls, another 200 feet above. It took a devious scramble to reach them. I found a series of strange, half-collapsed walls and rooms stretched along a knife-edged ridge; not the sort of place most people would choose to live! And farther along this airy architecture, I found a small panel of exquisitely drawn figures, scratched in pencil-thin lines on orange bedrock shale. Four or five eerie human faces had the bug eyes and horrified open mouths of Munch's "The Scream." One figure hung upside down (in Australian aboriginal art, a death hex, but it could mean anything here). Another had an upright torso with an inverted head. The whole panel resonated something pagan and ominous.

I wanted desperately to linger and look for more of this art, but the others down at the boats were getting impatient. The boys who had told Richard all about the chancel knew nothing about the high structures or the engravings on the orange schist.

Not a half mile downstream, we pass into another hot zone, where the dust is fine and the land parched. The beetling gorge is ovenlike and cooks us to the bone. The setting contrasts from the start of the expedition, where we were wrapped in greenery, and waterfalls squabbled from every ravine and breach. As if to punctuate this transition, a small herd of camels appears on the eastern bank, a breed we never anticipated on this journey. They flutter their large lips at us and then stretch their necks down to drink in long, steady gulps.

At a western bend, we come upon a large herd of piebald goats and sheep, and John Yost insists we pull over. As the senior camp cook, John has led the charge to escape from our freeze-dried repertoire, and within minutes he's negotiating for a white-fleeced yearling sheep for 170 birr (about $35). The owners agree to terms, then push the animal, wheelbarrow fashion on its forelegs to a slaughtering bench in the shade. Its hind leg tied to the tree trunk, the animal, from the noise it makes, seems well aware of its fate. It kicks and bicycles and pops its eyes. With John's river knife they slit its throat with the precision of surgeons, silencing its anguished bleats. Its long, gory dewlap hanging loose, the animal collapses on its knees as if at prayer, and then folds into meat.

Now, at camp, after an hour's preparation by John, we're supping on garlic lamb stew, freshest meal in a fortnight. We slip to sleep with bellies full, and a pot of dreams to pursue tomorrow.

# CHAPTER 28

# THE HOT ZONE

"One generation passeth away, and another generation cometh; but the earth abideth for ever."

—Ecclesiastes 1:4

*September 20*

The river creams along at a steady five miles per hour now, which is a good thing, as with this heat the trip would be unbearable without the breeze the river creates. The river corridor widens and narrows and opens back again to reveal terraced temples against the sky, sculpted by wind and water from the rock laid down millions of years ago. On one wall there are classical columns and cornices composed of horizontal slabs that remind me of Frank Lloyd Wright's prairie houses; on another wall there are schists that resemble Henry Moore sculptures, polished like black marble by the palms of the sweeping water. In one canyon the walls have thin, colorful beds that bend sinuously in every direction. "It's like somebody's drug fantasy on canvas. I've never seen anything like it in nature before," John offers.

As we ride the river's back, I regret this all seems so transitory. On the silty riverbank a man with a whip lashes at his slow-moving ox as it drags a single-shafted wooden plough. The twisted yoke and beam, culminating in a short iron point, scratching the alluvial topsoil for a millet planting resembles a scene from an Egyptian fresco. The shriveled trees here look as if they are the rags of time, wrung in the mangle of drought, shrunk and discolored by the sun. But in the crook of one bleached and sapless tree there is a bush flamed with yellow flowers, like sunshine caught in a net. Passing a dark, polished, sensuous-looking wall laced with white-flowering, sweet-scented lianas, I feel I want to arrest everything for a moment or two. This is a new feeling, as in the past I always wanted to move, to keep going, to escape. Always I've sought the broad view, the long lens, but I see the river can bring its passenger closer to the details of life. Now I want a hundred lidless eyes to study each gorgeous detail. Now my heart wants to stop, and to know this place where time seems honest and primitive. What I will be left with is some fractured memories, perhaps a scar or two, an album of photos, a website, and a movie, in which all that happens in these weeks, and over the years it took to get here, will be reduced to perhaps fifty minutes.

## September 21

A boy with legs so long he walks like a giraffe leads a detachment of our expedition to the village of Meda. As we climb up out of the great canyon, through high, sharp elephant grass, the first signs of distant hillside cultivation and columns of blue smoke betoken the presence of farmers. We emerge from the tall grasses, then hike over broken, ploughed land. As we walk, the silence is broken only by the unmelodious clinking of several water bottles attached to my pack. The village rests on several hills, yet the mountains a day's walk away make the Rockies look like a bread board. The phantasmagoric spires and towers of the Simiens could be the artist's inspiration for the Emerald City or a petrified version of a retro-future metropolis from a Ridley Scott storyboard. And they stretch to eternity, seeming not so much to end as to vanish in the blue haze. Between two freestanding phallic spires, a thin waterfall plummets. Distances and measurements are impossible to calculate, but the falls looks to be higher than Venezuela's Angel Falls, at three thousand feet reputedly the world's highest.

Pasquale Scaturro, Everest veteran and solo climber of Aconcagua, set out from camp alone, in sandals, after most of the rest of us had laced our boots and started up the canyon rampart. Yet when I finally step over the last rise to the village, the first face I see is Pasquale's. He must have raced up the sheer canyon wall to arrive ahead of us. While waiting for us, he was escorted around the village and taken to a rock house where a man lay in sickness. With his rudimentary grasp of Amharic, Pasquale listened to descriptions of the illness and then offered to return to the rafts to fetch some antibiotics and vermifuge. But then we show up, and he gives us the tour along the village paths filled with streams of loosely superintended animals.

Pasquale hustles me over to Beta Maryam on the edge of town, the church from whence the Ark is supposedly brought to the altar at the hot springs upstream during the annual Timkat celebration. The humble tabernacle is backdropped by the granite cores of extinct volcanoes, sprouting like vast gray cactuses in the sky. The setting makes me drunk on the view. I walk into the first circular keep; nobody is there. Then to the circular slate-roofed main church, the k'ene mahlet. A slender, white-bearded man with the heavy beak of a parrot is guarding the padlocked entrance. I ask him to open the door. A pair of eyes occluded with cataracts look at me as though I were a ghost, or some form of theophany. To our great surprise he goes ahead and unlocks the church.

We step inside and in the dim light walk around the sanctuary. The atmosphere is musty, the air warm, like the exhalation of some giant beast. The ecclesiastical paintings within are peeling with damp and decay. In the paintings Christ and his Ethiopian disciples are depicted as white men, and they are attended by the half-naked figures of female saints. When I get to the curtain that shields the Ark of the Covenant from the gaze of laity, I ask the priest if he will show me what lies behind. He looks hard at me, and must think I am from a holier world, and he briefly pulls back the curtain. But another door, a locked one, sits behind, blocking entrance to the mak'das, the innermost sanctum. Suddenly there is commotion outside, and the priest rushes out. There is yelling and angry banter. Then the priest rushes into the chamber, face pinched and red. He grabs my sleeve and pulls me outside, where several richly robed priests wave prayer sticks at me. They usher me out of the compound, and I stop at the entrance and demand to ask a question. By this time Daniel has rushed over to the fuss and offers to translate. I ask the priests if I can pay them to let me see the tabot.

They wait for a translation, then simultaneously shake heads no, and start to push me away. I stop and have Daniel ask if I offer a million birr, more money than the village will ever see in several generations, to the priests, will they let me open the final door? But my offer falls on ears tuned only to the rhythms of tradition. Without a pause they say, "Yellum! Yellum!" No amount of money would allow me to look within. And they send me down the path.

The Ark of the Covenant, if legends are true, contains things money cannot buy. Throughout history it has been used to turn back and destroy invading armies, and just plain bad people. Even in modern times. Some believe the Ark was used when Menelik II defeated the Italian invasion in 1896 in the most notable victory of an African over a European army since the time of Hannibal. It is true the Nazis sent expeditions in search of the Ark, believing it would help them win the war. Some even theorize the Ark may have been used by the ragtag TPLF (Tigre People's Liberation Front) in their overwhelming of the largest army in Africa, Mengistu's 600,000-strong government forces, in Tigre in 1989, and if so, it may have been carried down the Tekeze, through Meda, which was the scene of heavy fighting and much bloodshed, and a place where the Dergue was turned back.

Of course, we would never see the Ark of the Covenant. Was there true value in gazing on the relic? Or was the worth in the mystery, the power of its myth, and the hold it exercises upon human imaginations in countless lands and through the centuries? These were the enduring things—the magic and the imaginings, the inspiration and hope. Better to hold fast to them than to physical prizes; better to aspire and win nothing than to succeed and later be ashamed, or melted to oblivion by the powers of the Ark.

Pasquale takes us to a cool, spacious tukul set in its own palisaded yard on the other side of the village. The walls of this house are made of slabs of slate cemented with wattle and daub and framed with two concentric rings of posts, pierced by two staggered doorways. Goats and chickens pick their way in and out, mainly in the narrow space between the two rings. Inside are four massive wooden pillars supporting the dark thatch above. Across the back is stretched a partition of sackcloth, over which from time to time a shy child peeps. Stools, gourds, and large clay dishes lay scattered about. A woman squats by a stone hearth, making coffee over a flat-cake dung fire. We are waved in and sit on the hard, mud floor, as it is more comfortable than the stools.

We rinse our hands ceremonially as she pours water over them into a bowl. It is impossible not to notice her shoulder blades, upon which are rows of small cicatrices, painfully made by rubbing salt or earth into small cuts. She bends into a crude cupboard and produces several tiny cups, flower-patterned and handleless, which she then fills with fresh coffee. With pleasurable anticipation I raise mine to my blistered lips. We're all thirsty. I take a sip and spit it out in a hose. The coffee is heavily salted, done supposedly to bring out the coffee flavor, but for me it does the opposite.

Then a fellow villager peeks in and asks if we would care to attend a funeral. The sick man Pasquale had met earlier just passed away.

At almost the same moment, from the other side of the village, a soft cadenced chanting and drumming rises up—an eldritch, heart-stopping resonance that is at first so faint and so muted that I can barely make it out.

We thank our host for the coffee, and walk to the edge of Meda to join a funeral procession in progress. (With no refrigeration or preservation capabilities, burials take place quickly.) We learn the dead man was about forty years old, had been a freedom fighter with the TPLF for five years, and had returned to Meda a hero. A week ago he was stricken, but there are no clinics or medical assistance within a three-day walk. Now he lay on a funeral bier, a miniature four-poster bed, wrapped in white cotton.

A group of holy men in tattered vestments stand by holding ceremonial umbrellas, fringed at the edges and decorated with crosses, crescent moons, and other sidereal objects. Some are carrying long processional staves, while still others are waving wooden prayer beads. The odor of frankincense wafts from a smoking censer suspended in a fine net of silver chain, waved drowsily by one priest as another reads Ge'ez scriptures from a huge book of goatskin parchment. Another man blows a crude, single-note tin trumpet with a sound so evocative it causes the hairs at the nape of my neck to prickle and stand erect. Another man, wrapped in a homespun tunic and jodhpurs, is striking the stretched skin of a kebero with a quiet but insistent beat. Involuntarily, I feel my own body responding to the rhythm. A few yards down the path the rest of the village keens and wails like ambulances. Children press their hands together like butterfly wings. Every few minutes the women parade in a sobbing treble circle; then the men do the same.

As the procession moves down the path, I walk alongside a middle-aged woman in a black mantilla. In midstride, without warning, she lets out a guttural moan, then collapses like a kicked tent into a dead faint. As Eric and I push through the throngs of women to help, she starts to jerk and twitch, her eyelids fluttering. Eric splashes water on her face and tries to make her drink, but for long minutes she remains in a seizure state. When she comes around, still in a daze, the other women lift her to her feet and usher her onward in the cortege.

The funeral march continues, stopping in the shade of parasol-shaped thorn trees every few minutes for scripture readings and more antiphonal chanting. The word spreads quickly: people from nearby villages begin to file into line to pay homage. The crowd seethes and eddies like a foaming sea. The wood-posted bier is lifted over a flagstone fence to the church, forbidden to women. With a logic truly Abyssinian, only men are allowed to enter Beta Maryam, the church of the Virgin Mary. Final rituals are performed. Then the body is carried to a cemetery, lowered into a shallow grave, and covered with slate stones. Finally, the crowd debouches into a square in front of the church and pays respects to the surviving father and brothers (we donate 50 birr to the brother who would care for the surviving children). Then ninety liters of sorghum tella are passed around.

Sitting in the scant shade of an acacia after the conventicle, I can't help but compare what we witnessed with the Western version. In the West public pieties, the rituals by which the living seek to comfort themselves, obscure the truth about the dead and the act of dying, and the social connections to such. Death in this part of Africa comes frequently and publicly. What might in the Western world have been long, complex obsequies are starkly simplified here. There seems such a deep sense of community, of collective grief and purging. Everyone shares the sorrow and anguish; there is no effort to disguise the raw reality and emotion of the moment. It is an emotional moment for me, too: I think of my own father and his surgery.

I had decided that if something happened to my father while I was on this journey, I didn't want to know. I asked loved ones not to contact me, as though this were a remote expedition a century ago, or even a year ago. If he were to die, and I missed the funeral, I hoped it would be well attended, but watching today's ceremonies, I wondered. Like most Americans, my father moved many times throughout his life, made friends in many places. But now he lives in a desert condominium, and many of his neighbors have never met him. More families live in my father's complex than in the village of Meda, but there is no similar sense of community; there will be no geographical union of sentiment when he passes. The news, and the sympathy, will instead be spread along the path of people he has touched around the country, around the world; a network made up of individuals who share not every day in common, only a common confluence with a man.

Before leaving, we are invited into another home. One woman hands out fresh eggs. "Sinteno? [how much?]" I ask, and try to pass her some birr, but she refuses. Another hands out beakers of sour tella. I know better this time, and palm the drink, pretending to sip. Eric is feeling bold and quaffs the local beer.

As we are leaving the village, a small woman breaks from the ranks of mourners and runs to us. On her back is a syrupy-eyed, skinny child who looks about six months old, though the woman says he is three years old. She makes gestures suggesting a stomach problem. Pasquale takes pity on the woman and begins to ask a series of questions about her son's conditions. The conversation continues for quite some time. I had traveled with Pasquale around Ethiopia and was impressed with his enormous charity and concern for the well-being of those who cross his path. In every city and one-story town it seemed there was someone who was Pasquale's friend and whom Pasquale had helped by buying a bicycle, setting up a business or school, or sending money or anodynes. I hike back with Pasquale to camp, where he rifles the medical kit and pulls out small dosages of Septra, Cipro, and Erythromycin and gives them to a Meda villager who had walked with us to the river, along with instructions on giving small doses to the child. Then he asks the villager for his own address, to send a thank-you gift for his efforts. But the villager says nobody in Meda has ever received a letter, and there are no addresses. So Pasquale writes down the man's name, and the name of his father, and his grandfather, and promises to mail something to the nearest administrative district. Perhaps eventually, proper recognition for a random act of kindness will be delivered.

It rains hard all night, and I huddle beneath a tarp covering the computer, satellite gear, and the blue folding tables and chairs that make the *Mungo* camp. Several villagers from Meda who hiked down to visit crawl in with me. With no prophylactics or cures, the villagers risk malaria and other river-borne diseases whenever they leave the cool highlands plateau, but our presence here is just too bizarre to ignore.

CHAPTER 29

# LORDS OF THE FLIES

"You were once wild here. Don't let them tame you."

—Isadora Duncan

*September 22*

With the morning, the tarp is pulled back, and camp looks as new and shiny as wet paint. Jonathan Chester fires up his laptop and begins to acquire the digital photos he took the day before. Several are of shots of the villagers with us, and they scream and holler and laugh like fast water when their images scroll on the liquid-crystal screen.

George is feeling peppy today, and as a breakfast of Yost toast is being battered, he grabs a climbing rope and maunders off down the beach hung with slings, lifelines, bright new *jumars,* and daisy chains of carabiners to a seventy-five-foot-high travertine natural bridge. He climbs up the back side, anchors his rope, and begins to jumar down rock that looks like the inside of a sugared Easter egg into a fissure. I come across George hanging like a fruit bat, and yell up as to what he's doing: "You must be feeling better—you look ten feet off the ground." "Actually, about forty feet," George, the literalist, calls back. He yells down he's looking for sand flies in the cracks and crannies, but I know he's just crazy, doing it for the fun.

After breakfast, the stress that comes from long trips in the field flares a bit, and little things take on undue importance and severity. We have a rigid regimen for cleaning utensils and dinnerware, to maintain as much as possible good health in a place inherently unhealthy. Every plate and cup must be dipped in a prewash bucket, then a heated wash bucket, then a rinse, and finally a Clorox-treated bucket. When one of the film crew refuses to adhere to the system, a shouting match ensues with Greg Findley, the kitchen master. When it almost escalates into a fight, Greg grabs the Clorox bucket and pours it over the filmmaker's head, whose face twists into the smile of a camel thief. And that douses the tension, for now.

There are days on the river that have a deeper texture. This is a day of birds. We see Goliath herons and soaring fish eagles, Technicolor hummingbirds and kingfishers, sand martins and pied wagtails, carmine bee-eaters and red-winged starlings with feet curled like commas. Bart, one of his cameras permanently to his face, gyrates on his rowing seat, snapping hungrily away. The sky has a nacreous quality, like the inside of a shell, and it portends rougher weather.

We also hit some real rapids, which thrills us all, perhaps most especially the film team. I take the oars at a couple. On the Zambezi there is a belief that if a hammerkop flies in front of a boat, it will flip in the next rapid, and more often than not, it is true. Now a well-headdressed hammerkop draws its wings just over my brow. Signs and omens notwithstanding, I'm ineluctably drawn to the turbulence. As I slide down the long tongue, I break out in shouts of exultation. Decades shed, and I feel like I'm twenty-two. This is the way the world was meant to be—everything else is a mistake! Spreading streamers of spray seem to hover in the air above me like the burst of a Fourth of July rocket, and I feel the delicious shock of inundation. The raft shudders from the impact of each successive wave, and recovers just in time to meet the next one, wham, wham, wham. All I can see between drenchings is a crazy kaleidoscope of whitewater, black cliffs, and blue sky. It's that giddy, dangerous feeling, as though it is late at night on a back road with a logging truck bearing down. Running rapids is the physical expression of intellectual passion. It feels great to be pitching through whitewater in Africa again. I wish Lew were here to share this moment with me. I wish my father could see me now. At the eddy below, I step out of the raft onto the shingled beach to wait for the other rafts to follow. The stones at my feet are bright and smoothed by a million years of river flow. I pluck one rounded rock, a polished piece of white quartz the shape of a smile, off the beach and drop it in my pocket.

In the afternoon the river reverts to a fast, brimming smooth ride, and we seem but pilgrims meandering toward the Grail. Terraces of alternating scrub and cliff soar above us like an opulent wedding cake. We pass some villagers on the left bank. *"Tanastalin!"* I shout (Amharic for "hello"). Silence. *"Salaam alaykum,"* I try. Then one boy sets off running down a long spur to the river. He speeds along the beach and along a limestone shelf, and, astonishingly, he keeps pace with us as we move quietly along, a successor to Abebe Bikila, the Ethiopian marathon runner who won gold medals in the 1960 and 1964 Olympics. He causes a tiny, irrational crumb of alarm, although he is alone and carrying only a slender spear tipped with a point of iron. Suddenly, he stops, and favors us with an inscrutable stare as we slip out of his life.

*September 23*

I awake to the upending whooping distinctive to Mike Speaks when the first pot of coffee has boiled, and to the local villagers when they yell to one another across the river. The news of our approach is being passed on: "Ferenji are coming down the Tekeze." Although we might outpace shifta, we cannot escape being picked up by this Ethiopian Distant Early Warning System. Unseen eyes watch us all the time, and at every bend we are anticipated.

Now there is the sound of birds, their dainty songs complicit with the river. Then a shot shatters the birdsong from the western bank. I spring up and see Jonathan Chester scrambling out of his tent looking to the source of the noise.

My first thought is shifta firing at camp, but we haven't seen an AK-47 in days. Mike may have furthered the illusion by standing guard on his raft, his camera monopod strategically slung over his shoulder to appear more menacing than it was. I creep over to Mike, who says the sound was the snap of a whip made by a villager moving his goats.

Later George Fuller tells me that of all the ways to die on an African river trip, a shifta shot is his preferred, "as long as he's a good shot"— quick and easy, unlike most of the diseases with which George is so well acquainted. And it fits into George's neo-uber-existentialist cosmology: shifta happens.

A few hours downstream, we hear a whistling, and see a rock hyrax scrambling over the granite. As anyone who has visited backfield Africa knows, the rock hyrax is the closest living relative to the elephant, though it looks like a furry loaf of bread with feet. I am enthused to see the elusive mammal, another to add to the list. George, though, is dismayed.

He explains that rodents and rock hyrax are reservoir hosts for a particularly vile disease called leishmaniasis. The disease is transmitted to humans by biting sand flies. Kala-azar, the visceral form of leishmaniasis, is a slow, chronic disease characterized by fever, weight loss, engorgement of the spleen and liver, and the development of immune deficiencies, just as with AIDS. Typically it takes eighteen months from the sand fly bite to death, and unknown numbers of Ethiopians are infected.

George studied kala-azar, as well as schistosomiasis and other parasitic and insect-borne diseases, along the Lower Tekeze, near the Sudanese border, from 1972 to 1976. What he saw there convinced him that this river expedition was a bad idea. Nobody lives at the bottom of the Tekeze. Those accustomed to the bright horizons of the plateau fear to go down to the place they regard with superstitious awe, and malaria is the chief reason. But to villagers, one fever is like another. George now conjectures that perhaps the man who died in the village of Meda died of kala-azar, as he had spent time as a rebel in the Tigre People's Liberation Front in the belly of the Tekeze.

The experience at Meda stays with us. Eric Magneson has the I-drank-tella-in-the-village blues and has been vomiting throughout the day. John Yost and Lewis Wheeler both have eye infections, as though they saw too much.

With all the incumbent dangers on this river, I wonder what Daniel Mehari, our interpreter, feels about the journey. He has gone with the flow since we began, never a word of complaint or concern, although he told me later, "When I first came here I was so scared. I imagined so much danger. My wife was afraid of malaria and asked how I could go to a place like this. I am very close to my six-year-old son, and he was worried for me. But now I really feel comfortable; even with the meals."

We camp at a beautiful site, with a ribbon waterfall at our backs and bent baobabs rimming the hills, looking like old men of the river. A local shepherd boy whittles a flute from a bamboo stalk and plays a haunting tune that unfolds like a prayer. There is but one downside: the camp is hopping with sand flies, the biting variety, so I pull on my socks for the first time in weeks.

It is Pasquale's birthday, and so after our freeze-dried turkey teriyaki dinner we have a surprise bash, with a Dutch-oven cake, and fireworks concocted by Mike Speaks using kerosene and cloth. Pasquale exudes a pure gladness of place and time. He is at peace here. As I sit back and watch the celebration, I wonder if there might be another universe, somewhere where the lights are kept when they go out here. I listen to

Pasquale's deep and easy laugh, and think that if there is one person here who embodies the spirit of Lew Greenwald, it is Pasquale. They would have been friends. Maybe the light has reappeared here.

As I am helping Jonathan Chester erect his tent, I suggest he forgo the rain fly, as it rained the evening before, and it never rains on consecutive nights. But an hour later the skies flash and boom. Almost every night throughout this expedition I have slept outside, near the spaghetti of wires, cords, and cables that connect us to the world beyond this canyon, and every night I have slept fitfully, as though the night currents were arching through my cerebellum, conducting bytes and bits of worried thoughts. But this storm drives me indoors, and as I lie in Jonathan's tent, I listen as the wind surreptitiously pools all sounds, sucking up every noise until there is only the sound of my breathing. I am in awe of the elements, struck with a kind of stupor, a total oblivion of where I am and of every other sublunary concern. It is the best sleep I've had on the trip.


*September 24*


Sometime in the afternoon we slip the rafts up a serpentine side canyon and meet a waterslide. On our original expeditions we would find respite from the heat, the bugs, the rapids, the fear in a series of slides we would plunge down in all manners of styles and techniques. Here is a clear tributary in an Edenesque setting with a series of fluted slides perfect for slithering, skimming, and tobogganing. Africa has a way of reconstructing time. Now we turn back the clock, and for hours slide and giggle and splash and bathe and wallow in the brilliant water. We have found the Fountain of Youth. Butterflies, tiny and yellow, flit around us like the lights of collapsing stars. John and I break out into a bellowing, off-key rendition of "Summertime." Whoever said the soufflé can't rise twice?

It's late in the day, and Jim is looking for the perfect campsite. It has become an obsession. Virtually every night of the trip, after several stops and look-arounds, he has delivered—a wide beach, scenic, near a clear tributary for bathing and drinking water. Jim is proud of his record. But this afternoon pickings are slim. Beach after beach Jim pulls over, ships his oars, stomps up the slope, looks around, circles his arm indicating we need to continue, and strikes back to the boat for more. We've done this a dozen times this afternoon, and everyone is getting tired and impatient. Some are calling Jim "the General," with unflattering overtones. Cirrus clouds, dark as plums, are rolling toward us. Finally, I take the initiative and pull over on the northern shore where I see a tributary. It's clear, the beach is long, though littered with the remains of bonfires. Otherwise, it's perfect. Jim pulls in behind me, marches up, looks around, squints at the bonfire scars, and circles his arms in a gesture that means we will continue.

"What's wrong with this place?" I protest. Jim doesn't answer, just plods back to his raft. I follow, push off, and a few minutes later, with tropical savagery the storm breaks over us. Jim pulls over on the southern bank on a mudpan that looks like cracked china, and races up to the scant shelter of a tree with a trunk that appears to be made of cables tied in a Gordian knot. We all follow and huddle together like moorland sheep under the branches as the downpour lashes. In minutes the river turns the color of café au lait. It is suddenly so cold I'm shivering. For the first time this trip I curse Jim Slade. If he had listened to me, we would be on a decent beach, tents erected. Then, as quickly as it came, the storm stops, and the bruised clouds heal. Jim calls camp on the narrow wet beach, where there is no tributary water and barely enough space for our group. I point out the larger beach across the river, but Jim is adamant. We're all tired, wet, and fraying a bit. It's not worth fighting over, so I step down to the rafts to unload.

We perch our tents like guillemot nests on the thin strip of mud and sand. In the wake of the storm, the sun briefly peeks through the clouds, hissing like a blowtorch, shimmering as though dipped in a bowl of crystal.

Because there is no side stream, and because of the nasty habits of the crocodiles, we're forced to bathe on shore, showering with buckets of muddy water drawn cautiously from the river. It is to be our last benison.

Tonight insects arrive in numbers never imagined, coating everything like snow. David Roberts and I try to type with mosquito net hats drooped over our heads, and others slap the bugs with towels. Bart creates a diversion by cooking popcorn in the Dutch oven, my favorite snack, and one we cooked many times during Ethiopian nights on rivers past. Someone finds a bottle of Ethiopian red wine, thick as Robitussin, that has survived the journey, and we pass it around to numb the ordeal. After a few sips, we sit back ignoring the buzzing hordes and drift back to earlier times. Bart, Jim, and George reveal they had taken acid on the Omo, and after all these years I am surprised. I had taken my share of hallucinogenics in the sixties and seventies, but the Omo seemed to me to be too spectacular, too phantasmagoric, too inherently trippy to ever want to miss anything with mind-altering drugs. The same with the

Tekeze experience; it in and of itself is an altered state, an enhanced reality. But, I remind myself, it is one about to end, and the flinty reality of the civilized life will be back. The transition will probably begin tomorrow, as the map shows the take-out bridge just a few bends away. I put down my cup of wine, and wander back to my bag to lie back and watch the Milky Way. The sky is a net so heavily weighted with stars it seems to droop above me. By standing on tiptoe it seems I could steal one of the lights and set it, twinkling, on the beach.

CHAPTER 30

# THE INFINITE VOYAGE

"It is possible to believe that all the past is but the beginning of a beginning, and all that is and has been is but the twilight of the dawn."

—H. G. Wells

*September 25*

A bruptly, the river expedition ends.

Before the sun has won its daily battle against the canyon shade I awake to the haunting hoots of a Verreaux's eagle owl perched on a branch above my head. A skein of mist unrolls across the river. For a few short moments everything seems to exult in living. We move about our morning tasks silently, like ghosts cleaning house, packing for the final time. Jim Slade limps a bit as he moves from beach to boat. A nasty blister has formed where his sandal strap crossed his foot, most probably from the tough hike to and from the village of Meda on the canyon plateau. Jim had hoped to wear his black "hiking sneakers," a weathered, worn-in pair he'd used to hike all over the world. But they have gone missing.

In the soft pool of early light we push into the current, on a river angry-red with the blood of sediment and silt flushed by the squalls of the past few days. The river flows quite fast at the edges, while in the deeper middle it bubbles up like thick porridge. The normal seethe and suck of the river is now an audible roar. We round a bend and hear baboons barking on one side of the river. Monkeys scamper down the other. A couple of green-backed crocodiles hover in the eddies, bringing the trip's total to 250, about one per mile. A baobab bows a farewell.

A gray-blue column of smoke, laden with rosy sparks, rises from the right bank. People are stoking a bonfire to make charcoal, which indicates we are near a road, as charcoal is traded to the cities as cooking fuel. I contemplate pulling out my Minolta for a parting shot but instead grab my DC50 Kodak digital camera and make the shot. I had lugged my complement of film-camera gear all the way from Seattle but never shot a single celluloid frame throughout the expedition. Without really noticing I have gone digital.

Then we slip circumspectly around a gravel bar into sight of gray, twisted slabs of metal scattered like pieces of a plane crash along the river. This is the old Tekeze Bridge, blown up by an air strike by Mengistu's government forces in 1989—a vain effort to prevent the Tigrean rebels from marching south to Addis Ababa. Now, in place of the wreckage, an unassuming Bailey bridge is slung across the river, once again allowing vehicles to travel between south and north, from the interior to the Red Sea.

This is also where British ambassador to Ethiopia Douglas Busk crossed the Tekeze on a mountaineering expedition in 1956, the year my father was in Tehran, the year we went camping. Upon reaching the far shore of the Tekeze, Douglas Busk wrote, "In the remote future this little known river will provide vast possibilities of electric power for industries as yet undreamt of and the control of its waters will contribute benefits to people we shall not live to know." He was, of course, thinking of a dam, and I can only hope his vision of the future here will not come true.

We hove to at 8:40 A.M., and land on the exposed beach downstream of the bridge, carefully picking our steps. We had been warned of one final danger to worry about: land mines at the take-out.

There is, of course, no cascading water from fire floats, no gun salutes, no champagne. Instead, we all wander over to one another and give the SOBEK handshake one more time, maybe the last time. I finger the good luck bracelet, engraved with Coptic crosses, that our houseboy Abba gave me in Addis twenty some years ago, and which I have worn ever since.

As we go through the derigging process, we all glance downstream: the river hums a barely audible refrain, but we hear its message. The Tekeze has been a nice, polite flower, and yet a funeral bloom for time.

We barely tilled its garden, touching less than three hundred miles of its course. Several hundred miles of unrun, unexplored Tekeze remain, beckoning us onward to the Sudanese border, to the Nile itself. But not for us; not now.

The last time the five of us traveled together was the Omo River in 1973. If fate had taken a different turn, Lew Greenwald would be washing the boats and tying the oars with us now. Perhaps this is our lost covenant found. We vowed to run the Tekeze; I promised Lew that. Our code was to explore new places and celebrate old friendships. Our ark was a raft, and we made good on our pact.

Anatomizing friendship, of course, like translating a poem, risks leaving behind the unanalyzable spirit of the thing. But, I did think for a moment that friendship is the experience that draws one to another and draws again. It isn't made of the tests we devise to prove ourselves right or wrong. It is most preciously the frame in which we see ourselves with others, and for us the banks of wild rivers have been those frames. We joke now that if we congregate again in twenty-three years we'll be in our late sixties and early seventies. About the only waterways we might explore together would be the canals of France. Then again, the Tekeze downstream looks pretty inviting, and we've all guided vigorous septuagenarians on exploratory rafting adventures. Someone mentions the Kabul River in Afghanistan; there's a rumor the Onyx River, running through the dry valleys in Antarctica, might have a thirty-mile runnable stretch in a good January. So much water, so little time.

As we're emptying our dry bags, Jim sees his lost sneakers pour out of one. He grabs his much-missed footwear, archly spews some choice words, and moves on. Thinking about the land mines, we all keep to a small perimeter and step gingerly up to the road. There transportation waits, arranged with perfection by Abadi Haile, our Good Samaritan in Africa, our Kurtz.

By eleven we're climbing into the bus, parked by a watchtower riddled with bullet holes. A flatbed truck behind is packed with the rafts and gear. A local boy who helped load our gear waves good-bye as his grubby T-shirt postures: "What if the world had turned its back on Einstein? Einstein was a refugee."

In minutes we're engaged in a noisy first-gear wending up the escarpment on a road the Italians built a half century ago. The suspension is sagging and the chassis groaning. It is a 150-mile trip up a narrow road that twists and doubles to the plateau. It will take nine and a half hours to reach the ancient castellated capital of Gondar, where we will spend the night, and then continue to Bahar Dar on the shores of Lake Tana, source of the Blue Nile. From there we'll catch flights back to Addis Ababa and connect to our homes.

The scenery on this drive is splendid, including a poster of actress Jennifer Connelly that pastes the front of the bus. Out the windows, the ever-amazing spires and buttes of the Simien Mountains prove there is magic on earth. The unrelenting horizontal quality of the race from the Nile turns abruptly vertical here. This is a land where the only meaningful directions are up and down. We drive by a field in which a Soviet-made T-55 tank lies derelict, its turret blown askew, its gun barrel drooping impotently. Out the other window we can see smashed military lorries, burnt-out armored personnel carriers, and more gutted tanks. These all belonged to the Mengistu government forces, and were destroyed by the locals seeking freedom, perhaps with the help of the Ark of the Covenant.

We sip the tart Asmara beer, and I am fascinated to watch the beads of condensation skitter down the sides of the bottle. We share cheese and *muz* (sweet bananas), and talk about the rich history we shared together exploring wild currents of rivers run and lost.

We began in Ethiopia in 1973 with a simple, but seminal, bump and grind down the Awash River. We were the uttermost branch of a peculiar evolutional limb of boating. But that trip launched thousands of international raft trips, changed the face of adventure travel, inspired many river romances and relationships, and scores of kin of such. It changed the way many of us connect with the cultures and wildernesses of the world, with one another, with ourselves. As the bus driver chews his chat, and we pass the faded blue and yellow single-story storefronts of road towns, someone asks how many rivers SOBEK has explored. Tallying the total is an exercise never undertaken, so on the long, grinding bus ride we huddle and scribble to come up with the definitive list:

*First Raft Descents by Members of the Tekeze Expedition:*

AFRICA

| | |
|---|---|
| Zambezi River, Zambia/Zimbabwe | Mahajamba, Madagascar |
| Gabba-Birbir-Baro system, Ethiopia | Betsiboka, Madagascar |
| Awash River, Ethiopia | Kuhnene, Angola/Namibia |
| Omo River, Ethiopia | Tana, Kenya |
| Blue Nile, whitewater section | Kilombero, Tanzania |
| | Ruaha, Tanzania |

Luangwa, Zambia
Shira, Malawi
Kafue, Zambia

ASIA
Euphrates, Turkey
Coruh, Turkey
Great Bend of the Yangtze, China
Indus, Pakistan
Alas, Sumatra
Ayung, Bali
Sala Sadang, Sulawesi
Yarkand, China
Hunza-Gilgit, Pakistan
Zaskar, India
Kayan, Borneo
Boh, Borneo
Dar Jung Guo, China
Biritingi, Sumatra
Kunar, Pakistan
Swat, Pakistan
Ghizar, Pakistan
Tons, India
Yamuna, India

EUROPE
Reisa Elva, Norway
Alta Elva, Norway/Finland

NORTH AMERICA
Upper Youghiogheny, Pennsylvania
Tatshenshini, Yukon/Alaska
New Gorge, West Virginia

Kennicott/Nizina/Chitina, Alaska
Kongakut, Alaska
Hulahula, Alaska
Canning, Alaska
Tsirku, Alaska
Tkobe, Alaska
Chilkat, Alaska
Six-Mile, Alaska
Eau Claire, Quebec

OCEANIA
Bulolo-Watut-Markham system,
   Papua New Guinea (PNG)
Tsau-Jimi-Yuat system, PNG
Wahgi-Tua system, PNG
Motu, New Zealand (NZ)
Mohaka, NZ
Clarence, NZ
Hast, NZ
Tasman, NZ

SOUTH AMERICA/CARIBBEAN
Manso, Argentina/Chile
Bío-Bío, Chile
Roosevelt, Brazil
Baker, Chile
Toa, Cuba
Quijos, Ecuador
Aguarico, Ecuador
Sereno, Chile
Apurimac, Peru
Tambopata, Peru

It is a catalog we are proud of, even as we know it is but a scratch in the body of possibilities. But in the silence that washes over us after we register the last name in the SOBEK roll call, it seems we are all of a single current. It seems we were born upon the rivers, that our blood flows with the silt between the banks, and that we will meander forever to the delta of our dreams.

# EPILOGUE

"We shall not cease from exploration
And the end of all our exploring
Will be to arrive where we started
And know the place for the first time."

—T. S. Eliot

We check into the Lake Tana Hotel in Bahar Dar, and after a couple green bottles of beer I muster up the courage. I go to my room and dial the international operator. It takes forever to make the connection. Finally, a familiar voice. "Mom . . . it's me. . . . How's Dad?" A long silence. "He's okay," she practically yells. "He made it through the operation. They say he'll be out of the hospital in a few more days. . . ." I am happier than I ever thought I would be. This time I'm going to go home and kiss my father, hold him, and tell him I love him, no matter the misadventures that hurt him, that hurt me. I won't tell him about the Tekeze, or Africa, or what I saw and learned. I know these types of travels left a scar on him, and he would rather not hear of my own. I accept that. I'll just say I understand, and I'll thank him for a little camping trip so, so long ago. And I'll take my own son, Walker, camping, just the two of us, by a rushing river.

〜〜〜

Two days we spend cleaning and organizing our gear, eating fat french fries and guzzling cold beer. John Yost leaves for the States—he has to get back to work—but the rest of us go to bed early on the second night.

Under the moon in lunar eclipse, in the murkiness of predawn, Jim Slade, Bart Henderson, George Fuller, and I drive the twenty miles to the Blue Nile Falls, or, as known locally, Tissisat ("water that smokes").

It is an otherworldly ride down the wide carriageway and round the roundabouts, for it is Maskal, the Ethiopian Christian holiday celebrating Saint Helena's finding of the true cross of Christ. Bonfires licking long poles, representing the wood of the cross, litter the landscape, and reviews of white-robed revelers carry torches that burn holes in the darkness.

At first light we reach the village near the famous falls and see a whorl of mist spiraling hundreds of feet into the air, looking like smoke from a massive brushfire. We pay our entrance fees, step across the seventeenth-century Portuguese bridge, and wade through the cloacal mud to a promenade overlooking the grand cataract. In Africa, this sheet of falling water is second in scale only to Victoria Falls on the Zambezi. The Scottish explorer James Bruce, in his search for the source of the Nile, came upon this sight in 1770 and described it thusly:

> The river . . . fell in one sheet of water, without any interval, above half an English mile in breadth, with a force and a noise that was truly terrible, and which stunned and made me, for a time, perfectly dizzy. A thick fume, or haze, covered the fall all around, and hung over the course of the stream both above and below, marking its track, though the water was not seen. . . . It was a most magnificent sight, that ages, added to the greatest length of human life, would not deface or eradicate from my memory.

When James Bruce returned to Scotland and published volumes of what he saw in Ethiopia, his uncannily accurate descriptions seemed so outlandish to British cognoscenti that he was dismissed as a fraud and publicly ridiculed. A further irony: after the years he had spent wandering the wilderness of Abyssinia, enduring endless risks and surviving countless dangers, Bruce died in 1794 when he tripped and pitched over his head, falling down the stairs of his home in Larbert. Now, standing before the immense panorama, watching the water spout and bloom like gargantuan brown mushrooms and the mist shape and move like a time-lapse sequence of clouds, I am struck by how accurate James Bruce had been and how little the sight has changed in more than two hundred years.

The other great waterfalls of the world—Niagara, Iguassu, Victoria—are all scarred with hotels and tourist boutiques and scenic flights. Here there is nothing save the raw, deep voice of nature and an architecture supported by the brilliant beams of rainbows.

Looking down from a muddy hill I can trace the course of the Blue Nile as it twists through the gorge below the falls, over cataracts that would kill anything that breathes. The spray flung up from this gorge creates a perpetual soft rain that blows across my face. At my feet a forest of wet green reeds waves from side to side, like seaweed at the bottom of the ocean. Looking above the falls I can see a *tankwa,* a papyrus reed boat, upon which fishermen are propelling themselves with bladeless bamboo poles. I see flocks of little black birds with pointed pinkish wings flying directly into the spray and landing on the slippery rocks at the very lip where the water makes its horrifying plunge. Unconcerned, they fly off again through a rainbow nearly circular, hanging in the spray like a whirling firework.

It was the Blue Nile, after all, that brought me to Africa in the first place. To locate its source—*Quaerere caput Nili*—had been the hope of many great captains and geographers of the classical age: Herodotus, Cyrus and Cambyses of Persia, Alexander the Great, Julius Caesar, Nero. The first European actually to find it was Father Pedro Paez, a Portuguese Jesuit missionary, who was taken there by the Emperor Susenyos in 1618. The first Briton to make his way to the source, perhaps in search of the Ark of the Covenant, was the Scot James Bruce. I had been enthralled by the writings of Bruce and of Alan Moorehead, whose book *The Blue Nile* swept me into a world beyond the pages of *National Geographic.* I started a correspondence with Moorehead, who lived in Switzerland in the late 1960s, and before he died he sent me a note urging me to travel to Ethiopia to see firsthand the stories he had told.

The second chapter of the book of Genesis refers to the rivers that flow through the Garden of Eden: "And the name of the second river is Ghion; the same is it that compasseth the whole land of Ethiopia." The Blue Nile, sweeping out from Lake Tana in a wide loop, does indeed encompass the ancient land of Ethiopia. And the two springs regarded as the source of that great river are known to this day as Ghion. So, perhaps, Lew took the right river trip, one that carries him still to Paradise.

In a place like this it is easy to understand how we live historically. We are aware of the continual becoming, which is also to say the continual unbecoming, of our lives. Being on the river Tekeze allowed me to understand that nothing need ever be lost, unless the link of feeling that connects us to the past is broken, to be repaired, badly, by the crude glue of thought. For me, Lew has never gone away.

Ever since that Christmas, the last time we spoke, when I promised Lew we would run the Tekeze together, his spirit has traveled with me: down the California rivers, on exploratories, across Africa, around the world. He died much too young, but for two years he lived a life full and deep and rich, with laughter and connection and warmth. It was a short, happy life, but it perhaps was better than the path down which he was headed before he took that journey on the Colorado. As we wander about Tissisat Falls, soaking in mist and memories, Jim Slade points out where they had launched on the ill-starred expedition in 1975. It is the first time I have seen the black basalt walls and the raging currents that were the last images in Lew's eyes. He had endorsed the river dream; swallowed it whole. He ran the Blue Nile. He had said before he left that the next trip on his list was the Tekeze. And now, at last, I have completed a piece of his dream.

I reach in my backpack and pull out a stone I found on the Tekeze, a beautifully polished piece of white quartz. I toss it into the boiling waters of the Blue Nile, to roll with the spirit of a friend. Now it is time to go home. . . .

RICHARD BANGS—adventurer, river explorer, author, and producer—is a founding partner of SOBEK Expeditions, now Mountain Travel★SOBEK, the adventure travel firm. He has written more than five hundred magazine articles and eleven books, among them *Rivergods* and *Riding the Dragon's Back*. He lives in Redmond, Washington, where he works for the Microsoft Corporation and Expedia.com.